Brushes with Faith

Brushes with Faith

Reflections and Conversations on Contemporary Art

Aaron Rosen

CASCADE *Books* · Eugene, Oregon

BRUSHES WITH FAITH
Reflections and Conversations on Contemporary Art

Cascade Books
An Imprint of Wipf and Stock Publishers
199 W. 8th Ave., Suite 3
Eugene, OR 97401

www.wipfandstock.com

PAPERBACK ISBN: 978-1-5326-4931-8
HARDCOVER ISBN: 978-1-5326-4932-5
EBOOK ISBN: 978-1-5326-4933-2

Cataloguing-in-Publication data:

Names: Rosen, Aaron, author.

Title: Brushes with Faith : Reflections and Conversations on Contemporary Art / by Aaron Rosen.

Description: Eugene, OR: Cascade Books, 2019 | Includes bibliographical references.

Identifiers: ISBN 978-1-5326-4931-8 (paperback) | ISBN 978-1-5326-4932-5 (hardcover) | ISBN 978-1-5326-4933-2 (ebook)

Subjects: LCSH: Art and religion | Christianity and art | Judaism and art

Classification: N72.R4 R70 2019 (print) | N72.R4 (ebook)

Manufactured in the U.S.A.   07/22/19

To my son Arthur
His aunts Whitney and Katrina
And his uncles Ross and Isaac

Contents

II. Conversations

Illustrations

Front Cover: Sam Winston, *Erasure of Blind Drawing*, 2016. Photo: Andy Sewell / Sam Winston. Image cropped.

Back Cover: Jacqueline Nicholls, *Day 41. Aaron Rosen*. From "To have and to hold," Omer drawing series, 2013.

7.1. Dan Leon, Matthew Lloyd, Shahed Saleem, *Friday Saturday Sunday*, visualization of ongoing architectural project, 2018. Courtesy of and © Dan Leon, Matthew Lloyd, and Shahed Saleem. | 52

8.1. R. B. Kitaj, *Eclipse of God (After the Uccello Panel Called Breaking Down the Jew's Door)*, 1997–2000, oil and charcoal on canvas, 91.3 × 121.8 cm, The Jewish Museum, New York City, NY. Purchase: Oscar and Regina Gruss Memorial and S. H. and Helen R. Scheuer Family Foundation Funds, 2000–71. Photo by Richard Goodbody, Inc. Photo Credit: The Jewish Museum, New York / Art Resource, NY. © R. B. Kitaj Estate. | 54

8.2. Paolo Uccello, *Miracle of the Desecrated Host* (Scene 2), 1465–69, panel, 43 x 58 cm, Urbino, Italy, Galleria Nazionale delle Marche. Photo courtesy Galleria Nazionale delle Marche. | 55

9.1. Siona Benjamin, *Exodus: I See Myself in You*, 2016, 7 panel polyptych (gouache, acrylic, and gold leaf) with sculpture (mixed media, wood, paint, and cast resin), 200 x 300 cm total dimensions, installation view, Riverside Church, New York, NY, *Stations of the Cross* exhibition, 2018. Courtesy of and © Siona Benjamin. | 59

9.2. Siona Benjamin, *Exodus No. 2*, 2016, gouache, 22K gold leaf, and mixed media on museum board mounted on wood panel, 53 x 41 cm. Courtesy of and © Siona Benjamin. | 60

9.3. Siona Benjamin, *Exodus: I See Myself in You*, 2016 (left panels detail). Courtesy of and © Siona Benjamin. | 61

10.1. Adel Abdessemed, *Bristow*, 2016, steel, bollard, 174 x 35 x 28 cm. Courtesy of and © Adel Abdessemed. | 65

10.2. Adel Abdessemed, *Untitled*, 2014, CNC-machined polyurethane, graphite on 3D printed nylon, scalpel blades, 140 x 125 x 90 cm. Courtesy of and © Adel Abdessemed. | 67

10.3. Adel Abdessemed, *Décor*, 2011–2012, razor wire, 4 elements, 210 x 174 x 41 cm; 207 x 174 x 41 cm; 218 x 174 x 40.5 cm; 205 x 174 x 37 cm. Courtesy of and ©Adel Abdessemed. | 70

12.1. Leni Dothan, *Mine*, 2012, mother, child, knife, 00:23' video in loop. Courtesy of and © Leni Dothan. | 77

12.2. Leni Dothan, *Mother and Child in a Window*, 2016, mother, child, wooden structure, duratrans print. Courtesy of and © Leni Dothan. | 79

12.3. Leni Dothan, *Middle Ages/Mother and Child*, 2017, duratrans print. Courtesy of and © Leni Dothan. | 80

13.1. John Edmonds, *Untitled (Du-Rag 3)*, 2017. Courtesy of and © John Edmonds. | 85

13.2. John Edmonds, *Tête de femme*, 2018. Courtesy of and © John Edmonds. | 86

13.3. John Edmonds, *Untitled (Head 1)*, 2018. Courtesy of and © John Edmonds. | 86

14.1. Eva Petrič, *Collective Heart*, 2016, 1097 x 579 cm, Vienna, Austria, St. Stephansdom, found, collected, and donated antique laces from around the world. Courtesy of and © Eva Petrič. | 91

14.2. Eva Petrič, *Hematoma*, 2012, lace, 299 x 299 cm, projection, sound ("Missing Lullaby"), Buenos Aires, Argentina, Centro Cultural Borges. Courtesy of and © Eva Petrič. | 94

14.3. Eva Petrič, *Soul*, 2014, combination of analog and digital photographs of organ explantation in light box tower. Created in collaboration with the Vienna General Hospital (AKH). Courtesy of and © Eva Petrič. | 95

15.1. Sam Winston, *Erasure of Blind Drawing*, 2016. Photo: Andy Sewell / Sam Winston. Courtesy of and © Sam Winston. | 99

15.2. Sam Winston, *Blindfolded Text Drawing*, 2016. Photo: Andy Sewell / Sam Winston. Courtesy of and © Sam Winston. | 102

15.3. Sam Winston, *Darkness Visible*, 2017, installation view, Southbank Centre, London. Photo credit: Pietro Martini. Courtesy of and © Sam Winston. | 103

Acknowledgments

My first debt in this book is to the artists who joined me in conversations, invited me into their studios, and offered their friendship. On a practical note, I would like to thank them for the generous permission to reproduce their works, without which this book would be aesthetically impoverished. A number of the essays in this book first appeared in print elsewhere and I am grateful to the following magazines, publishers, and organizations for permission to reprint my work in adapted form: October Gallery (Ch. 1); Douglas & McIntyre and the Jeffrey Rubinoff Foundation (Ch. 2); Rizzoli (Ch. 5); Frame Publishers (Ch. 7); *Art & Christianity* (Ch. 8); Opalka Gallery, Sage Colleges (Ch. 9); Hå gamle præstegård (Ch. 12); *Jewish Quarterly* (Chs. 2 and 11); Hannah Barry Gallery (Ch. 10); *The Brooklyn Rail* (Ch. 22); and *Poetics Today* (Ch. 24).

The nature of this book, which spans some of my very first professional scribblings to my latest, means many friends and colleagues with an eye for forensic accounting will be able to recognize debts to their insights and assistance. As I prepared this manuscript, it was a pleasure to recall conversations with the following people, which shaped this book in ways small and large: Dua Abbas, Devon Abts, Tahnia Ahmed, Douglas Adams (Z"L), Diane Apostolos-Cappadona, David Ariel (Z"L), Hannah Barry, Christopher Brewer, David de Bruijn, Sherri Cornett, William Danaher, Jr., André Daughtry, Nausikaa El-Mecky, Sage Elwell, Rachel Fendler, Michelle Fletcher, James Fox, Philip Francis, Renata Homem, Graham Howes, Robert Katz, Ezra Konvitz, Catriona Laing, Ayla Lepine, James Lindon, Thomas Marks, Glen Milstein, John Moody, Sashareen Morgan, Jacqueline Nicholls, Lex Paulson, Ralph Peterson, Brent Plate, Sally Promey, James Purdon, Ben Quash, Melissa Raphael, Chloë Reddaway, Joanne Rosenthal, Maryanne Saunders, Daniel Siedell, Eliyahu Stern, Casey Strine, Peter Tolton, Gary Waddingham, Giles Waller, Lieke Wijnia, Tijana Zakula, and Eric Ziolkowski.

Above all, I thank my wife Carolyn. From our first dates in the Ashmolean to the Cloisters, the Tate, the Rijksmuseum, and just the other day the Detroit Institute of Arts with Arthur, all art—all that is good—leads back to you. As Frank O'Hara writes, "I would rather look at you than all the portraits in the world."

Introduction

Every book contains the beginnings of other books, as yet unwritten. We are lucky if we get to write some of those books ourselves. When I wrote *Art & Religion in the 21st Century*, I was conscious that I was sketching out the contours of an emerging field, rather than drawing definitive borders. Like an enthusiastic but imperfectly informed cartographer, I knew my extrapolations would need to be verified in the future, by myself and others. In the past few years, I have set out to refine and supplement the survey I offered in *Art & Religion* with a series of essays and in-depth interviews with individual artists. The result is *Brushes with Faith*, a collection that endeavors to offer a more granular look at what is happening on the ground in contemporary art, as artists engage ever more deeply with religious imagery, themes, practices, and questions.

The division of this volume into "Reflections" and "Conversations" is not meant to be binary. Instead, each section echoes aspects of the other. The essays are, for the most part, born out of long-running conversations I have had with the artists in question. And the interviews, distilled from hours of recorded conversations, have an almost epistolary feel, furthered by an editing process in which the artists and I each tinkered with the texts. Beneath these formal similarities, however, lies a simple fact with somewhat complicated implications. The majority of artists I write about in this book are friends, whether new or old. We have collaborated, kvetched, and challenged one another frequently. Indeed, as I type these sentences I look around my living room and see some of their works hanging on the wall. So much for scholarly objectivity, you might say! My hope, however, is that what I lack in distance, I make up for with the kind of details and disclosures that can only be conjured through intimacy and reciprocity.

Artists are, with good reason, wary when it comes to revealing the thoughts and processes behind their works. As a result, interviews and essays tend to repeat the same anecdotes about artists' experiences, calcifying into a veritable litany over time. Aside from being expedient, this strategy can be a form of self-protection, helping artists navigate around topics that might seem to determine or domesticate the meaning of their work, and potentially paint them into a corner as a particular "type" of artist. Recognizing that good art thrives on multivalence, savvy artists tend to avoid proffering any material that might be fashioned into an interpretive master key, unlocking an authoritative reading of their work.

So how does one create opportunities for more enlightening dialogue, especially on a subject—religion—that many artists steer clear of in public fora? In my experience, being a theologian has, surprisingly, proven to be an asset. If many artists resist talking to art critics and art historians about religious connections in their work, perhaps it is because they perceive a genuine risk, with comparatively little advantage. If there is a common bond between Jewish, Christian, and Muslim artists across the globe, for example, it exists not in any shared style, theme, or process but rather a mutual reluctance to be identified by these very labels, and the stereotypes they engender. As a theologian, I am sensitive to the histories and effects of religious typologies, and indisposed to apply them uncritically. At the same time, standing outside the art world's corridors of power—more prone to haunt the cloistered halls of divinity schools than art fairs and biennials—means that I am free to point up religious connections without scaring off skittish collectors, or otherwise impacting an artist's market value. Taken together, these factors make for a reliable confessor—one hopes!—to practitioners with spiritual inclinations.

Yet I also like to think that theologians bring something else to the bargain. The best artists have voracious appetites for new material, and religion—in all its permutations—constitutes a profound, inexhaustible, yet often untapped resource. And so it is not uncommon to find myself playing Virgil in the face of some rather eccentric queries from artists, like this missive, received in the middle of the night from John Edmonds, one of the artists featured in this book: "I'm doing research about symbolism and dreams . . . angels, demons, spirits . . . I'm on a quest for knowledge and feel a big change coming on . . . is there something you recommend that I read?" I love these kind of exchanges, and not just for the opportunity to moonlight as a demonologist. With admitted self-interest, what inspires me most about working with artists is engaging them in discussions about process; what the novelist Philip Roth called "shop talk."[1]

1. Roth, *Shop Talk*.

As an academic, there is something genuinely instructive about how artists approach research. Rather than the determinism that handicaps so much academic inquiry, whereby we often set out to prove a precogitated conclusion—and thereby satisfy the requirements of a grant, tenure application, or research assessment—artists tend to follow a far more organic, open-ended route. And more often than not, they are delighted when the bread crumbs lead them along an unlikely route. They can afford to get lost in the woods. And, as the philosopher Walter Benjamin reminds us, getting lost is an increasingly rare skill.[2] If the interviews in this book involve some detours, I invite you to read them in this spirit, not so much to forage for clues in order to interpret a specific painting or installation, but to enter the process of artistic creation, redolent as it is with theological implications.

Implications for whom? This collection is not aimed exclusively at academics, though I hope scholars of theology, religious studies, and visual culture will all find materials of use here, particularly when it comes to original accounts of artists who have previously received limited attention. The intersection between art and religion is too important a topic to be left only to those with specialized training. We need to create conversations that are as free as possible from disciplinary jargon, and I hope this volume serves as an open invitation to more people to join this dialogue. It is meant to awaken questions on key existential themes—from origins to death, destruction to transformation—rather than propose definitive theories. If such unabashedly open-ended topics might scare off some academics, I trust they will be received well by some of the people I spend the most time with these days: artists and clergy.

One concern of mine, which crests into view regularly in these essays and interviews, is pedagogy. As both an educator and curator, I am increasingly interested in where, and how, we can create spaces for greater literacy about contemporary religion and art, and especially their points of intersections. There are some universities where this dialogue is taking place at an advanced level, and I have been privileged to teach at three such institutions, Yale Divinity School, King's College London, and Wesley Theological Seminary. Examples of art schools which prize theological education are rarer, though some innovative initiatives have appeared in recent years, such as the Institute for Doctoral Studies in the Visual Arts, which grants PhDs to practicing artists who wish to delve into philosophical and theological questions more than a traditional MFA allows.

2. Benjamin, *Berlin Childhood*, 53–54.

There are also an increasing number of nonprofits devoted to advocating for artists and arts education within individual traditions, such as Art + Christianity in the UK, the Jewish Art Salon in the US, and Eleven, a Muslim arts collective in Australia. Numerous museums have taken up religious themes in recent exhibitions, such as *Heavenly Bodies: Fashion and Catholic Imagination* (2018) at the Metropolitan Museum of Art, New York City, which energetically stretched the contours of art history in new directions. Other curatorial initiatives have broadened the very definition of the museum itself. In 2017, for example, fourteen Dutch churches and two synagogues declared themselves "The Largest Museum of The Netherlands," embracing a new model for conceiving both religious heritage and spaces for contemporary exhibitions.

For my own part, with my collaborator Catriona Laing, I have co-curated the public arts project *Stations of the Cross*, which has traveled from London to Washington, D. C., New York City, and Amsterdam. The exhibition—staged in fourteen secular and sacred locations across each host city—uses the themes and iconography of the Passion as a lens to focus upon contemporary issues of social justice. The project incorporates existing masterpieces and monuments as well as commissioning new works, including several from artists in this book. Visitors are guided through this pilgrimage via smartphone, with GPS-enabled maps and podcasts by leading artists, clergy, and intellectuals. Reconfiguring the ways in which we experience public spaces—both physically and virtually—has an almost unlimited potential to generate new ways of seeing religion.

As encouraging as it is to see more universities, museums, and cultural organizations taking up questions of religious identity, much more needs to be done to engage with intersectional issues of sexual, ethnic, socioeconomic, and other differences. Indeed, one of the persisting problems in theology more broadly is the way in which religious identity is still largely treated as a form of difference that supersedes or contains other diversities, like a series of matryoshka dolls. In practice, this leads to a tremendous hermeneutic audacity, by which viewers arrogate to themselves the capacity to decide that a given work, for example, is first and foremost a statement of the artist's faith, and only secondarily or tertiarily a product of their experience as a person of color, or as gender non-conforming. We must be careful, then, that our desire to elucidate religious questions in art does not inadvertently lead us to mute other, equally important questions, or to treat them in isolation. Learning to listen more acutely in multiple registers can in fact often yield richer insights than training our ears first and foremost for what might seem demonstratively religious. Artists rarely make for good ambassadors or apologists, and we do a disservice to them, as well as ourselves, when we expect otherwise. I am reminded of the Jewish writer Franz Kafka musing in his diary: "What have I in common with Jews? I have hardly anything in common with myself . . ."[3]

The artists examined in this book hail from across the globe, from my own countries of the United States and Great Britain to Germany, Slovenia, Algeria, Israel, India, and Nepal. Some expressly define themselves as Christian, Jewish, Muslim, or Hindu, while others employ practices from Buddhist, Taoist, and other traditions. While I take advantage of this diversity of perspectives, bringing together artists engaged with similar questions or themes, I do not attempt to position individual artists as representatives of a particular religious, national, or other group. My goal is not to produce a definition of what Christian art is, for instance, but rather to indicate the many, indeed innumerable, things that it *might* be. In theological parlance, I take a cataphatic approach, preferring to affirm possibilities rather than eliminate them.

The potential for an artist to reveal theological insights through his or her work is not determined by the surety of their religious convictions. Indeed, I would wager that a spirited atheism can generate a more convincing canvas—both aesthetically and theologically—than lethargic belief. Herein lies the double meaning I intend by the title of this book. For some artists, the power of their convictions seems to radiate from the images they produce, as if their brushes bear the literal force of their faith. For others, their encounter with the spiritual is seemingly coincidental, like two strangers passing one another in the train, reading the same obscure book. And, for a few, the encounter provokes trepidation, like a close brush with death. Whether fortifying or disturbing, these brushes with faith challenge and invigorate the artists in question, and—I trust—those of us who study the results.

3. Kafka, "Selections from Diaries," 259.

Part I

Reflections

Origins

1. Govinda Sah: Divine Eyes

> It is a strange thing how little in general people know about the sky. It is the part of creation in which nature has done more for the sake of pleasing man, more for the sole and evident purpose of talking to him and teaching him, than in any other of her works.
> —JOHN RUSKIN, *MODERN PAINTERS*[1]

The sky was the insipid color of skimmed milk as I poked my way through the faintly dystopian premises of an industrial park to meet Govinda Sah at his South Wimbledon studio. Surely, I thought, an artist who grew up in southeastern Nepal, not far from the foothills of the Himalayas, then lived in the Kathmandu Valley, must feel uninspired gazing out at this less than dramatic vista. From the home of the world's highest peaks to the penultimate stop on the Northern Line seemed a rather precipitous decline in natural wonder.

Looking out the artist's studio window, I posed a rather cynical question to him: had he found inspiration in England precisely because of such banality? Had the dreary indignities of British winters forced him to look inwards to conjure the kinds of sublimity he once had on his doorstep? Impervious to sullen self-indulgence, Govinda refused to take the bait. With infectious enthusiasm, he insisted that there was something truly remarkable about English skies. Where I saw fog, Govinda spied clouds capable of racing across the horizon, an unusual phenomenon in the deep valleys of his homeland.

Clouds have long been a source of inspiration for Govinda. In his student years, he recalls painting *en plein air* in the early morning, watching the rising sun melt away the mist around Kathmandu, with molten clouds bubbling up like froth over the face of the mountains. He was just as enraptured by the cloud studies of John Constable and the stormy seascapes

---

1. Ruskin, *Modern Painters*, Vol. 1, Part 2, Section 3, Chapter 1.

of J. M. W. Turner, which he saw reproduced in the art books he assiduously saved up to buy. After earning his Bachelor's Degree in Fine Art in Nepal and an MFA in Bangladesh, he moved to London in 2007 to pursue a second MFA at Wimbledon College of Art. Stepping into Tate Britain, he realized for the first time that Turner was English. He recalls:

> I hadn't bothered to read the text in those books, but just went straight to the pictures! When I first saw the actual works, it was as though I was filled with the spirit of this artist who taught me so many things. What Turner did was really extraordinary, and I consider myself—honestly—to be one of his disciples . . . Later, when I saw Constable's paintings at the National Gallery, I realized I was living in the place which produced these two great masters . . . it definitely confirmed how right I was to come to England. That's karma, if you like!

During his studies in London, Govinda's disparate sources of inspiration began to coalesce into a singular vision. The insights he had gleaned from his studies of nature, both in Asia and Europe, fused organically with the images he admired from past art. Indeed, some of the appeal of Govinda's paintings lies precisely in our inability to disentangle the two. As Ruskin observed, our mental picture of clouds is replete with "blue and white reminiscences of the old masters."[2] Govinda does not just paint clouds, he paints what we *believe* they look like, observed through the prism of the art historical past.

Yet it would be a mistake to think of Govinda's paintings simply as skyscapes. In recent years, Govinda has become just as interested in cosmology as meteorology. While never simply illustrative, many of the paintings Govinda has produced this decade evoke the extraordinary phenomena witnessed by the Hubble Telescope. *Apocalypse* (2010) and *Illusion and Truth* (2011) blast outwards like supernovae, while *Begin* (2010) and *Untitled* (2012) crackle like nebulae, an effect he achieves through his signature process of blending acrylic and oil paints—an anathema to most painters! At times, Govinda makes cosmological connections explicit in his titles, as in *Birth of a Star* (2010; **Fig. 1.1**). On several occasions, the artist has spoken at international conferences dedicated to exploring the intersections between art and science, and enjoyed fruitful conversations with astrophysicists.

2. Ruskin, *Modern Painters*, Vol. 1, Part 2, Section 3, Chapter 1.

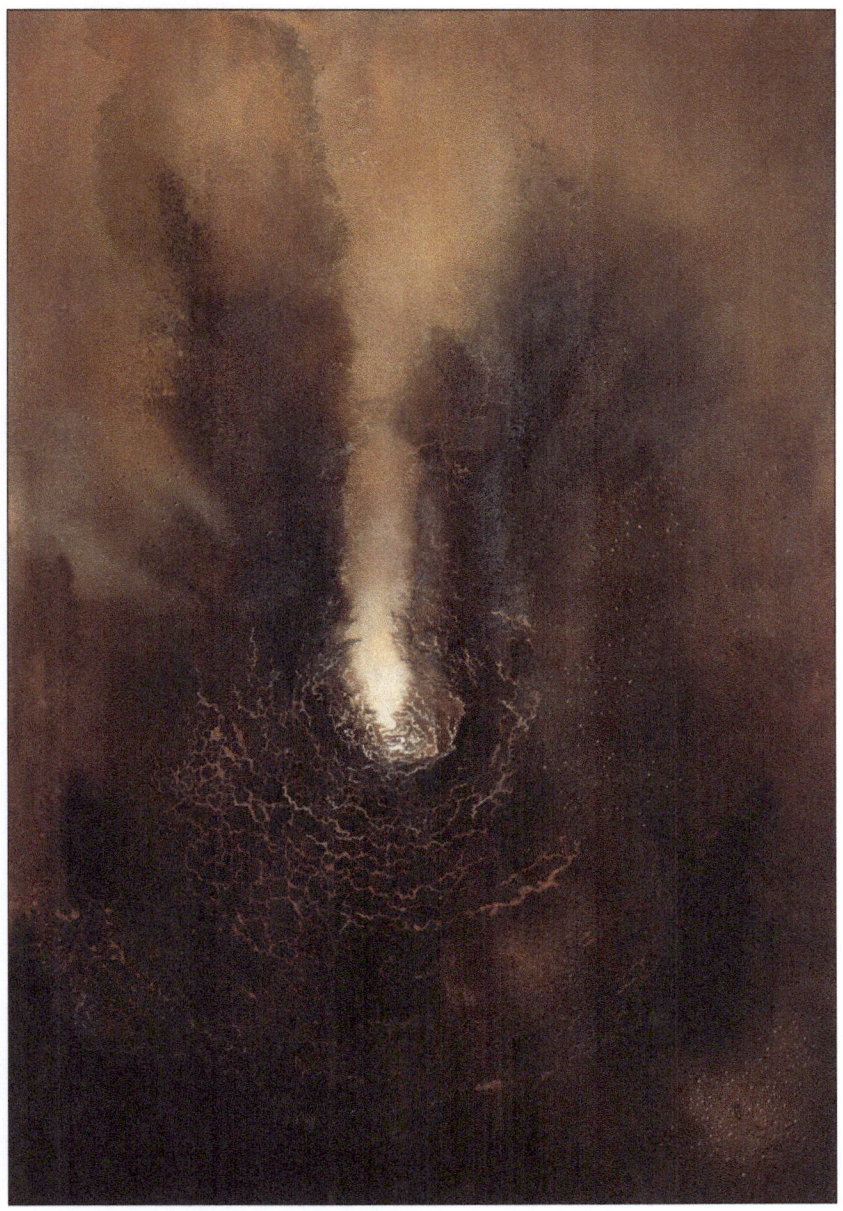

Figure 1.1

Rather than obviating the need for artistic depiction, recent discoveries have required the imagination of artists more than ever. This was powerfully demonstrated recently when a team of scientists announced that LIGO had for the first time detected gravitational waves, as theorized by Albert Einstein, in the form of minute variances in space-time from the collision of black holes a billion light-years away. For many people, the only hope of grasping some sense of such esoteric phenomena was through the rendering of artists. One could easily imagine Govinda being tasked to depict such phenomena, and indeed his canvases with cut-away centers strikingly evoke, among other things, the nullity of black holes. But what I suspect inspires scientists the most about Govinda's work is not how his images parallel their discoveries, but how they anticipate spectacles yet to be experienced, or even imagined.

Guided by what the painter Wassily Kandinsky called the artist's "inner need,"[3] Govinda imagines a cosmos of boundless possibilities. The questions he asks in his work are just as much those of the theologian as theoretical physicist. And indeed, Govinda does not see a radical difference between the two disciplines, which both pursue truth, as they understand it, at the outer reaches of human conception. "Knowledge exists outside all of us," comments Govinda, "and for me, painting is the activity by which I reach out to discover it. The truth isn't within us: it surrounds us."[4] While many contemporary artists shy away from talking about truth, preferring instead to speak of culturally constructed meanings and the incertitude of signs, Govinda feels completely at home with such diction, unabashedly invoking theological concerns. His titles confirm these interests, including *Illusion and Truth* (2011), *Salvation* (2011; **Fig. 1.2**), *Transcendence* (2013), and *Infinity/Depth* (2018; **Fig. 1.3**). What is notable in these names, and even more so in conversation with the artist, is his deep yet eclectic approach to religion. He moves nimbly, without anxiety, between Western and Eastern points of reference, invoking Milton's epic Christian poem on the one hand, and the Buddhist concept of *maya* (illusion) on the other.

This equanimity owes a great deal to the religious milieu of the artist's native country. Nepal's 2011 census confirmed Hinduism as the faith of an overwhelming majority of Nepalis at 81.3 percent, with Buddhism at 9 percent and much smaller percentages adhering to Islam or ancestral

---

3. Kandinsky, *Concerning the Spiritual in Art*, 32–35.
4. Govinda Sah interviewed by Gerard Houghton, *A Sense of Wonder*, unpaginated.

religions.[5] Despite these numbers, which suggest clear divisions between Hinduism and Buddhism, a strong connection with the Buddha runs across religious boundaries. Siddhartha Gautama, as the Buddha is otherwise known, is believed by many to have been born in the region, and is worshiped as a divinity by many Hindus in Nepal. Growing up, Govinda recalls, no one he knew overtly identified themselves as either Hindu or Buddhist, and if there was a difference it was best measured by a spectrum of beliefs, rather than dogmatic boundaries. The lives of his family and community were saturated with religion—witnessed in a widespread commitment to social duties entailed by *dharma*, and a range of devotional practices—but untroubled by definitions.

Figure 1.2

5. National Population and Housing Census, 2012.

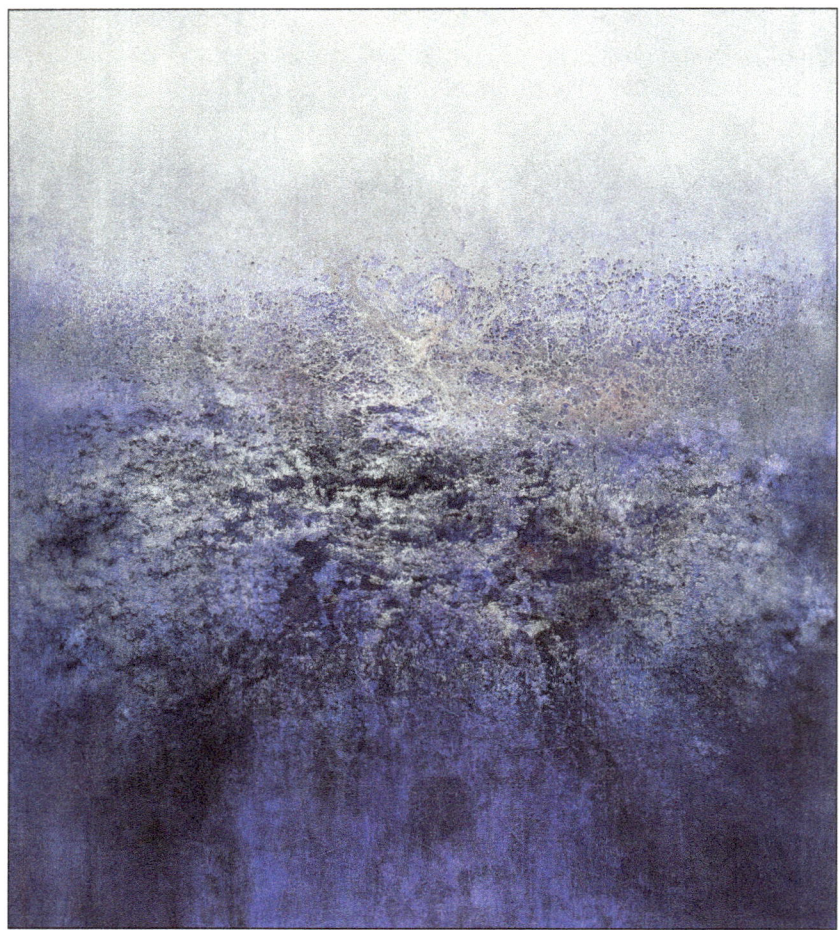

Figure 1.3

Govinda remains proud of this religious inclusivity, a part of his national heritage that he believes was violently compromised by Maoist rebels, who fomented Civil War in Nepal from 1996–2006. In his first mature paintings, Govinda painted interiors of local temples and sculptures of gods, whom he sometimes pictured levitating against the kind of swirling backgrounds that would later occupy the foreground of his work. Govinda intended these devotional images, he recalls, as icons of tolerance and resistance, defying Maoist ideology, which offered vague promises of social improvement while encouraging violence that made progress impossible. However, Govinda did not paint religion as a panacea. While his depictions of rituals affirmed traditional order and observance over and against in-surrection, they also critiqued false piety, questioning how best to follow religious imperatives in a changing society.

In the mid-2000s, during a time of tremendous change for both Nepal and the artist himself, the imagery of Govinda's can-vases began to evolve. The figures of divinities and devotees that once populated his paintings began to disappear and the celestial dramas of his mature work began to take shape. As overtly religious symbolism faded from his canvases, however, metaphysical questions increasingly percolated to the surface: Why is there something instead of nothing? Why, and when, is there order instead of chaos? Is divinity immanent or tran-scendent? Intuitively, Govinda began to shape responses to these questions in the technique and structure of his canvases. In *The Shadow is Darker than Black* (2014), he trades sackcloth for canvas, covering it with chalky black paint. From a distance, it appears solid, but on closer inspection the perforated surface allows tiny pinpricks of light to poke through like a con-stellation. What appears to be a painting about absence becomes, paradoxi-cally, a piece about presence.

In another technical innovation, Govinda recently completed a series marked by streaks of smoke, deftly breathed onto the canvas like brush-strokes. In one of Govinda's largest works to date, *In Between* (2015), smoke billows up from the bottom of the composition before igniting into a lumi-nous shower of color, like the grand finale in a display of fireworks. Even when he paints tempestuous skies and cosmic explosions, Govinda seems to find himself drawn, ineluctably, towards an underlying order. The celes-tial forms that unfurl across his compositions do so with axial symmetry, evoking the structure of mandalas, the cosmic "maps" common in Nepal-ese art. Occasionally, Govinda begins his canvases with a grid. Even as he pushes himself toward the unknown, it seems Govinda cannot imagine a universe without logic and purpose.

These blasts of astral energy might also be interpreted as signals of divine presence. In the Bhagavad Gita—the Hindu Scriptures that Govinda keeps by his studio window—the warrior Arjuna beseeches Lord Krishna to reveal himself in his universal form. Krishna subsequently bestows Ar-juna with "divine eyes" (11.8), whereupon the Gita reveals:

> If hundreds of thousands of suns rose up at once into the sky, they might resemble the effulgence of the Supreme Person in that uni-versal form. At that time Arjuna could see in the universal form of

the Lord the unlimited expansions of the universe situated in one place although divided into many, many thousands (11.12–13).

If gods no longer occupy the center of Govinda's canvases, as they did in much of his earlier work, divinity has by no means disappeared. It is simply everywhere instead of somewhere, transcendent instead of immanent.

Govinda identifies God with Nature, but not in the dry, deterministic manner espoused by Spinoza.[6] Divinity for Govinda is not merely another way to describe the mechanisms of the universe, but an active, palpable presence in the world around us. Clouds, he tells me—in a way that seems to stretch beyond metaphor—are the earth "inhaling and exhaling." Nature can also be violent, as the artist knows all too well from the devastating earthquake which struck central Nepal in April, 2015, while Govinda was visiting family. When he was finally able to return to London, Govinda recalls that for months he had trouble believing the earth was solid under his feet. In his dreams, he continued to feel the aftershocks with terrifying proximity. Govinda regards such natural disasters as reminders that the earth has its own life, and its own furious way of recalibrating and reasserting its power in the face of human-made changes. Although Govinda has been painting cracks in his canvases for several years—with such illusionistic prowess that from a distance they often look like flaking paint—the Gorkha Earthquake lent these fissures a jarring immediacy. The cosmic explosions in Govinda's canvases are, at the same time, seismic convulsions. The entire universe seems to rattle and rumble with terrifying power.

This sublime imagery has a venerable provenance. In *Modern Painting and the Northern Romantic Tradition*, Robert Rosenblum hypothesized a common thread connecting Turner, Caspar David Friedrich, and other titans of nineteenth century landscape painting to twentieth century Abstract Expressionists such as Mark Rothko and Clyfford Still. Rosenblum lavishes special attention on Augustus Vincent Tack, whose craggy forms, like Govinda's, defy easy divisions between abstraction and figuration. In Tack, Rosenblum notes both "thundering chaos" and "awe-inspiring symmetry," a binary that serves just as well to describe the tensions at play in Govinda's work.[7] For Rosenblum, such qualities are born out of an attempt "to find, in a secular world, a convincing means of expressing those religious experiences that, before the Romantics, had been channeled into

6. Spinoza, *Ethics*, Part IV, Preface, 188.

7. Rosenblum, *Modern Painting and the Northern Romantic Tradition*, 198.

the traditional themes of Christian art."[8] Visually, Govinda fits perfectly into Rosenblum's genealogy, extending the tradition of the Northern Romantics into the twenty-first century. But what about the cultural dynamic sketched by Rosenblum? Coming from a country replete with religious imagery, from traditional *thangkas* to mass-produced posters, Govinda's problem was never how to *find* the spiritual, but rather how to *share* it. The impulse to "seek the sacred," as Rosenblum puts it, assumes that the sacred has been either hidden or lost.[9] For Govinda, neither is true. The sacred surrounds us. We need only learn to look with "divine eyes."

2. Jeffrey Rubinoff: A Tribe of His Own

The reclusive artist, toiling in obscurity on the edges of the earth, has become the white whale of the contemporary art historian. Every year a fresh tide of doctoral theses attempt to pluck some artist from the unknown in order to raise him or her up as an unheralded genius, worthy of elevation into the canon. But the truly great artist, working beyond the gaze of the all-seeing eye of the art market, remains an almost mythical species.

When I received an invitation to meet the Canadian Jewish sculptor Jeffrey Rubinoff on Hornby Island, part of the archipelago of Gulf Islands accessible from Vancouver only by a series of ferries—or a rattling sea plane in my case—I suspected I was on a futile quest. I hoped to see some killer whales frolicking in the sound, and the frosted mountaintops for which British Columbia is famous, but I reckoned the artist's work would be inoffensive at best. While the orcas eluded me, I found something even more remarkable: the entire oeuvre of a major artist, almost completely neglected by critics and scholars, gathered in a single site.

Up a pebbly, unmarked driveway, branching off the appropriately rustic-sounding Shingle Spit Road, the Jeffrey Rubinoff Sculpture Park opens up unexpectedly through the trees. Bounded on one side by a mountain ridge and on the other by a sweeping vista of the shoreline, the park has been reclaimed from the forest—which continually threatens to reabsorb it—in order to accommodate a sprawling field replete with streams, ponds,

8. Rosenblum, *Modern Painting and the Northern Romantic Tradition*, 195.

9. Rosenblum, *Modern Painting and the Northern Romantic Tradition*, 218.

and shaggy outcrops. Carefully nestled into position in order to respond to the landscape, Rubinoff has erected over one hundred steel sculptures, ranging from colossal geometric abstractions to willowy, naturalistic forms, which together span more than forty years.

Habitually clad in dungarees, braces, and galoshes, the artist—now in his late sixties[10]—has only recently started giving public tours of the park to Hornby's eclectic mishmash of draft-dodgers, farmers, and tourists. Rarely leaving his estate—to the extent that a sighting of the sculptor in the island's single pub is a bit of an event for the island's 1,000 permanent residents—Rubinoff has lived and worked on site for several decades. In the large, weather-beaten barn at the center of the property, Rubinoff works in complete isolation, operating a personal steel foundry with cranes, presses, saws, and other heavy machinery adapted for single use. Adding to the mystique, no one is allowed inside the studio except his wife, Betty, whom he sometimes permits to watch during casting, when he fears he might ignite himself working with metals heated to over 1,000 degrees Celsius.

Rubinoff's steadfast, singular focus is more evocative of the artistic titans of a bygone era. His language, too, belongs to an earlier generation. Isolated from the prevailing winds of postmodernism, he is an unrepentant modernist, unabashedly invoking grandiose concepts of tradition, destiny, and essence to describe his works. "Art is the map of the human soul," he asserts with the surety of a biblical prophet.[11] "Perfection is the spiritual essence of Art."[12] On the one hand, such pronouncements serve to draw a line in the sand—quite literally for this island hermit—between himself and the contemporary art world. But his insistence on art as a sacred pursuit is more than just an indictment against the moneychangers whom he believes have taken up residence in the temple of art. Rubinoff fervently believes that good art must tap into the fundament of the universal, revealing truths about the human condition.

Rubinoff's spiritual convictions seem more appropriate to the manifestos of the early twentieth century. Indeed, his thinking bears a strong affinity with Wassily Kandinsky, who proclaimed in 1911: "We have before us the age of conscious creation, and this new spirit is going hand in hand with the spirit of thought towards an epoch of great spiritual leaders."[13]

---

10. The artist has since passed away, in 2017, at age seventy-one.

11. Rubinoff, *Art Beyond War*, 10.

12. Rubinoff, *Existential Realities of Post Agriculture*, 20.

13. Kandinsky, *Concerning the Spiritual in Art*, 57.

There is a critical difference between these artists, however. Kandinsky, writing well before the First World War, was certain that art and society were steaming ahead towards a utopian future. For Rubinoff, we are doing the very opposite, propelling ourselves further and further away from all that is good and pure. Born in 1945, in the immediate aftermath of the Second World War—"in the shadow of the Endgame" as he memorably puts it[14]—Rubinoff believes that we must look to the past for the "spiritual essence of Art," not to a future which may never come.

Rubinoff is obsessed with origins. Only by moving backward, he claims, can we recover an untainted vision of humanity, free from "tribalism."[15] He is convinced that if we are willing to peel away the accumulated layers of history—artistic, natural, and religious—we will discover a common point of origin that predates our particularities, and the conflicts they fuel. But the matter is never so simple for a Jew, and here Rubinoff raises unfashionable but important questions about Jewish identity. To what extent can Jewish particularity coexist with universality? Does the former always negate the latter? For the sculptor, as indeed for many other contemporary Jews, the search for the universal remains conditioned by Jewish questions of heritage and genealogy. Moreover, strategies for evading religious and cultural particularity—in Rubinoff's case, art-historical and evolutionary—often serve to reinforce it. Ultimately, I want to suggest, what makes Rubinoff's art most universal is actually his failure to circumvent his Jewishness.

Rubinoff has a deep appreciation of his family's Jewish history, especially the harrowing experiences of his grandfather and father in the Russian Pale of Settlement, in present-day Belarus. He himself grew up in rural Ontario, Canada, where his mother and father—who went on to make a fortune in real estate and hotel development—owned a large farm; "a dream for Russian Jewish peasants."[16] Although his parents were a strong presence in the Jewish community, they "picked [Jewish tradition] from a menu," according to the artist, and took observance with a grain of salt.[17] While Rubinoff's parents ensured he had a *bar mitzvah*, his formative Jewish experience came several years later. Like many Jews of his generation, he remembers being riveted by the trial of Adolf Eichmann in Jerusalem

14. Rubinoff, *Through the Lens of the Endgame*, 2.

15. Rubinoff, *Art Beyond War*, 9.

16. Personal interview with Jeffrey Rubinoff, Hornby Island, British Columbia, Canada, May 20, 2013.

17. Personal interview with Jeffrey Rubinoff.

in 1961, and the accounts he read by Hannah Arendt and others afterward. For Rubinoff, the toxic ideology of racial purity that led to the Holocaust was, above all, the malignant symptom of tribalism. "I regard tribalism," he writes, "not as a genetic inevitability but as a cultural pathogen."[18] But while he views Jews as history's greatest victims of tribalism, they are not immune to the illness either. Indeed, Rubinoff seems to have the Hebrew Bible in mind when he cautions against "any tribal mythology that harbors divine favor at its center."[19] The only sure way to stave off the maladies of tribalism, according to Rubinoff, is to rely on an equally powerful anti- dote: art. From Rubinoff's perspective, the Second Commandment—the so-called prohibition against graven images—is downright lethal if taken literally. Jews, perhaps more than any other tribe, need art. But, he cau- tions, they do not need *Jewish* art.

Rubinoff positively bristles when I ask whether he minds being called a "Jewish artist." Echoing the sentiments of Mark Rothko, Barnett New- man, and many of the other Jewish Abstract Expressionists he admires, Rubinoff finds the term "offensive."[20] And yet, Rubinoff's ideas about art remain stubbornly entwined with his thoughts about Judaism. While Ru- binoff makes no effort to establish a lineage of Jewish artists for himself— citing Donatello and Michelangelo as his precursors *par excellence*[21]—his *concept* of genealogy bears a palpable affinity with Jewish ideas of ancestry. What he impugns as "tribal" in a religious context, he hails as "original" and "authentic" when it comes to art history. Rubinoff writes:

> I realized that to make original art with artistic depth I would have to return to the lineage of the ancestors—the history of art by art- ists. So began a dialogue with the ancestors, artist to artist via the work itself.[22]

Like the Oral Torah passed down through the prophets, sages, and rab- bis, Rubinoff presents art history as a sacred transmission between great artists. According to Rubinoff, artists alone—unmolested by critics or historians—have perceived the "encoded spirit of art manifest in the es- sence of liberation and originality passed from generation to generation

---

18. Rubinoff, *Art Beyond War*, 9.

19. Rubinoff, *Art Beyond War*, 9.

20. Personal interview with Jeffrey Rubinoff.

21. Rubinoff, *Through the Lens of the Endgame*, 8–9.

22. Rubinoff, *Art Beyond War*, 3.

of artists."[23] The universal "spirit of art" becomes the birthright of an elite sect of artistic geniuses for whom—paradoxically—originality is itself inherited. Thus, while Rubinoff claims to reject Jewish tradition, he seems desperate to form his own tribe to fill the vacuum. It hardly seems like a coincidence that when Rubinoff makes his regular pilgrimage to Italy to "revisit the ancestors," he insists on paying his respects, above all, to Michelangelo's *Moses* (1513–16).[24]

While the Old Masters have done the most to shape Rubinoff's sense of art history, formally he takes his inspiration from the recent past of postwar British and American sculpture. In his work from the early seventies, Rubinoff frequently included pyramids of COR-TEN steel, recalling Barnett Newman's iconic *Broken Obelisk* (1963–69). In *Series One* (**Fig. 2.1**), which Rubinoff considers his first major suite of sculptures, he turned to Newman's contemporary, David Smith. He took off where Smith left off in his late *Cubi* series (1961–65), emulating the brushed texture of Smith's stainless steel polyhedrons. At the same time, there is a strong indication of Rubinoff's rapidly growing confidence and ingenuity in these works, as he attempted to introduce a greater sense of motion than his predecessor, welding together blocks that cascade to the earth in multiple directions. Rubinoff has made a point of tracking down and studying as many of Smith's sculptures in person as possible. Tellingly, during his 1993 visit to Israel he claims that his greatest highlight was not his trip to the Wailing Wall, or any other religious sites, but rather seeing Smith's *Cubi VI* (1963) at the Israel Museum.[25] Rubinoff would freely admit that he discovered his roots in the hills of Jerusalem, but ironically these roots turned out to be artistic rather than Jewish.

After exploring mechanical structures in *Series Two*, in which the shimmering sculptures seem to take inspiration from the very instruments which forged them, in *Series Three* Rubinoff pared his vocabulary down to flat sheets of COR-TEN steel. Here he utilizes some of the same rusted, planar forms as Sir Anthony Caro. However, Rubinoff achieves a sense of springiness and lift absent from Caro's sculptures in the same period. Rubinoff also began to develop the hallmark of his mature work, creating sculptures that impress viewers with their weight and scale without

23. Rubinoff, *Through the Lens of the Endgame*, 13.
24. Personal interview with Jeffrey Rubinoff.
25. Personal interview with Jeffrey Rubinoff.

overwhelming them; drawing them in, rather than threatening to crush them in the fashion of Richard Serra's tilting arcs.

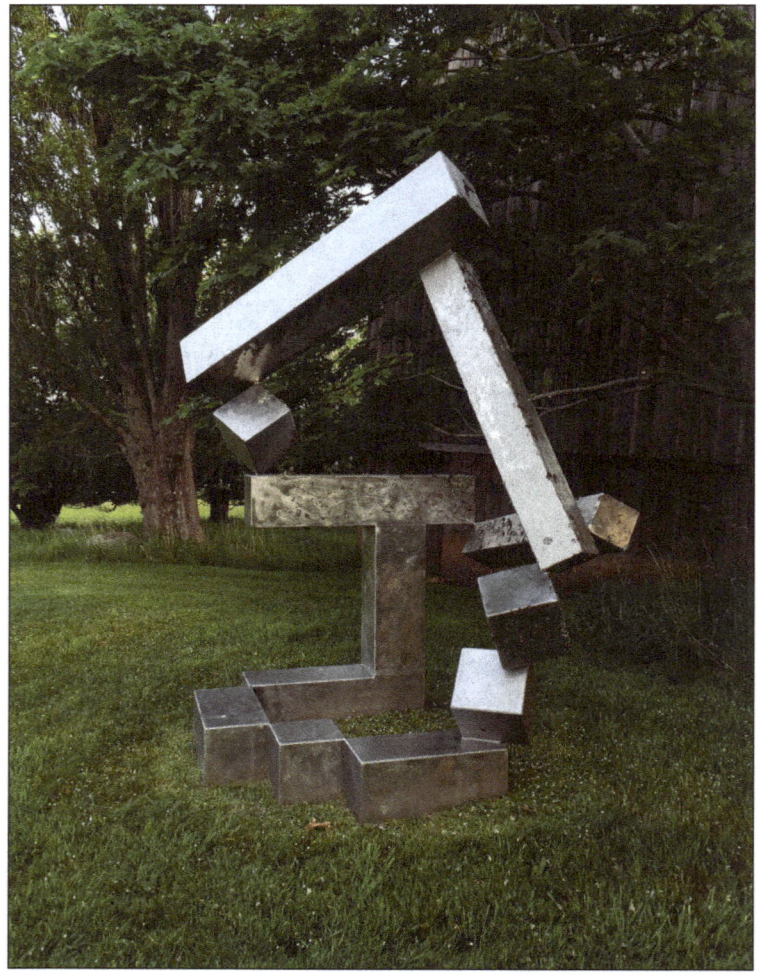

Figure 2.1

In *Series Four*, probably Rubinoff's most accomplished grouping, his components became even heavier and more individualized, while the relationship between forms becomes increasingly complex. Although their shapes evoke comparisons with everything from grinding teeth to engine turbines and defunct artillery, the works remain steadfastly abstract (**Fig. 2.2**). Unexpectedly, however, Jewish history intrudes into these ostensibly universal structures. Rubinoff was stunned to learn after constructing *Series Four* that much of the steel used in these works derived from Krupp, the German conglomerate favored by Hitler for the production of armaments, which relied extensively upon Jewish slave labor. For Rubinoff, the realization that the Holocaust could penetrate "even here," in his remote Arcadia of Hornby Island[26]—half a world and half a century away from Nazi Germany—sounds a call to vigilance against "Resurgent Tribalism." At the same time, his sensitivity to these connections bears witness to the artist's deep, albeit reluctant, Jewish bonds.

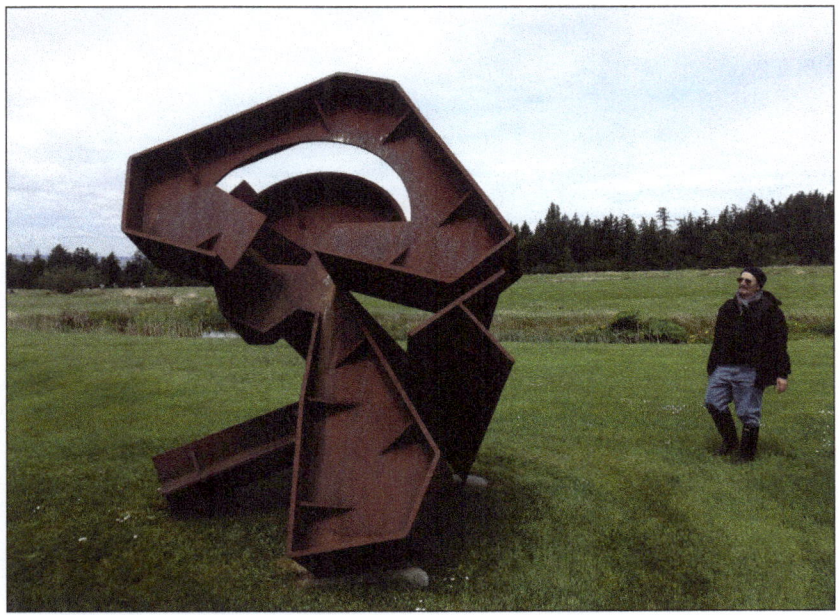

Figure 2.2

Over the past two decades, Rubinoff's genealogical impulse has increasingly driven him toward the prehistoric past in pursuit of a universal reference point. "Since 1989," Rubinoff writes, "I have been extending the history of art deep into evolutionary history";[27] a project which eventually led him to Charles Darwin's *On the Origin of Species* as "a handbook for creativity in

---

26. Personal interview with Jeffrey Rubinoff.
27. Rubinoff, *Through the Lens of the Endgame*, 4.

the studio."[28] While Rubinoff previously eschewed figurative imagery, fearing that this would solder his works to specific interpretations, the presumed universality of the deep past relieved these anxieties. In *Series Six, Seven,* and *Eight,* Rubinoff crafted his first explicitly figurative pieces, even giving them individual names for the first time, like an excited naturalist cataloguing a hoard of freshly discovered specimens. In fact, two works from *Series Six, Burgess 1* (**Fig. 2.3**) and 2, directly reference the Burgess Shale in the Canadian Rockies, home to an important trove of middle Cambrian fossils. Not only does evolutionary history provide a new source for Rubinoff's art, the subject also allows him to penetrate deeper into the history of art. Where he began his career exploring the late cuboid works of Smith, in his own later work Rubinoff draws upon Smith's early, Surrealist works. It is tempting to see a playful one-upmanship in Rubinoff's Cambrian sculptures, as if he is determined to do Smith's *Jurassic Bird* (1945) one better, proposing a Paleozoic precursor to Smith's Mesozoic creation.

In 1959, Smith argued that modern artists, including abstractionists, were just as concerned with nature as artists had always been. What had changed, he speculated, was the artist. "Identifying himself as the artist," Smith wrote, "he becomes his own subject as one of the elements in nature. He no longer dissects it, nor moralizes upon it; he is its part."[29] Nature, in other words, is a domain of self-revelation. Similarly, while Rubinoff sets off on his voyages into natural history in order to tell us something about the origins of our species, ultimately he reveals just as much about his own origins—or, more precisely—his *approach* to origins. What most excites Rubinoff about the study of our biological roots is the hope that we might uncover an ur-text that reveals our artistic and ethical gifts in their purest, most powerful form. Speaking about the human genome, his eyes glitter as he declares: "The text is there!"[30] Whether Rubinoff is conscious of it or not, there is a deep similarity here to the way in which he talks about Jewish heritage. "I'm not sure what Jewish culture is," he told me in an unguarded moment, "but there's something you carry around with you."[31] While Rubinoff might worry that such connections dilute the universality of his message, I would wager the opposite. After all, there's nothing more universal than the story of an individual grappling with his religious and cultural identity.

28. Rubinoff, *Art Beyond War,* 9.
29. Smith, "Tradition and Identity," 767.
30. Personal interview with Jeffrey Rubinoff.
31. Personal interview with Jeffrey Rubinoff.

Rubinoff may not want a tribe, but it wouldn't be the first time a Jew got something he didn't bargain for in the wilderness.

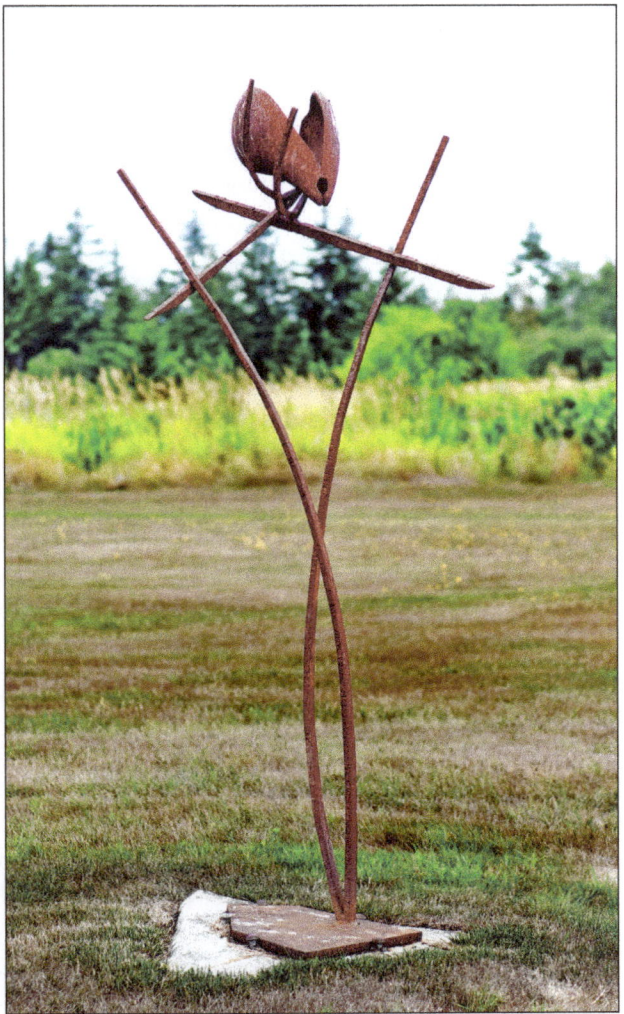

Figure 2.3

3. Carole Berman: Garden Carpets of Eden

"I am drawn again and again to the place of creation, a place of being and becoming," writes Carole Berman.[32] In the decade I have known her, I have watched her carefully sift through traditions, stories, and histories to reach just such a place. Like an archaeologist uncovering the strata in an ancient *tel*, nothing is too small to note, record, and preserve. In this essay, I want to explore how Berman's self-investigations—often arising out of intensely personal imagery from dreams and memories—consistently lead her to important sites of religious and cultural intersection.

For many years, Berman has been at work on a series of paintings and sculptures exploring the Foundation Stone in the Dome of the Rock in Jerusalem. In Jewish tradition, this stone is the place where Creation began, where Abraham nearly sacrificed his son, and where Solomon built the First Temple. According to Islamic tradition, it is also the place from which Muhammad made his Night Journey into heaven to meet Abraham, Moses, and Jesus, leaving behind a footprint in the rock. After years examining the Foundation Stone, the legendary site of Creation, it seems only natural that Berman's search for origins has recently taken her into the garden of Eden, a subject she alluded to in early works such as *In the Midst of the Garden* (2001; **Fig. 3.1**). Paradise, like the Foundation Stone, is the patrimony of multiple faiths, and Judaism, Christianity, and Islam each offer a wealth of traditions concerning Paradise. For Christians—especially since Saint Augustine—Eden has been viewed preeminently as the site of original sin. And it is this Eden, both beautiful and damned, which has dominated Western art. Berman's Paradise owes more to Judaism and Islam. While both recognize the eating of the forbidden fruit as a sinful act, neither turn this sin into an ontological condition. There are debates in both Judaism and Islam about where the Garden (*ha-gan*, in Hebrew, *al-jannah* in Arabic) might exist. Beyond geographical speculation, however, they seem to agree that the Garden holds not just primordial but eschatological significance. We might have left one garden, in other words, but another awaits us in the afterlife. Jewish and Islamic writers have each sketched enticing visions of this paradise; a resplendent oasis said to be flowing with streams of water, wine, milk, and honey. It is this garden, a place of both past and future, which seems to inspire Berman's paintings.

---

32. Personal correspondence with Carole Berman, November 5, 2017.

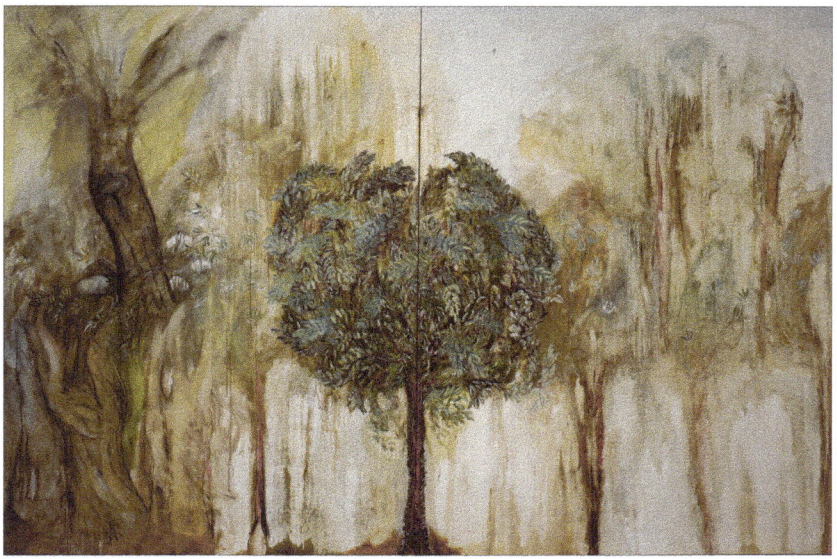

Figure 3.1

Where dreams provided a path to the Foundation Stone, childhood memories offered Berman an entry into Eden. The home of her maternal grandparents had a beautiful garden, and it was here, the artist recalls, that she had her first intimation of paradise. Photographs of this immaculate garden—with a rose garden, fountains, and statues—lie at the center of *Gold Carpet Painting* (2016) and *Green Gold Carpet Painting* (2016). Indeed, even interior scenes from her grandparents' house abound with freshly cut flowers from the family garden, as seen in *Red Carpet Painting* (2017) and *Vase Carpet Painting* (2016), turning indoor and outdoor alike into a veritable Arcadia. At times, these photographic flowers seem to pollinate the rest of the composition, lending inspiration to the floral abstractions that blossom in the margins. At other times, the painted flowers seem to take seed inside the photographs, playing the part of volunteers, as gardeners say. There is a witty interplay between different media, perhaps best seen in *Red Carpet Painting*, in which the artist paints a lotus atop a photograph of a garden carpet—all part of a canvas that itself becomes a carpet. Rather than sharp distinctions between foreground and background, these elements interweave on a single picture plane, reminiscent of Henri Matisse's classic *Red Studio* (1911). This playful referentiality extends across the series at large. If one looks carefully at the central photograph in *Vase Carpet Painting* there is a drawing of Solomon and Sheba by the young Berman, proudly positioned on her grandparents' mantle. These same archetypal lovers return, twenty-seven years later in *Conference of the Birds* (**Fig. 3.2**). Chronological as well as spatial distinctions fade away in Berman's carpet paintings. The past becomes lovingly, eternally present. And it is this timelessness, even more than the lush, verdant designs of these works, which makes them Edenic.

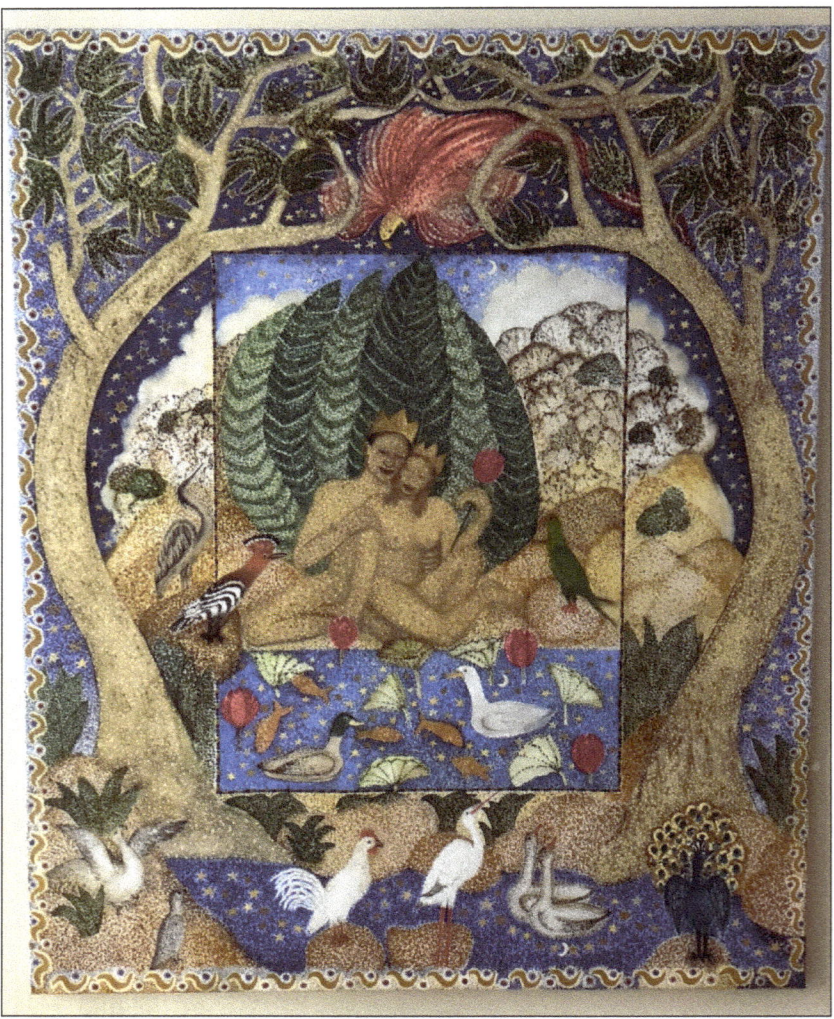

Figure 3.2

The motif of the garden carpet allows the artist to braid together different strands of memory from different periods in her life. As a child, she grew up playing on the vibrant Oriental rugs that adorned the homes of her grandparents and parents. Later, while working at Sotheby's in her twenties, she developed a deep and formative friendship with Jack Franses, the auction house's renowned textile expert, who specialized in Islamic carpets and tapestries. Franses's passion left an indelible imprint, and throughout her life Berman has continued to visit the Victoria & Albert Museum's textile collections for inspiration. Indeed, both *Gold Carpet Painting* and *Red Carpet Painting* draw inspiration from specific masterworks in the museum's Islamic galleries. Carpets have even entered her dreams, including one she still recalls from decades ago, in which she found herself climbing up an infinite chain of rugs—a sort of Jacob's ladder—reaching up and over the Himalayas. She did a painting inspired by this dream early in her career, and while she has only recently returned to painting images of carpets, she did create some paintings in the 1990s inspired by the Cluny tapestries. One might even argue that Berman's dotted brushwork owes a greater debt to the extraordinary stitching of Persian carpets—sometimes populated by as many as 8,000 knots per square inch—than the pointillist paintings of Georges Seurat.

Craftsmanship, of course, is but one aspect of a Persian carpet. The classic garden carpet does not just fill space, as people are accustomed to thinking about rugs in the West, it *creates* space. The classic carpet design takes inspiration from the *chahar bagh*, or fourfold garden, favored by the Savafid dynasty in early modern Iran; a famous example of which lies in the lush central square of Isfahan, the dynasty's opulent capital. Such lavish gardens, replete with splashing water features, ample shade, and fragrant fruit trees, were themselves intended to anticipate the perfect pleasures of the afterlife. Seen in this context, the garden carpet is nothing less than an ideal image—or, better yet, map—of paradise. By painting garden carpets, Berman adds her own layer to a rich and complicated mimetic trail. If this route seems circuitous, that is—in fact—the point. Eden, Berman suggests, is not the property of a single religious or cultural tradition. Rather, it is to be found by creatively following the clues and traces embedded in multiple traditions. This comes out forcefully in *Shulamith* (**Fig. 3.3**), inspired by an historic rug in the Albert Hall Museum in Jaipur, India. Berman paints Shulamith as a woman of color, inspired by the lover's proud declaration in the Song of Songs: "I am black and beautiful" (1:5). Naked yet unabashed, Shulamith is encircled by a cloak with soft, curving folds reminiscent of Henry Moore's *Mother and Child: Hood* (1983) in St. Paul's Cathedral, London. She is framed by the arch of a Safavid mosque, with a Persian *ewer* playfully positioned beside her. In a single "carpet," Berman subtly interlaces Jewish, Christian, and Islamic references to form an inviting picture of Paradise, open to all.

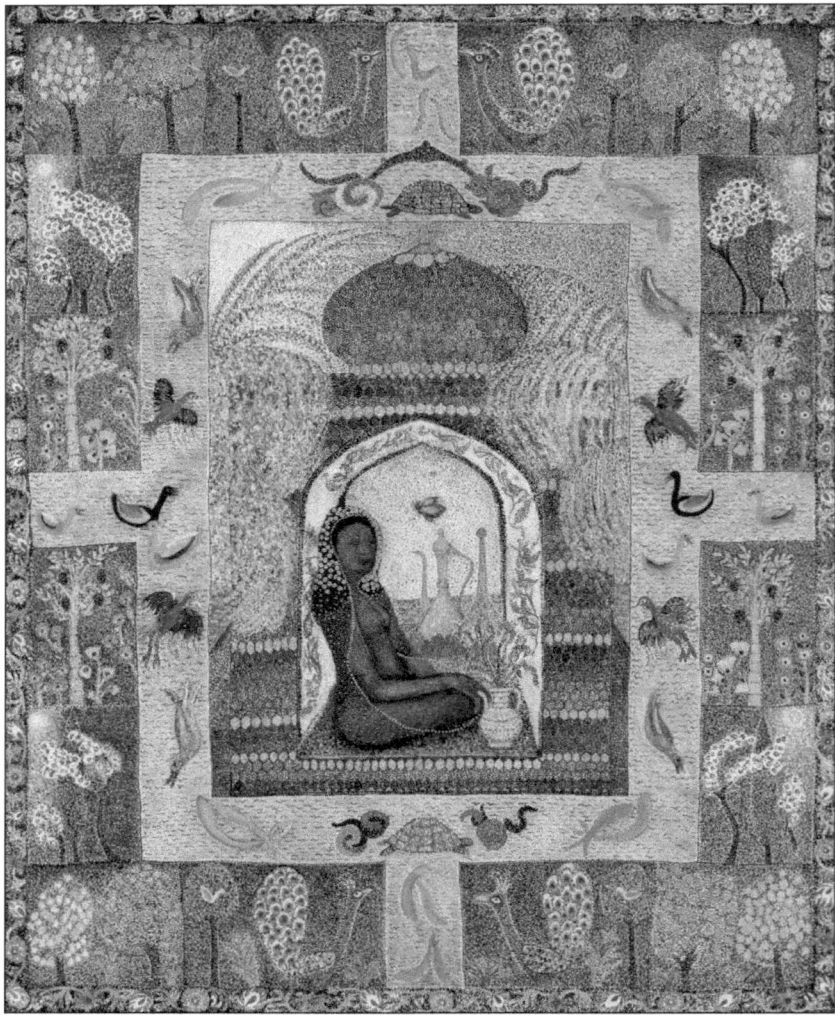

Figure 3.3

This empyrean vision reaches its apogee in *Conference of the Birds* (2017). A nude King Solomon and Queen of Sheba sit at the edge of a water garden, attended to by a "Conference of the Birds," to use the title of Farid Attar's poetic masterpiece from medieval Iran.[33] A striped hoopoe, a wise figure in this Sufic narrative of self-discovery, leans towards the couple, while the mythical phoenix looks on from the firmament. Lotus flowers, symbols of enlightenment in Buddhism, blossom in the pond. And indeed, the figures, wreathed by petals, almost seem to bloom themselves; their sinuous limbs intertwining like serpents. Erotic knowledge, stripped of any disdain, appears as an authentic method and expression of spiritual understanding. The couple might also be read as Adam and Eve. If they do constitute this primal pair, however, there are some important differences. In Genesis, Eve is created from Adam's rib (2:21–22). Here, Adam's fingers—coiled around his partner's midsection—seem to double as her rib cage. Perhaps it is Adam, we might speculate, who derives his existence from Eve. Either way, the figures are entwined in an inseparable embrace, unconcerned by any potential for expulsion. In an image ripe with intertextual associations, love is at least "as strong as death" (Song of Songs 8:6). In Berman's paintings, the human condition is something to be celebrated rather than condemned. Paradise, she hints, is more accessible to us than we think. And more original to us than sin.

33. Attar, *The Conference of the Birds*.

Materials

4. James Balmforth: Material Witness

The hour of the appointment with Matter, the Spirit's great antagonist, had struck . . . —PRIMO LEVI, *THE PERIODIC TABLE*[1]

In the 1960s, Gilbert and George cheekily declared themselves living sculptures. James Balmforth is not one for such coy declarations. And yet, if he would hesitate to call himself a living sculpture, one could say—more seriously—that he lives sculpture. I cannot think of another artist working today in England who is so closely connected to his materials. Every time I see Balmforth—and I suspect one could catch him during breakfast and it would still be the same—he seems to have just emerged from some solitary skirmish in his studio, slicing, soldering, hacking, or riveting some piece of metal. Still, Balmforth is wary of the heroic trope of the modern sculptor. Balmforth is not, nor does he set out to be, Anthony Caro or Richard Serra. He does not wrestle his materials into submission so much as expose their vulnerabilities. There are no mythic victories to be had in Balmforth's studio. The most he delivers, to take the title of one his sculptures, is "myth interrupted."

In this essay, I want to take a close look at how the artist probes not only his chosen materials, but the dynamics of materiality itself. To my mind, Balmforth is a sculptor who breaks things as much as builds them. Or, perhaps even more accurately, he builds things *by breaking them*. On one level, his practice evokes parallels with Auto-Destructive Art, as theorized by Gustav Metzger in the late fifties and early sixties. In his manifesto of March 10, 1960, Metzger decrees:

> Not interested in ruins, (the picturesque).
>
> Auto-destructive art re-enacts the obsession with destruction, the pummeling to

---

1. Levi, *The Periodic Table*, 34.

which individuals and masses are subjected.

Auto-destructive art demonstrates man's power to accelerate disintegrative

processes of nature and to order them.[2]

While Balmforth shares this fascination with disintegration, his creations have a different emphasis. For Metzger, formulating his practice at the height of the Cold War, under the imminent specter of nuclear winter, art could only be truthful if it spoke a language of impermanence, and useful only if it spurred political action. Like Metzger, Balmforth's deconstructions deliberately invite metaphorical interpretations. But where Metzger prophesies extinction, Balmforth discloses entropy, ineptitude, and failure. He does not so much warn us of the end of the world as document its decline.

To delve deeper into the significance of Balmforth's work, it is helpful to think of his works not only as artistic creations but scientific experiments. I have in mind here the reflections of the Italian chemist and writer, Primo Levi. Perhaps more lucidly than any other modern writer, Levi illuminates the imaginative, poetic dimensions of scientific research. In *The Periodic Table*, Levi interweaves autobiographical passages and short stories into chapters inspired by the unique properties of elements, from argon to carbon. Talking to a fellow chemist, recounting tales of their trade over many decades, Levi declares himself unmoved by "the grand chemistry, the triumphant chemistry of colossal plants and dizzying output, because this is collective work and therefore anonymous."[3] Instead, he writes:

> I [am] more interested in the stories of the solitary chemistry, unarmed and on foot, at the measure of a man, which with few exceptions [has] been mine: but it has also been the chemistry of the founders . . . who confronted matter without aids, with their brains and hands, reason and imagination.[4]

The same might be said of Balmforth, for whom "reason and imagination" are similarly entwined. At the heart of his practice lies a naked, earnest encounter with *hyle*—palpable, intractable *stuff*—which Levi would have instantly recognized. And it is the integrity of this engagement, the confrontation with matter in its grimy, unvarnished glory, which lends Balmforth's work

2. Metzger, *Damaged Nature, Auto-Destructive Art*, 59.
3. Levi, *The Periodic Table*, 203.
4. Levi, *The Periodic Table*, 203.

its depth. If he succeeds in disclosing existential truths, it is not, in the first instance, because he goes looking for them. It is because he is willing, like the patient chemist—"unarmed and on foot"—to let matter speak first.

What I want to offer is, in a sense, a lab report. If Balmforth's studio is a laboratory, and his works constitute the fruits of his research, it remains to the critic to evaluate the artist's methods and results. For some writers, Balmforth's methods *are* his results. This approach is important. Balmforth's formal innovations—the way in which he has adapted and transformed the tools and techniques of contemporary sculpture over the past decade—are notable. But what interests me most are those moments in which the artist bears witness to something larger. On the one hand, the corrosions and defacements in Balmforth's work render our world visible at its most broken and banal. And yet, if we look closely, these indignities do something else, too. Like a chemist seeking to isolate and identify a mysterious substance, Balmforth subjects his materials to a battery of tests. Destruction is not an end in itself, I want to argue, but rather a method for discovering what is ineradicable and irreducible: beauty.

From the start of his career, Balmforth has instinctively probed for paradoxes, now a defining characteristic of his oeuvre. His most successful early works centered, ironically, around the concept of failure. In *Movement Towards Diminishing Object* (2009; **Fig. 4.1**), Balmforth placed a roughly hewn chunk of Quartzite on a plinth, with a channel cut part way through the center. Inside the plinth he secreted a motor, which drags a plastic chain through the channel, fostering the illusion that the feeble chain is in fact biting through the rock, progressively cutting it in half. In reality, the motion of the chain is not only futile but self-abnegating. The rough contours of the stone gradually scrape and abrade the plastic chain, until—presumably—it will finally snap. Partially severed, and strapped to the plinth like a sacrificial victim, we expect the stone to be the eponymous "Diminishing Object." What Balmforth provides, however, is a more subtle allegory. The exertions of the captor only serve to emancipate the captive. Failure for the chain leads to freedom for the stone.

The same year he created *Movement Towards Diminishing Object*, Balmforth produced another, even grander monument to futility. *Failed Obelisk* (2009) takes the somber form of an Egyptian monolith and comically transforms it into a wobbling icon of impotence, whose pointed top awkwardly springs from its shaft. The artist explains:

Intended as powerful symbols of permanence, control, stability and a connection to the divine, the Obelisk now fails in its function, affirming instead that everything, including power itself, is constructed and transient, and that the partition between presence and absence remains precarious.[5]

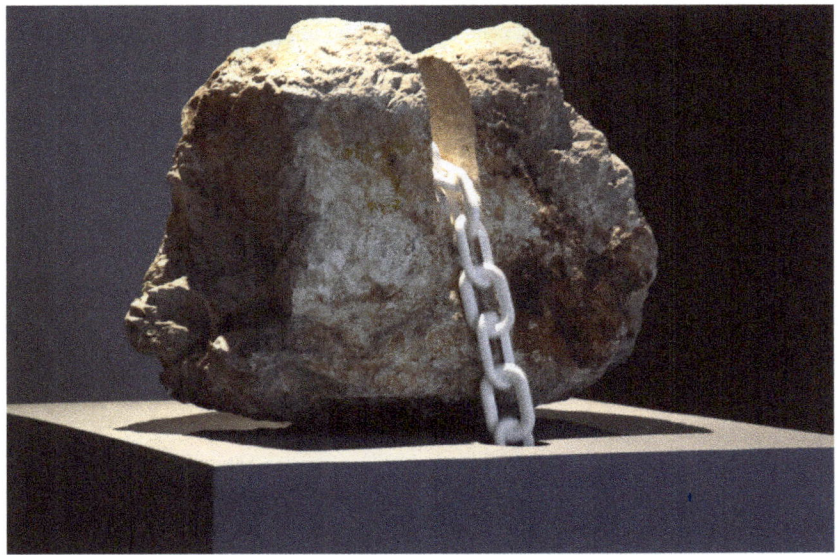

Figure 4.1

In Balmforth's withering critique, not only do the eternal aspirations of the ancients seem suspect, but those of the later empires that have appropriated them. One can only imagine the embarrassment of the Lateran Obelisk in Vatican City, Cleopatra's Needle in London, or the Luxor Obelisk in Paris prematurely popping their tops. Nor would America's capital seem so self-confident were its Washington Monument to start wiggling in the wind. Where Barnett Newman's *Broken Obelisk* (1963–67) elicits pathos, Balmforth's *Failed Obelisk* manages only self-mockery. And yet, perhaps even in this moment there is a measure of dignity. However debased, the obelisk stands ready to accept its humiliation, long after the myth of perfection has fractured and fallen away.

If failure is explicit in *Broken Obelisk*, it is implicit—though no less present—in *Gallium Dagger* (2012; **Fig. 4.2**), which I displayed in my 2015

5. Personal correspondence with James Balmforth, October 11, 2014.

exhibition, *Sacrifice*, at the Jewish Museum in London. While it may look like steel, the dagger's blade is cast in gallium, a curious metal whose existence was predicted by Dmitri Mendeleev before its discovery in the late nineteenth century. Used today in various high-tech creations, from solar panels for the Mars Rover to Blu-ray discs for home entertainment, gallium melts at an unusually low temperature, such that holding this blade in one's hand would be enough to turn it soft and squidgy. Balmforth explicates the reasoning behind the piece:

> A dagger is a symbol of power, but by casting the blade of the dagger in gallium, it now harbours a hidden vulnerability to that which it was designed to influence. With human contact now necessitating a sacrifice of its own, a balance is introduced in the act of exchange between object and subject, creating a new relationship based on mutual affectivity.[6]

The dagger retains its unblemished perfection only so long as it is remains unused. To commit an act of violence—its ostensible purpose as a weapon—would be to expose its fatal flaw. The line between beauty and failure turns out to be razor thin.

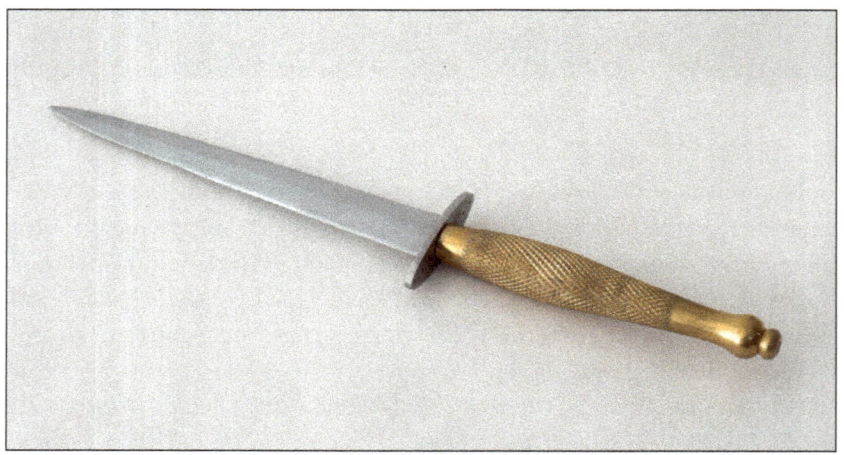

Figure 4.2

While Balmforth has designed a number of his works to fail, as we saw above, he is equally fascinated by the processes of collapse and decay. In a series of works created between 2010 and 2011, Balmforth took to combining

6. Personal correspondence with James Balmforth, August 1, 2015.

rusted steel and brightly colored, self-consciously lumpy blobs of plastic. This unusual marriage constitutes, to my eyes, a kind of *kintsugi*. Following this centuries-old tradition in Japan, potters repair precious pieces of broken ceramics by filling cracks with resin mixed with gold dust, creating shimmering veins which call attention to, and even glory in, the presence of imperfections. Balmforth's *Advance from Disjunction* (2010), and other works of self-conscious mending, such as *Symmetry Collapse* (2014), could be seen as a bold extension of this thinking. Where traditional practitioners of *kintsugi* use precious materials to enhance a shattered object, Balmforth uses mundane adhesives, testing whether we can find beauty in brokenness without embellishment. In *Advance from Disjunction*, the artist joins the legs of a large, rusted chair with deliberately ungainly globules, as if daring the viewer to reject his shoddy sculpture. We might do well to add a question mark to the title: can we "advance from disjunction"? Or are we prepared to see only damage?

Ideas can collapse as well as objects. In *Myth Interrupted* (2011), Balmforth coats a cast-iron lion in lipstick-red plastic. Beside the beast lies a corroded, uncoated wing, which looks as though it has just fallen from the sculpture. Compared to its glossy twin, proudly soaring from the lion's shoulder, the broken wing feels heavy and lifeless. The installation seems to embody not one but several fractured myths. On the one hand, the winged lion recalls Daniel's vision in the Bible, in which the creature represents one of four monstrous powers which shall come to rule the earth. Daniel recounts:

> I, Daniel, saw in my vision by night the four winds of heaven stirring up the great sea, and four great beasts came up out of the sea, different from one another. The first was like a lion and had eagles' wings. Then, as I watched, its wings were plucked off, and it was lifted up from the ground and made to stand on two feet like a human being; and a human mind was given to it. (Daniel 7:2–4)

Perhaps Balmforth's beast will shed a second wing and sprout "a human mind." Or maybe this rusty feline is destined for a less apocalyptic role, like the brazen lion in Venice's Piazza San Marco. The winged lion is a relic from the ancient Middle East, later repurposed and added to by Christian sculptors, who transformed the "pagan" symbol into an emblem of Mark the Evangelist, the patron saint of Venice. Perhaps what Balmforth wants to interrupt, and call attention to, is the very process of myth-making. Every story and every symbol—however corroded—has the potential to be reborn.

There may be no more powerful example of the reinvention of symbols than the crucifix. Historically associated with the most demeaning form of public execution devised by the ancient Romans, in Christian hands the crucifix became an abiding image of triumph over death and the promise of salvation. While, by his own reckoning, he did not intend it to be such at the start, Balmforth created his own crucifix in *Intersection Point* (2015; **Fig. 4.3**). I had the privilege of displaying the work in Methodist Central Hall Chapel in the exhibition *Stations of the Cross*, held in fourteen venues across London in 2016. Hundreds of people prayed before Balmforth's cross in the weeks leading up to Easter. For many, its "X" shape evoked the way Jesus shouldered the cross as he walked, and repeatedly fell, on his way toward Calvary. In Balmforth's sculpture, the image of the stumbling Christ dovetails, unexpectedly, with that of a collapsed building. Combing through the wreckage of Coventry Cathedral after the Blitz, and the World Trade Center after 9/11, survivors looked desperately for symbols of hope. In the simplest of forms—two intersecting pieces of wood or metal—they recognized the cross, and with it a promise of redemption. What began for Balmforth with an act of destruction, scarring a pair of metal beams with plasma, led to an unexpected "intersection point" with faith.

In different forms, beauty surfaces again and again in Balmforth's work, emerging unexpectedly from the midst of failure, wreckage, and refuse. And yet there are rarer moments, which I want to turn to now, in which Balmforth seems to seek out beauty more directly. In these cases one can almost sense the artist testing how close he can get, or how much beauty he can tolerate. In a video entitled *The Consumptive Sublime* (2009), Balmforth films a parade of exquisite flowers steadily passing across a pitch-black background. A focused beam of light settles upon each stem. For a second, this tiny pinprick of light seems to freeze each flower in a moment of angelic perfection. What reveals beauty, however, also destroys it. The white light bears a scorching heat, and one by one the flowers wincingly succumb, bending and collapsing as their stems start to smolder. Like the early modern masters, who included incipient signs of decay in their most lavish still-lives and landscapes, Balmforth delivers the message of death: *et in arcadia ego*. The term "consumptive sublime" was initially coined in reference to nineteenth-century idealizations of addiction and melancholia.[7] Balmforth reappropriates the phrase to offer a cultural diagnosis tailored to the twenty-first century: we have gotten better

---

7. Dijkstra, *Idols of Perversity*, 29. Cf. Lawlor, *Consumption and Literature*, 189.

at destroying beauty than discovering it. And—worse yet—begun to savor the sublimity of this destruction.

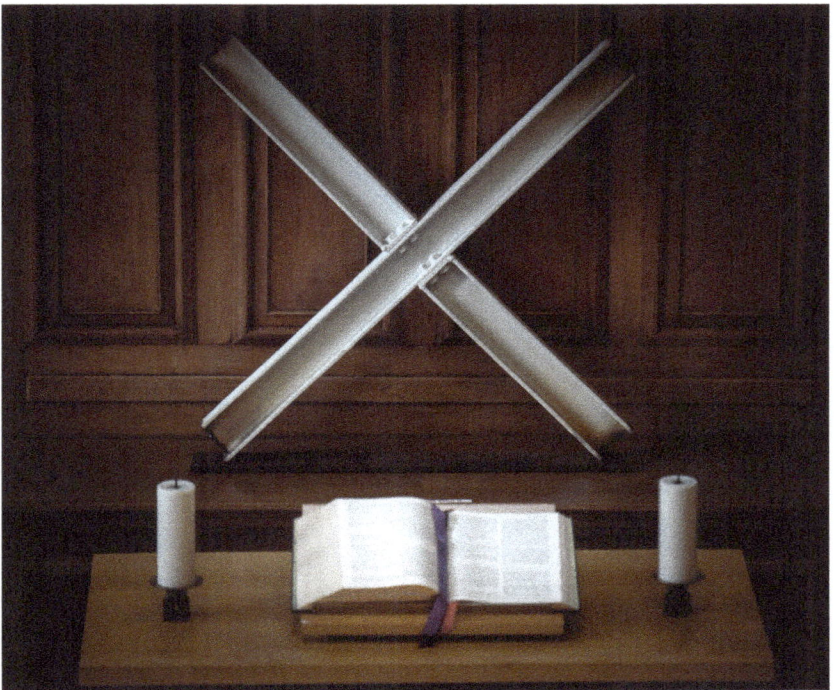

Figure 4.3

Hope is a precious commodity in Balmforth's work. It is there, to be sure, but carefully guarded, even hermetically sealed. In *The Beauty Yet to Come* (2010), Balmforth took a number of rough gemstones and placed them inside a rotating metal drum with water and polishing compounds. As the mechanical drum revolves, it produces a loud, grating rattle. The title of the installation issues a messianic promise, which Balmforth places in dynamic tension with the practicalities of the piece. In order for the avowed beauty of the gemstones to be unveiled, a number of things would have to take place. The work would have to be purchased by a patron who would run it for days on end, and then split it apart to deliver its contents. Only the destruction of the work of art would emancipate or verify the "beauty" of its contents. And of course beauty itself is a matter of faith. The clatter of gemstones could, in the end, turn out to be merely pebbles. It is only "those who have not seen and yet have come to believe," as Jesus tells the incredulous Thomas (John 20:29), who can truly see the potential of *The Beauty Yet to Come.*

There is something noble, even quixotic, about Balmforth's artistic quest, thermic lance in hand, confronting his materials alone in an old utility room in a neglected corner of the Peckham Car Park. As contemporary as his works may be, they emerge from a fidelity to materials, and a belief in earnest, difficult, unbounded encounters, which is almost embarrassingly traditional. To return to the words of Primo Levi, Balmforth's practice could be summarized by a single, overarching impetus: "to know matter and to confront it."[8] For many of the great sculptors of the past, respect for material meant reverently coaxing images out of wood, clay, stone, or metal—sanding, polishing, or stroking figures into life. Balmforth, by contrast, shows his respect for his materials through his willingness to be firm, harsh, and at times even destructive with them. The results can sometimes seem modest— a deformed sewing machine in *Internal Reasons* (2012), or a charred steel pole in *Interference Point* (2015)—but they are hard won. Objects which might otherwise be neglected, or quietly shuffled away to the refuse heap, gain a new fierceness and beauty in survival. It would be too easy to find despair or delight in destruction. Balmforth discovers dignity.

5. Gary Baseman: Walking through Walls

Everyone carries a room about inside him. —Franz Kafka[9]

In the title of a 2011 exhibition, Gary Baseman asked viewers to imagine "Walking through Walls." Now, in the title of his retrospective at the Skirball Cultural Center, he has declared that "The Door is Always Open." Even for an artist already known for crossing boundaries, Baseman seems increasingly intent upon removing obstacles. But what are these barriers? And, even more importantly, what lies behind them?

In the first instance, these barriers are artistic. "Throughout my career as an artist," Baseman reflects, "I have heard others tell me what I could and could not do, but my need to experiment creatively made me

8. Levi, *The Wrench*, 53.

9. Kafka, *The Blue Octavo Notebooks*, 1.

cross a lot of confining lines."[10] Not only does Baseman's "Pervasive Art" leap partitions between genres—painting, photography, and performance, to name a few—it also defies artificial distinctions between high and low art. Yet as much as Baseman wants to dissolve art-historical boundaries, the divisions he is most concerned with are internal. "A few years ago," he wrote recently, "I decided that I personally wanted to live my life by walking through walls. I did not want to be held back anymore by societal restraints or by my own anxiety about accomplishing my dreams."[11] In crossing such boundaries, Baseman explains, "I wanted to be like my father, a Holocaust survivor, who was able to charm guards and move through work camps and other checkpoints to find food for family and friends, and who spent three years in the woods with Russian Paratroopers."[12] The act of boundary crossing is closely caught up, for Baseman, with questions of Jewish identity. In fact, I would suggest, Jewishness is also a destination for him. While the artist has never made a secret of his Jewish identity, it is only recently that he has unlocked its creative potential. The door may have always been open—a phrase Baseman borrowed from his father—but he still had to find his own way in.

Baseman was born in 1960, a self-admitted accident separated by at least a decade from his older siblings. His parents were almost a generation older than those of his peers; kind and supportive, but too chronologically and culturally removed to be chummy. Both parents were born in what is now northwestern Ukraine, where they belonged to Jewish communities which were all but wiped from the map by the German Wehrmacht and local collaborators during the Shoah. Baseman writes of his parents:

> They were simple, but they had this complex and tragic history that they hardly shared with their kids. They surrounded them-selves with friends who were also Holocaust survivors . . . [with whom] they always spoke in Yiddish, which they never taught their children. It was like they wanted to keep part of their lives secret, or they were just protecting their children from something so painful.[13]

If the artist only sensed the contours of this trauma as a child, he felt its sublimated effect in his parents' concern for social justice, and his early

10. Baseman, *Walking Through Walls*, unpaginated.

11. Baseman, *Walking Through Walls*.

12. Baseman, *Walking Through Walls*.

13. Personal correspondence with Gary Baseman, August 28, 2012.

sensitivity to prejudice, whether towards Jews or other minorities. Overall, Baseman felt more of a cultural than a religious attachment to Judaism, describing his Jewish upbringing as "fairly secular" despite the fact that he had a *bar mitzvah* ceremony, went to synagogue on the holidays, fasted on Yom Kippur, and observed the Passover seder at home.[14]

As an adolescent, Baseman remembers sporadically incorporating Jewish elements into his creations, including a film called *Super Pooper*, in his which his hero dons a costume emblazoned with a *shin* instead of Superman's iconic "S.'"[15] The image of this flatulent Jewish adventurer is surprisingly canny, picking up on the origins of Superman himself, who was created by the Jewish duo Joe Shuster and Jerry Siegel. If Baseman's juvenilia anticipated some of his later Jewish interests, these remained largely dormant into the middle of his career, as he established himself in multiple fields, from animation to commercial design. When he began to focus his energies on painting at the turn of the millennium, religious themes and iconography proliferated across his panels. And yet Judaism was notably absent, even as he summoned imagery from Christianity, Hinduism, Buddhism, and Greek mythology. In his 2005 work, *For the Love of Toby* (**Fig. 5.1**), for instance, Baseman imagines his eponymous character floating to the heavens, guided by angels like the Virgin Mary during her assumption. Overhead, a giant shining eye evokes the Eye of Providence, familiar from the American dollar bill, or the eyes of the Buddha, painted on Nepalese *stupas*. In *Mystic Toby* from the same year, Baseman's co(s)mic hero has six limbs, like the dancing Shiva, while several other works figure Toby as a kind of goofy Christ-child, receiving visits from equally doltish magi. Perhaps the most revealing image in this extensive series is *Toby's Roots* (2005; **Fig. 5.2**). Barely touching the ground beneath Toby's trunk-like body, these dangling roots palpably evoke the artist's tentative efforts to reach back into his cultural heritage.

In his 2007 exhibition "Hide and Seek," Baseman delved further into interreligious iconography, inspired by sources ranging from Michelangelo's *Pietà* (1499) to the hellscapes of Bosch and Bruegel, cheekily referenced in *The Battlefield Between Goo and Evil* (2007). Baseman also introduces a new character, a blobby simian creature called Chou Chou, "who takes away negative energy and hate, absorbs it and then oozes Creamy Gooey

14. Personal correspondence with Gary Baseman.
15. Personal correspondence with Gary Baseman.

Love out of his bellybutton."[16] While the touchstones in these works are seldom explicitly Jewish, Baseman was, nonetheless, beginning to home in on the central themes in his personal theology, from the transformative power of ritual to the balance between sacrifice and healing. Through his deepening dialogue with other religions—further stimulated by visits to shrines and temples across Asia—the artist had begun to shape and clarify his relationship to Judaism.

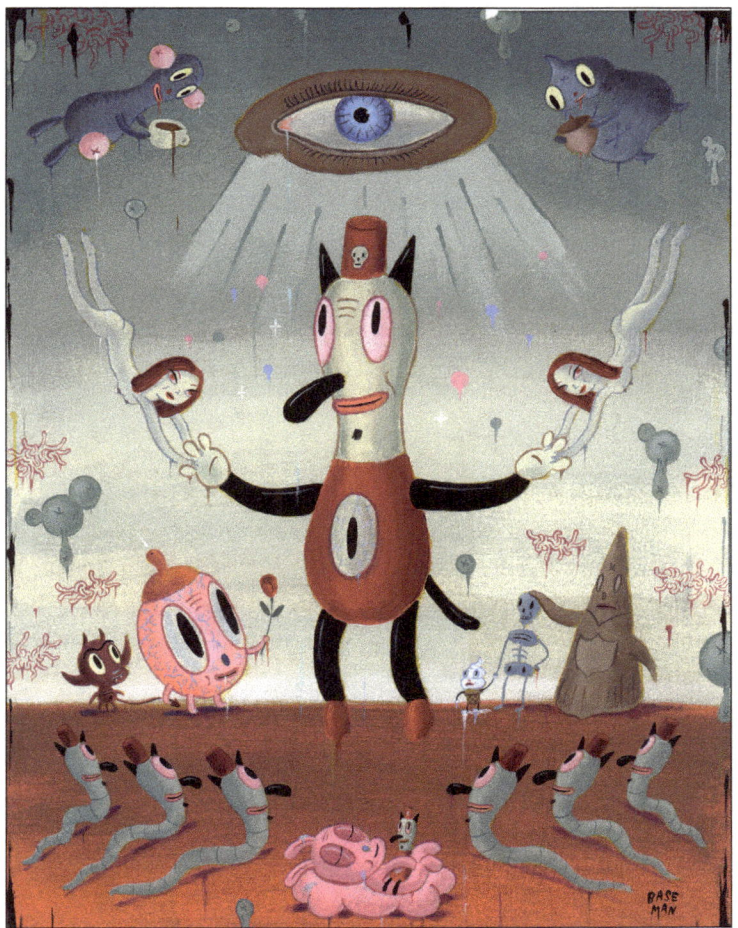

Figure 5.1

16. Personal correspondence with Gary Baseman.

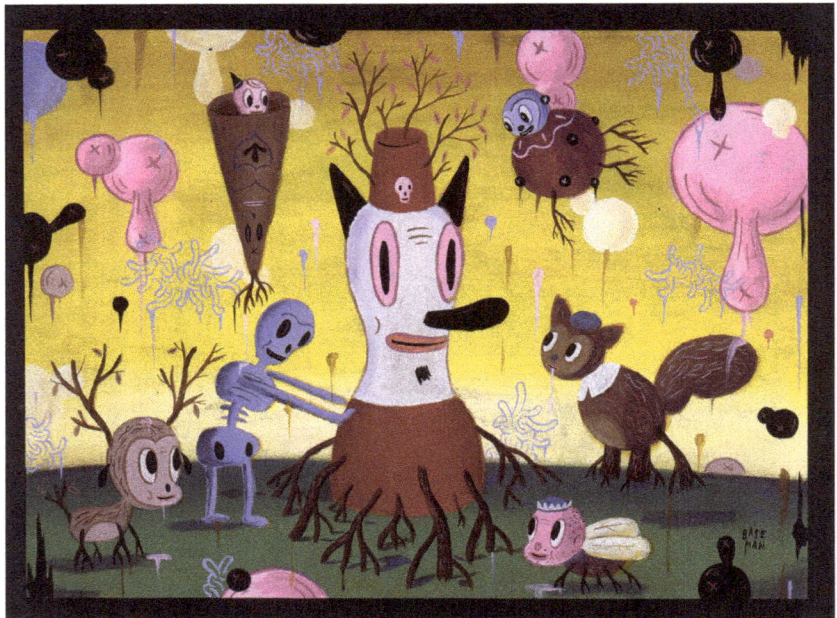

Figure 5.2

In 2009, Baseman's burgeoning sense of Jewish identity crested to the surface. Preparing the works for "The Sacrificing of the Cake," he suggests, "reminded me that I was Jewish after so many years."[17] Baseman's metaphorical cake—sacrificed, not sliced in connubial bliss—marked the end of his marriage in 2006 and an ensuing time of personal transition. The main protagonist in these works is a snake called "the Ooga," a creative transliteration of the Hebrew word for cake. While the Ooga might recall the Hindu *Naga* or the gorgon of classical myth, its clearest precursors are the crafty serpent that tempted Eve and the brazen serpent fashioned by Moses (Numbers 21:8–9). This engagement with biblical imagery coincided with Baseman's first visit to Israel since the age of twelve, an experience which felt "like a religious journey" to him;[18] a profound admission—despite its careful qualification—from an artist more comfortable talking about spirituality than religion.

With his "La Noche de la Fusion" exhibition, also held in 2009, Baseman was finally prepared to draw Judaism front and center. Yet rather than

17. Personal correspondence with Gary Baseman.
18. Personal correspondence with Gary Baseman.

sacrificing his cross-cultural interests in order to carve out a place for Judaism, Baseman reveled in the creative and spiritual possibilities of hybridity, exemplified in the exhibition's title, a blend of Spanish and French. Nowhere is this mélange more evident than in *Baseman Hooded Self* (2009; **Fig. 5.3**), which stitches together both Jewish and Christian symbols. On the one hand, this figure could be viewed as the latest incarnation of his cloaked magi, which crop up throughout his work, including his 2005 life-size installation, *Four Magis*. These shrouded figures not only reference the infant Jesus' mysterious visitors, they also resemble Christian penitents, especially the *Nazarenos* who process through Seville, Spain each year during Holy Week. Baseman accepts the fact that some viewers will mistake his hooded figures for Ku Klux Klansmen, insisting that this presents an opportunity to "[turn] something evil into something good."[19] There is also a deliberate wink here to one of Baseman's favorite precursors, the Jewish painter Philip Guston, also from Los Angeles. In his late canvases, Guston painted dozens of buffoonish Klansmen prowling the streets, looking for trouble. Guston liked to imagine what it would be like, especially as a Jew, to go "undercover" with these "hoods," as he dubbed them, bumping along in the presence of their casual evil. Baseman indulges in a similar fantasy, depicting himself clasping a severed, dripping head. Just as it did for Guston, the act of concealment allows Baseman to explore his Jewish identity from unlikely perspectives. Ironically, as several theorists have noted, masking can be a form of disclosure, making one hyper-aware of one's own identity. It is no accident, then, that Baseman sketches his self-portrait on a page from a Hebrew book, literally allowing us to see his Jewishness through his robe. In fact, this costume proved such an effective mode of self-representation that the artist donned a similar robe for his live performance, *Giggle and Pop!,* held outside the Los Angeles County Museum of Art on 12 June 2010.

This process of concealing and revealing—a "reveilation" to borrow a term from Mark C. Taylor[20]—continues in Baseman's latest work, this time with a new wrinkle. In *Beverly (In Memoriam)* (2011), the hooded figure is replaced by the silk-screened image of a little girl in a homemade ghost costume. The image is taken from a 1950s snapshot of suburban trick-or-treaters, one of thousands of vintage photographs in Baseman's personal collection. Baseman nicknames this anonymous girl Little Miss Boo, also calling her Muertita or La Petite Mort. Since she derives from a photo, the

19. Personal correspondence with Gary Baseman.
20. Taylor, *Disfiguring*, 94.

artist calls her "my very first non-fiction character."[21] The grainy, documentary character of this haunting image calls to mind Christian Boltanski's photographic installations, which memorialize the children who perished during the Holocaust. These associations reflect Baseman's growing sense of his legacy and responsibility as a second-generation witness to the Shoah, especially after his father's death in 2010. At the same time, the innocent Little Miss Boo is a capacious enough symbol to address other, individual losses, including the untimely passing of Baseman's favorite cousin, Beverly, loosely depicted on the right-hand side of the canvas.

On the heads of Beverly and Little Miss Boo, Baseman prints, respectively, the Hebrew words *emet* (truth) and *met* (death). Given the memorial theme of the piece, these words are fitting in their own right. However, they also endow the eerie Muertita with an alternate meaning, completing the transformation from magus to ghost to golem. According to Jewish legend, the golem was shaped out of clay by Rabbi Judah Loew ben Bezalel, the great sixteenth-century rabbi of Prague. After molding the giant's body, Rabbi Loew summoned it to life by inscribing the word *emet* into its earthen flesh. While the golem was intended to serve and defend the city's Jewish community, it soon began to run amok. At the last possible moment, the rabbi managed to scrub the aleph, the first letter in *emet*, from its forehead, leaving behind only *met*, at which point the golem crumbled to the floor. Sternly decreeing that the golem should never be reanimated, Rabbi Loew sealed the colossus in the attic of Prague's Old-New Synagogue where—legend has it—it still remains.[22] Of course, Baseman has never been too good with rules. Where others see barred and dusty gates, he sees permeable walls and open doors. Summoning golems may be risky business but the greater danger—I suspect—is to live in a world without them, without the old-new blend of Jewish magic that makes them possible. We need Baseman as a Jewish artist, but we need his brand of hopeful, devious magic even more.

21. Baseman, *Walking Through Walls*.

22. For a survey of the evolving golem tradition, see: Scholem, *On the Kabbalah and its Symbolism,* 158–204.

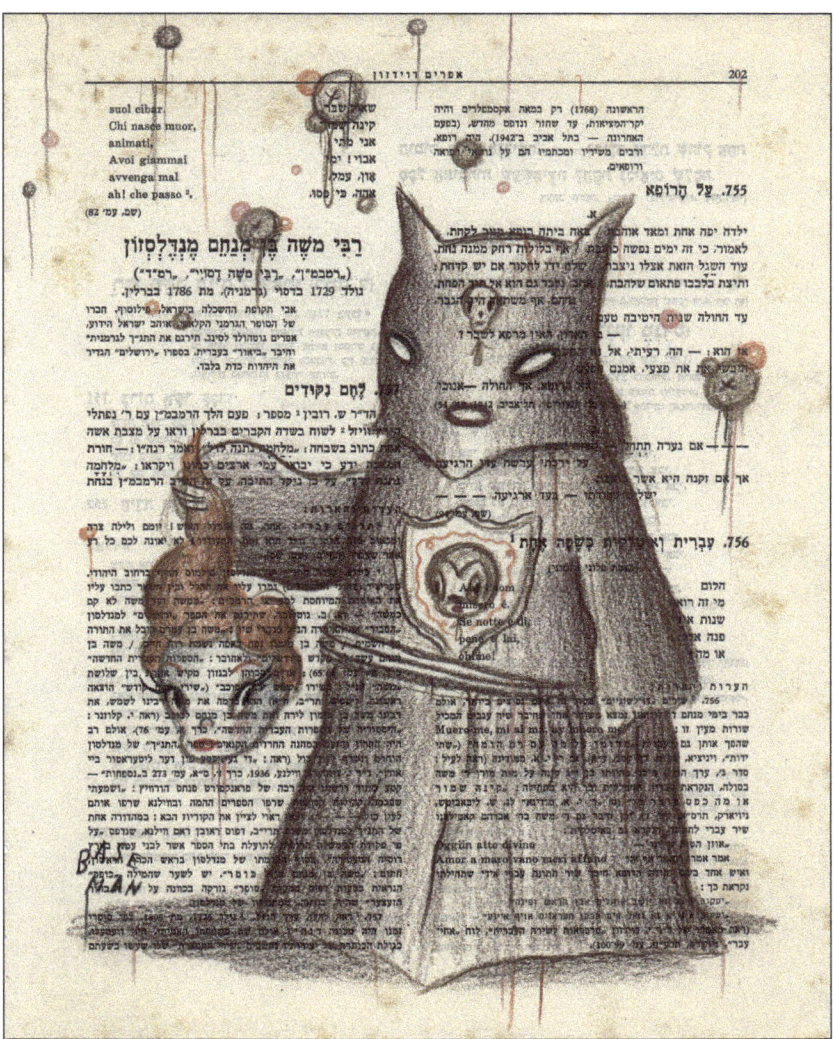

Figure 5.3

6. G. Roland Biermann: Revelations and Apparitions

The great painter Barnett Newman remarked once that "aesthetics is to artists as ornithology is to the birds."[23] The irony, of course, was that his comment, and his many essays, proved Newman was actually quite happy to put on his binoculars and train a critical eye on himself and other practitioners. G. Roland Biermann reminds me of Newman's words, and his works, on several levels. On the one hand, Biermann also belongs to that rare species represented by Newman, an artist equally talented at producing art and reflecting upon it. And Biermann is especially gifted when it comes to considering the religious iconography, themes, and implications of his works. To tinker with Newman's analogy, artists sometimes reveal themselves to be priests, capable of celebrating the mysteries of the divine, but they seldom turn out to be theologians, with a talent for exegesis. As both an art historian and theologian, writing about Biermann thus represents a formidable challenge: to keep pace with an artist eminently capable of illuminating his own work.

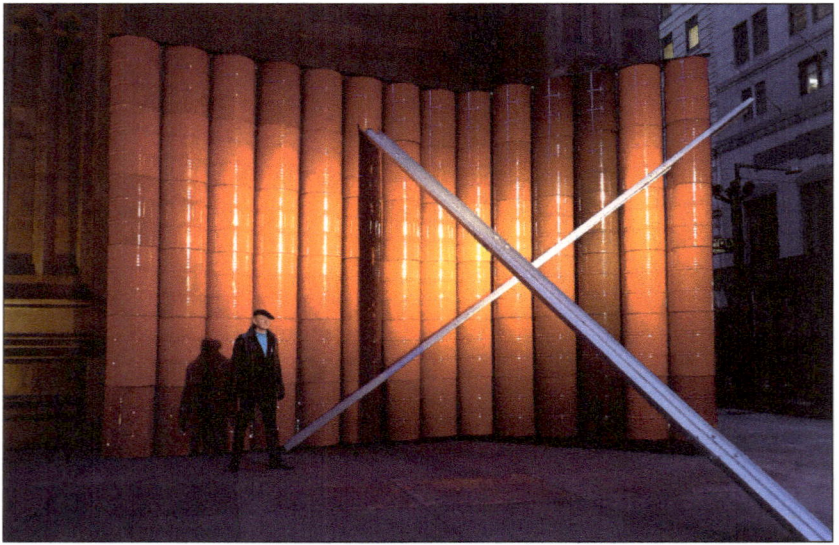

Figure 6.1

Fortunately, Newman offers a productive place to begin. The Abstract Expressionist is one of Biermann's favorite artists, and he has been captivated

23. Newman, *Barnett Newman*, xxv.

for years by *The Stations of the Cross—Lema Sabachthani* (1958–66), arguably Newman's magnum opus. Over the past several years, Biermann and I have spoken many times about his ambition to create his own stations, which culminated in the sculpture he produced for the Barbican terrace as part of my *Stations of the Cross* exhibition in London (2016); a work which has gone on to be installed in New York City (2018; **Fig. 6.1**). The centuries-old Christian practice of praying the stations, which commemorates the events of Jesus' Passion, holds an intrinsic allure for Biermann, who has been interested throughout his career in ritual and narrative structure. But Newman gave Biermann permission to think about the stations in a way that mapped even more closely to his artistic practice. What most intrigued Newman about the stations, the painter once said, was the challenge of capturing fourteen variations on a single theme. While traditionally the stations are comprised of a narrative sequence from Jesus' condemnation to his crucifixion and entombment, Newman saw all fourteen as permutations on one excruciating moment: Jesus' haunting cry from the cross, "'Eloi, Eloi, lema sabachthani?' which means, 'My God, my God, why have you forsaken me?'" (Mark 15:34). Newman's approach to the Passion, utilizing serial repetition to probe for a singular essence—both artistically and theologically—is precisely what compelled Biermann to create his own *Stations*.

Biermann ambitiously set out to express the *via dolorosa* as a cohesive whole. The backdrop of the piece is formed by oil barrels positioned in fourteen columns, with each band painted a different shade of red. The colors range from vibrant cadmium to burgundy and back to bright red, suggesting blood that runs, congeals, and quickens anew, referencing the death and resurrection of Christ as well as the miraculously liquefying blood of San Gennaro in Naples. These vertical "zips" (Newman's phrase) create a vast expanse of color, reminiscent of an Abstract Expressionist canvas. But Biermann interrupts this panorama with violent urgency. Two motorway crash barriers slice through the air, narrowly missing each another before piercing the wall behind. Jesus' fall on his lonely journey to Golgotha finds a contemporary echo in the everyday tragedy of a car crash. Symbolically, the barrels become containers of both blood and oil, an emulsion equal parts sacred and profane. This focus on bodily trauma returns Biermann to a theme he has examined before, as in *Apparitions 32* and *33*, which evoke the iconography of the Flagellation. Where Newman believed the *kerygma* of Christ was to be found in his final syllables, Biermann looks for meaning in the last shudders of Jesus' convulsing body.

Newman's *Stations* constitute a microcosm of his work at large. As Yve-Alain Bois aptly puts it, Newman's oeuvre functions like a "deck of cards," offering almost infinite variations within a deceptively simple format.[24] The same might be said of Biermann's corpus, which has continually progressed via series. The artist's studio practice resembles that of a scientist in a laboratory, alternating variables against a control, scrupulously testing and recording results. And yet, it is important not to miss the playfulness and subversiveness in his process. Speaking about his predilections for series, he says, "Sometimes they're sequential but not always. Sometimes they go along with what science promises, but sometimes they don't."[25] This is especially true in his *Snow + Concrete* polyptychs. "If you read them left to right," Biermann comments, "it seems like the snow is gradually melting and then rebuilding itself to its initial shape. So it's obviously something that scientifically wouldn't work, but one could also see it as a metaphor for the life cycle. On a larger scale it works."[26] And this is the key to understanding the artist's abiding interest in series. In each new group of works he establishes a seemingly ineluctable logic, coaches our expectations, only to undermine them. What interests Biermann in systems and patterns might seem, *prima facie*, to be how they ramify and self-replicate, but at a deeper level what truly fascinates him is how systems falter.

This meta-comment on the nature of systems, which runs throughout Biermann's work, takes on different points of emphasis in each new series, and indeed each new exhibition. In his video work *white cube/white wall* (2015; **Fig. 6.2**), he examined how both political and artistic hegemonies are constructed, dismantled, and reconfigured—often in tandem. A small, silent team of workers, clad in monochrome, stack and un-stack Styrofoam blocks in a curiously hypnotic performance. Created to coincide with the twenty-fifth anniversary of the fall of the Berlin Wall, Biermann's work manages to bring a fresh eye to events already saturated by representation. The choice of Styrofoam is a classic example of his penchant for injecting unexpected meanings into otherwise banal materials. Faced with depicting the impossible weight of history concentrated in the Berlin Wall, the artist chooses instead to expose the "unbearable lightness" of its memory, to reappropriate Kundera's phrase.[27] Viewed from on high,

24. Bois, "On Two Paintings by Barnett Newman," 4.

25. G. Roland Biermann interviewed by Aaron Rosen, "Divine Apparitions."

26. Biermann, "Divine Apparitions."

27. Kundera, *The Unbearable Lightness of Being*.

from a God's eye perspective, the act of constructing this wall—or perhaps any barrier—appears naïve, comic, and potentially even tragic. Indeed, we might recall the brilliantly nonsensical premise of a story by Kafka, in which the Great Wall of China is intended to form the foundations for a new Tower of Babel, laying the groundwork of a construction which, were it ever to be attempted, would crush humanity beneath it.[28] Biermann's "white wall," rendered in chunks of packing material, becomes a symbol not only of political but theological impotence. The false pieties of the art world, for their part, fare no better. The ideal of a pure "white cube" of aesthetic contemplation, fenced off from the impurities of history, proves impossible. For each act of creation, Biermann suggests, there is an equal and opposite act of deconstruction coming.

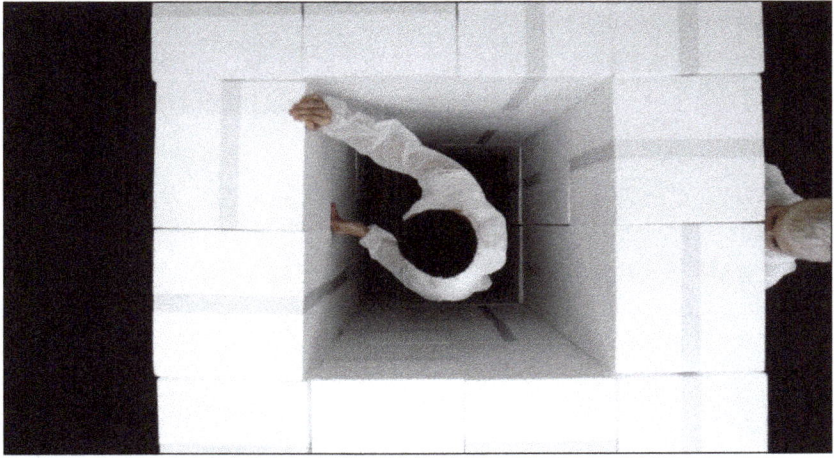

Figure 6.2

The interlacing ironies and wordplays of a work like *White Cube/White Wall* might strike some viewers as quintessentially postmodern. And there is certainly an element of cheeky pastiche that runs through Biermann's work, perhaps most evidently in *Apparitions*, in which he frequently riffs on the iconography of traditional Christian art. Lazarus, a recurring figure in *Apparitions* (**Fig. 6.3**), does not shed his bandages from the tomb but rather struggles free from a heap of cling-film, as if catching his breath after a sex game gone wrong. In *Apparition 17*, Biermann sticks plasters where we might expect to see stigmata. And in *37* he turns a deflated air mattress into

28. Kafka, "The Great Wall and the Tower of Babel," 25–26.

a rather flaccid crucifix. One of the most intriguing works in the series is *19*, which seems to reference the story of Belshazzar's Feast in the Book of Daniel, the subject of Rembrandt's masterpiece in the National Gallery, in which a floating hand inscribes a cryptic prophecy only Daniel can discern. Rather than a Babylonian palace, Biermann sets the scene in an abandoned tenement, with blackened, broken windows. A woman's hand scratches out a jagged line, in which we can almost hear the blood-curdling screech of fingernails scraping across a blackboard. With a sardonic touch, the artist suggests that what we so badly want to be prophecies might turn out to be gibberish, or the idle scribbles of a bored graffitist.

Despite the apparent irreverence in this series, David Jasper makes a compelling case when he claims:

> In no sense [is *Apparitions*] postmodern, for this work is rooted in story and antiquity, these photographs present a disturbing field for contemporary Christian theology, for its antique images remain in them, yet fleeting . . . separated from the assurances and foundations that would seem to guarantee their legitimacy . . .[29]

To me, Biermann's works seems to vibrate between the modern and the postmodern, and it is this intentionally ambiguous self-positioning that is one of his greatest strengths. He feels for the fractures of tradition with the seriousness of an

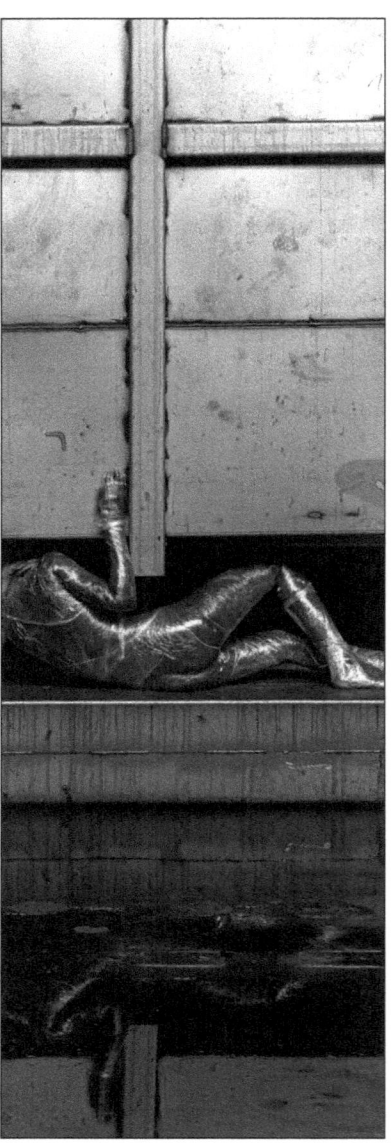

Figure 6.3

29. Jasper, *G. Roland Biermann*, 2005.

46

arch-modernist, yet enjoys juggling and juxtaposing references with a postmodern sleight of hand. Newman famously claimed at mid-century that "Instead of making *cathedrals* out of Christ, man, or 'life,' we are making it out of ourselves, out of our own feelings. The image we produce is the self-evident one of revelation, real and concrete."[30] To Newman's "real and concrete" revelations, Biermann responds with haunting, evanescent *Apparitions*. And yet, his dream is not so different. In his own way, he still sets out to make cathedrals.

30. Newman, "The Sublime is Now," 53.

Conflict

7. The Art of Reconciliation

What role does art play in religious conflict? At times, art has been at the epicenter of hostilities. In the eighth and ninth centuries, the Byzantine Empire was riven by fierce struggles over the place of art in Christian worship. Debates about the status of icons, and whether they drew people closer to God, or down the road to idolatry, led to decades of theological and political instability before iconodules (icon-lovers) finally won out. In the sixteenth century, the struggle between Reformers and Catholics became a war of images as well as words, reducing magnificent medieval sculptures like the shrine of Saint Thomas Becket to little more than rubble. In modern conflicts, art has rarely played so central and sustained a role. Even so, we need look no further than the attacks on the *Charlie Hebdo* offices in Paris—claimed as retribution for cartoonists' images of the Prophet Muhammad—for evidence that art continues to be a flash point for violence committed in the name of faith.

While art has sometimes kindled the fires of religious strife, more often it has served to fan the flames, or at least record them. Lucas Cranach the Elder helped shape the face of the Reformation through portraits of Protestant leaders as well as widely reproduced woodcuts excoriating the Pope. In the Netherlands, Reformers' iconoclastic fury ironically spurred an entire genre of prints devoted to depicting iconoclasm. Later, artists such as Pieter Saenredam painted immaculate images of bare church interiors. Visual art is no less revealing when it comes to understanding contemporary religious conflicts. During the Troubles in Northern Ireland in the late twentieth century, both Protestant loyalists and Catholic republicans created bold murals emblazoned with images of their respective martyrs. Recently, graphic novelists have turned an especially acute eye to religious and political conflicts. These run the gamut from illustrated histories, such as collaborations between Jean-Pierre Filiu and David B., to visual journalism by Joe Sacco, to autobiographical perspectives from Marjane Satrapi.

From even this brief account, it is clear that art has, at various times and places, served as both a catalyst and chronicle of religious conflict. But what about art as a source of mediation or resolution? In what ways might art de-escalate or diffuse religious violence? These questions are, if anything, even more challenging to answer. For starters, there are hermeneutic issues to address. Art can rarely be reduced to a single message that might be easily digested and communicated. Indeed, if that were the case, it would tend towards propaganda; hardly a helpful genre when it comes to reconciling divergent perspectives! The indeterminacy of art does not make it any less powerful, but it does make the results of creating and looking at art complicated to track. What *is* possible—and what I hope to do here—is suggest some of the ways in which art might open up new perspectives for audiences. I will not make the wider claim that art itself resolves conflicts, but rather that by challenging and adapting preconceptions about oneself and others it can foster the mind-set necessary for productive dialogue across religious divisions.

Art has the potential to do this in ways that often prove challenging for other modes of engagement. Most attempts at brokering interreligious and intercultural dialogue aim to resolve specific points of political and theological disagreement. However well intentioned, public fora that set out to tackle political disputes between Israelis and Palestinians, or to reconcile disparate passages from the Hebrew Bible and the Qur'an, tend to fall into predictably intractable patterns. The open-endedness of artistic encounters lends them the capacity to initiate fresh conversations, on grounds that are far less ideologically determined. This does not mean that substantive political and theological disagreements can or should be avoided in the long run. Rather, it means that we must be open to the value of more orthogonal approaches. Art can bring people to the table precisely because it does *not* promise to resolve specific grievances through debates or negotiations. Its very indeterminacy is its greatest resource, clearing a space for open exchange.

One of the most powerful ways in which art can enable discourse is by rendering visible the face of the Other. The anonymous French artist JR has explored this potential in multiple contexts. In a work from 2007 entitled *Face2Face,* he photographed Israelis and Palestinians on either side of the separation barrier between Israel and the West Bank at Bethlehem. Noting that Israelis and Palestinians usually only see each other through the distorting lens of the media, JR hung pictures on the wall of people who held the same jobs and would otherwise be neighbors. "[M]ost of the time people can't recognize who is the Israeli and who is the Palestinian, so they couldn't recognize who they were supposed to be," remarked the artist. "[T]hey're much more open than you think they are."[1] In 2014, JR's large-scale photographic installations inspired an artistic collective to travel to northern Pakistan—the site of numerous drone attacks by the United States—to install a massive photograph of a young girl who lost her parents and siblings in a drone strike. For drone operators, who only see the results of their strikes as microscopic blips on a video screen, the giant poster makes unmistakable the vulnerable face of "collateral" victims, even from a camera tens of thousands of feet in the air. The project aims to render clinical detachment impossible, as its emphatic title makes clear: *#NotABugSplat*. In both projects, the ostensibly simple act of presenting people with faces of their presumed enemies challenges religiously and culturally inculcated binaries of 'us' and 'them.' Coming *Face2Face* with difference might be the first step towards recognizing an Other, before whom our prejudices and preconceptions falter.

Not only are contemporary artists re-shaping how we see religious and cultural difference at the grassroots level, they are also witnesses to a new dialogue taking shape between leaders of different faiths. The British artist Nicola Green has documented a number of such encounters, spending years accompanying former Archbishop of Canterbury Rowan Williams, former UK Chief Rabbi Jonathan Sacks, and Pope Emeritus Benedict XVI in meetings with one another and other religious leaders around the world. In her wide-ranging project, *Encounters* (2018),[2] Green presents photographs and paintings inspired by intimate conversations with the figures above as well as the Dalai Lama, the Grand Mufti of Egypt, and others (**Fig. 16.1**). While in the past such encounters might have been stiff affairs contrived to generate politically expedient photo ops, Green's images reveal the depth of relationships being formed across historically deep divides. By paying attention to neglected factors in these encounters such as the gestures and even clothing of participants, Green presents a powerfully embodied perspective on interfaith dialogue. Refusing to see theology in a vacuum, she places faith fully within the context of material and sensory culture.

Not only can art create new ways of seeing and sensing others, it can open new spaces for encounters to occur. It is often assumed that the

1. JR, *The Colbert Report*, August 28, 2014.

2. Rosen, ed., *Encounters*.

optimal space for interreligious engagement should be as neutral as possible, scrubbed clean of any symbol or feature that might signal one faith or another. A group of British architects—Dan Leon, Matthew Lloyd, and Shahed Saleem—have drafted plans for a space that operates on the opposite premise: not only is it practically impossible to create a perfectly neutral space, it is undesirable (**Fig. 7.1**). Dialogue, they insist, thrives on difference. Leon, Lloyd, and Saleem each run their own firm in London, and they have all worked on commissions for religious communities in their respective faiths (Judaism, Christianity, and Islam). Together, they have crafted a plan for a conceptual pavilion—part work of art, part architecture—called Friday-Saturday-Sunday (FSS). It is designed to function as a mosque on Fridays, a synagogue on Saturdays, and a church on Sundays, while constituting a shared community space during the weekdays. As the space hosts worshippers from different faiths, seating and other features will shift, so that—for example—Muslims may kneel to pray, Jews can face a Torah ark, and Christians can install a Crucifix. For the architects, unity exists less in any single feature of the space than the hospitality involved in cyclically receiving and returning the space to others. "The underlying idea of our project," the architects write, "is not that differences should be disregarded, or that all faiths are or should be one. It is rather that these three faiths have an entwined and symbiotic series of relationships, and a history of tolerance and coexistence greater than their history of conflict."[3] Rather than presuming faith groups are inflexible, and conflict is inevitable, Friday-Saturday-Sunday is predicated upon the faith that communities possess both a capacity and desire for exchange. They simply require a space that facilitates it.

Art can also be a process, providing an opportunity for healing and transformation. In 2001, the Taliban used artillery and explosives to demolish the sixth-century Buddhas of the Bamiyan Valley in Afghanistan, claiming that they were false idols. Carved into cliffs in the Hindu Kush, these monuments once formed the world's largest standing sculptures of the Buddha. For centuries, Bamiyan was a flourishing site of Buddhist culture, with monasteries and sanctuaries clustered along the cliffs. Even after the area's conversion to Islam, the sculptures remained a source of regional pride. After the Taliban was driven out of the region, Afghans and international organizations such as UNESCO debated whether and how to attempt a restoration of the pulverized Buddhas. In 2015, a team of documentarians

---

3. Rosen, ed., *Religion and Art in the Heart of Modern Manhattan*, 237.

worked with local participants to project three-dimensional holograms of the sculptures into the empty, casket-like shells where they once stood. Although the future of the Buddhas of Bamiyan is uncertain, this installation illuminated one way in which to remember and honor Afghanistan's multicultural past, whilst projecting hope for the future. Such reparative, even redemptive uses of technology are not restricted to experts on site. In the wake of widespread cultural destruction across the Middle East by Daesh—the so-called Islamic State—archaeologists Matthew Vincent and Chance Coughenour founded Project Mosul to collect images of destroyed artifacts and architecture. Their effort has since evolved into Rekrei, an online platform which crowdsources images and integrates them into increasingly precise digital models using photogrammetry. The results not only provide a scholarly and educational resource but a mode of catharsis for those contributing images of their lost heritage. Perhaps it is possible to go even a step further. In the book of Ezekiel, God gives his prophet a vision of a new Temple, instructing him to measure its dimensions for the future (Ezekiel 40–43). Visualizing the lost wonders of Mosul and Palmyra may involve the latest technology, but the act channels an ancient hope that what is lost might yet be reborn.

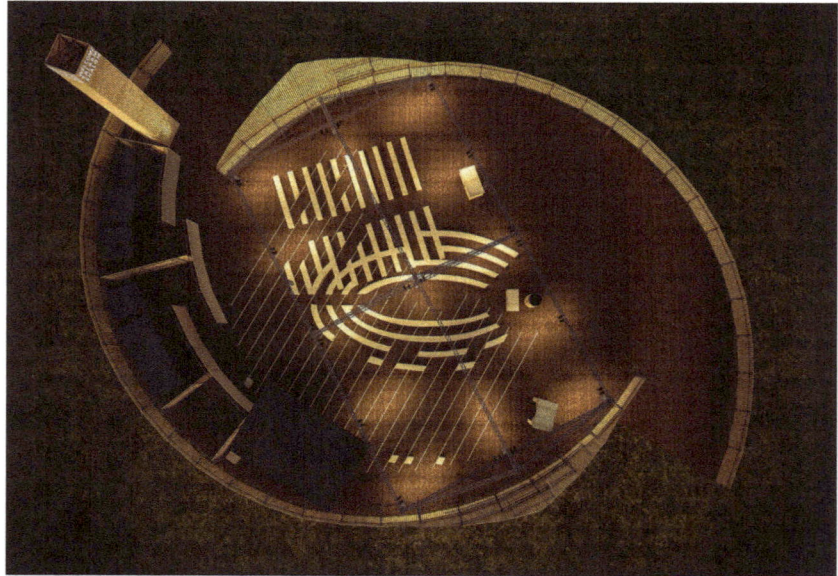

Figure 7.1

At the center of each of these examples is community. Art cannot hope to address religious conflict in an impactful and enduring way unless it opens out towards the wider public, to the people who mourn, endure, and even perpetuate violence. Those communities might be small, like the crowd who assembled to see spectral Buddhas shine against the Afghan night, or the Londoners working to implement Friday-Saturday-Sunday; separated, like the Israelis and Palestinians in JR's installation; or even virtual, like the people who gather online to share snapshots of decimated sculptures in Syria and Iraq. But however communities are constituted, art must reach them in palpable, engaging ways to enable dialogue that is anything more than merely wishful thinking and self-congratulation. Art is no more restricted to galleries than religion is to churches, synagogues, or mosques. If one is to prove beneficial to the other, they must agree to meet in public.

8. R. B. Kitaj: Repainting an Anti-Jewish Masterpiece

Western art history is littered with works, sometimes of impeccable skill, which might be termed anti-Jewish or anti-Semitic. Many of these works were unabashedly displayed in churches and cathedrals across Europe, often well into the modern period. With most now tucked away in ecclesial storage, or quarantined in museum vitrines, these images are largely regarded as an embarrassment. Art historians, including Dana Katz, have recently begun to take a second a look at such images, recognizing their value for understanding the societies that produced and preserved them. However, theologians have largely ignored this visual heritage of Christian anti-Judaism, assuming that little can be done except denounce it, or cite it as evidence of art's dubious seductions. I believe we might locate new, productive ways of approaching this kind of anti-Jewish imagery by turning to the resources of contemporary art. I want to take as my test case *Eclipse of God* (1997–2000; **Fig. 8.1**) by the Jewish-American painter R. B. Kitaj, which reimagines Paolo Uccello's *Miracle of the Profaned Host* (1468; **Fig. 8.2**), originally part of the altarpiece of the Church of Corpus Domini in Urbino, Italy.

Uccello's six-part predella tells the story of a Christian woman who is duped by a Jewish usurer into stealing the Eucharist in exchange for cash. The Jew boils and stabs the Host, only to discover—in a miraculous testimony to the efficacy of transubstantiation—that it begins to ooze blood. In the second panel, which forms the basis for Kitaj's canvas, blood has begun to seep through a crack in the wall, attracting the attention of the town's soldiers, who are about to break down the door to the Jew's home. In the ensuing scenes, the Host is rescued while the offending Jew, along with his wife and two children, are burned at the stake. Meanwhile, in the final scene the Christian woman—a victim of the Jew's perfidy—is forgiven from on high, receiving the Host from hovering angels on her deathbed.

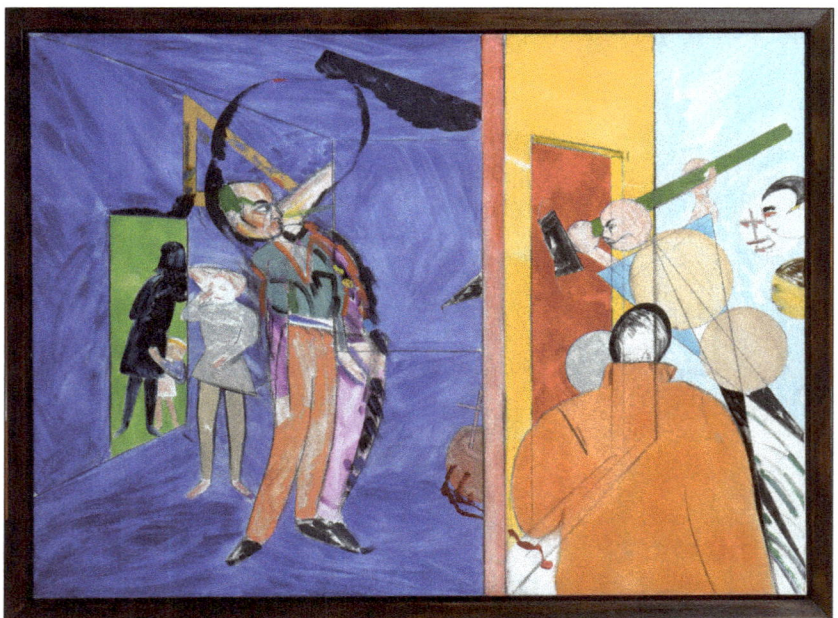

Figure 8.1

The inspiration for this narrative was a miraculous incident that purportedly occurred in Paris in 1290, but that was known by the fifteenth century in numerous popular Italian variations. Artistic representations of the legend of the profaned Host are rare in Italy, but the motif served a critical purpose in Urbino, where it was meant to justify the implementation of a new banking system, put in place to stamp out the practice of usury, an exclusively Jewish livelihood. The desecration legend also served to reinforce the broader policies of the local ruler, Duke Federigo da Montefeltro. As Katz argues, "Painting symbolically punished Jews for their alleged crimes in an attempt to preserve Christian social order."[4] In addition to clarifying the perimeters of tolerance *within* Christian society, the symbolic murder of Jews also deflected attention away from a much greater but less easily contained threat: Ottoman Turks. Together, these combined factors go some way towards explaining the exceptionally virulent tone of the piece, which takes the unusual step of showing the offending Jew's entire family burned alive. Uccello even makes a further, unprecedented move, by depicting the Jew's wife as pregnant. Thus, even the unborn Jewish child is designated as unworthy of reprieve, in sharp distinction to the Christian woman, whose theft of the Eucharist sets the drama in motion.

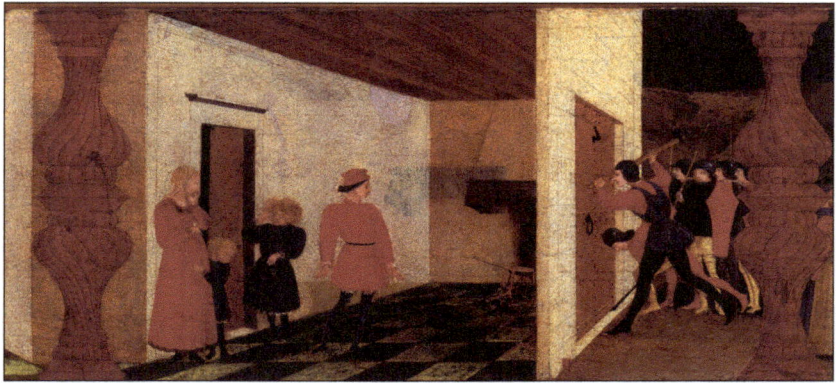

Figure 8.2

As Marilyn Aronberg Lavin remarks, all this violence is belied by the refined aesthetic of the piece, with its delicate figures rendered in what she calls "pure crystals of mathematical space."[5] For Kitaj, it is precisely this incongruous blend of beauty and barbarity that seems to have prompted his engagement with Uccello's masterpiece. More than a simple desire to avenge anti-Jewish imagery, Kitaj seems animated by a genuine reverence for the meticulous visual investigations of Uccello, whose *Deluge* (c. 1447) fresco he had previously used as inspiration for his 1990 painting *Greenwich Village*. Obsessed as he was with the history of painting, Uccello's biography probably also held an appeal for Kitaj. Well into the throes of what he called his "old-age style" when he painted the *Eclipse of God*, Kitaj may have felt a kinship with the elderly Uccello, whose style of painting was falling out of

4. Katz, *The Jew in the Art of the Italian Renaissance*, 12.
5. Lavin, "The Altar of Corpus Domini in Urbino," 1.

fashion at the time he executed the *Miracle of the Profaned Host*, regarded as one of the artist's very latest, if not last, paintings. Altogether, Uccello seems to occupy an ambiguous role in Kitaj's imagination, akin to that of T. S. Eliot, whose poetry was a major influence on Kitaj, and whom he frequently referred to as his "favorite anti-Semite."

The thrill for Kitaj, then, lies in a careful reversal of Uccello's perspective, beginning quite literally. Where Uccello plots the lines of sight in his panel to intersect just behind the Christian soldiers, causing us to identify with the soldiers' side of the story, Kitaj's composition directs the viewer to the threatening tip of the soldier's lance. The decision to turn Uccello's axe into a lance, and depict it penetrating the door rather than swinging towards it, further focuses our attention on the violence of the act being committed. As the lance pierces the fleshy red plane of the door, we are reminded that it is not so much the Eucharist being violated, but rather the sanctity of a Jewish home. Our sympathies are further aroused by the more personal, expressionist touch with which Kitaj renders the Jew and his family, opposed to the sharp, flattened geometry of the mob assembled outside.

There is also a strong personal element in Kitaj's picture, which extends beyond the artist's empathy for the Jewish victims of the kind of attacks depicted by Uccello. Kitaj was convinced that the scathing reception of his 1994 retrospective at the Tate had been motivated by English anti-Semitism, and he lashed out publicly at critics. At the height of this controversy—the "Tate War" as he called it—Kitaj's wife, the American painter Sandra Fisher, died suddenly from an aneurysm.[6] Blaming his detractors for Sandra's death, Kitaj declared that England, his home for over thirty years, was dead to him. After exhibiting the ferocious painting *The Killer-Critic Assassinated by His Widower, Even* at the Royal Academy Summer Exhibition in 1997, Kitaj departed bitterly for Los Angeles. For all its airy palette and light brush work, *The Eclipse of God*, begun soon after Kitaj's arrival in California, conveys the artist's sense of being under siege, even with a continent now between himself and his critics. The yellow barrier in the canvas might be read as the wall of Kitaj's yellow studio in the back yard of his new home in Los Angeles. And where the Jewish woman in Uccello's panel is clothed in vibrant red, in Kitaj's revision she's been turned an ashen black in memory of Sandra. A small child clings to her shade, perhaps reminding us of Kitaj and Sandra's young son Max.

6. Rosen, *Imagining Jewish Art*, 89.

Beyond Kitaj's own trials—which he casts in explicitly Jewish terms—the figures in Kitaj's painting also play a more emblematic role, symbolizing the long-suffering history of Jews in Europe, from the purported golden age of *quattrocento* Italy to the horrors of the Shoah. To all these accumulated tragedies, Kitaj's God—his name sketched on the cloaked figure in the foreground—stands witness. Tellingly, Kitaj positions the Almighty alongside the persecutors, watching impassively as they threaten to overwhelm their Jewish victims. While this depiction of the Divine might recall Exodus 33, in which Moses sees God from behind, the impending violence of the scene brings to mind the desperate plea to God in the Psalms: "Why do you hide your face?" (Pss. 44:24; 88:14). In a small canvas from 2005, one of several late works in which he takes up this theme of God's hidden countenance, Kitaj spells out this very question at the bottom of the painting, citing Psalm 44. Just as the Israelites suffer unjustly under their enemies in the psalm—which reminds God that it is not *they* who have forgotten their holy covenant—the Jews in Kitaj's *Eclipse* stand blameless, awaiting God's intervention. Translucent and inert amidst the tumult, God shows no signs of coming to the rescue. Whereas the Corpus Domini Altarpiece was meant to remind Christians of the "real presence" of their God in the sacrament of communion, Kitaj imagines a Jewish God who has become—at most—an absent presence.

To use the painting's title, borrowed from the eponymous book by Martin Buber, we witness *The Eclipse of God*. In this series of essays, first published in 1952,[7] Buber attempts to unmask the ways in which modern philosophy has marginalized God, making a genuine I-Thou relationship with the Divine seem unreal or impossible. Behind the task which Buber ostensibly sets himself, however, lies a further anxiety which he only hints at: that it is not merely humanity which has obscured God in modernity, but God who has shrouded himself from humanity. It is this second eclipse, as it were, which lies at the heart of Kitaj's canvas. By choosing to frame his work around this question of theodicy, the problem of God's presence in the face of evil, Kitaj makes it clear that his stated project of repainting Uccello and other artistic precursors "over again, after Auschwitz,"[8] extends beyond the merely polemic, beyond simply shifting accusations from Jews to Christians. For the Jewish viewer, Kitaj reassigns Uccello's masterpiece within a Jewish tradition of protest, of calling the Almighty to account in

7. Buber, *The Eclipse of God*.
8. Kitaj, "Jewish Art—Indictment & Defence," 46.

the spirit of Psalm 44. For the Christian viewer, who might be unfamiliar or uncomfortable with Uccello's image of Jewish persecution, Kitaj insists on the value of resurrecting this work as a cultural inheritance. If the Jewish artist is accustomed to approaching the artistic past from the outside, from a position of disjunction, Kitaj suggests that it is just as important for Christians to train themselves to be uncomfortable with their *own* tradition. To learn to look, in a sense, with Jewish eyes.

9. Siona Benjamin: Next Year in Nineveh?

We were fashioned to live in Paradise, and Paradise was destined to serve us. Our destiny has been altered; that this has also happened with the destiny of Paradise is not stated.—FRANZ KAFKA[9]

"Next year in Jerusalem." Every Passover, Jews around the world intone this deceptively simple formula, freighted with centuries of both diasporic disappointment and messianic hopefulness. While the Passover seder commemorates the ancient Israelites' emancipation from bondage, in the same breath it insists that freedom—true freedom—belongs to the future. It is this tension, balanced on the knife's edge of possibility, that Siona Benjamin probes so powerfully in *Exodus: I See Myself in You* (2016; **Fig. 9.1**), and the images which ripple out from it in her new exhibition, "Beyond Borders."[10] Above all, these works remind us of fetters that remain, escapes deferred to the next year and the next. Benjamin paints Jerusalems of the mind: paradises gained, lost, mourned, and imagined. Though she takes inspiration from the stories and rituals of Judaism, she conjures images capable of bearing the hopes and disappointments of Jews and non-Jews alike.

The works in this exhibition are haunted by the tragedies of recent events, especially the struggles of Syrian refugees who have fled the brutality of ISIS and Assad. Benjamin sees a contemporary Exodus unfolding in the journeys of these refugees, and she utilizes biblical imagery and symbolism to lend them dignity. This strategy sets her apart from many of the artists who have attempted to grapple with the catastrophe. A number of artists

9. Kafka, "Paradise," 29.
10. Opalka Gallery, Sage Colleges, New York, June 2016.

have repurposed the photograph of three-year-old Alan Kurdi, whose body washed ashore on the beaches of Bodrum, Turkey, in September, 2015, after the flimsy, overcrowded boat in which he and his family were traveling capsized. In Frankfurt, street artists spray-painted a giant image of the toddler onto a wall on the banks of the Main River, while an artist in India formed a giant effigy of Alan out of sand. More solipsistically, Ai Weiwei photographed himself lying 'lifeless' on the seashore. Like the young boy photographed raising his hands in the Warsaw Ghetto in 1943, Alan's image has—in just nine months—been appropriated to the point of paralyzing ubiquity. Acutely aware of the dangers of over-saturation, Benjamin honors the experiences of refugees not by merely recapitulating images of their suffering, but by inventing stories that speak to their dreams.

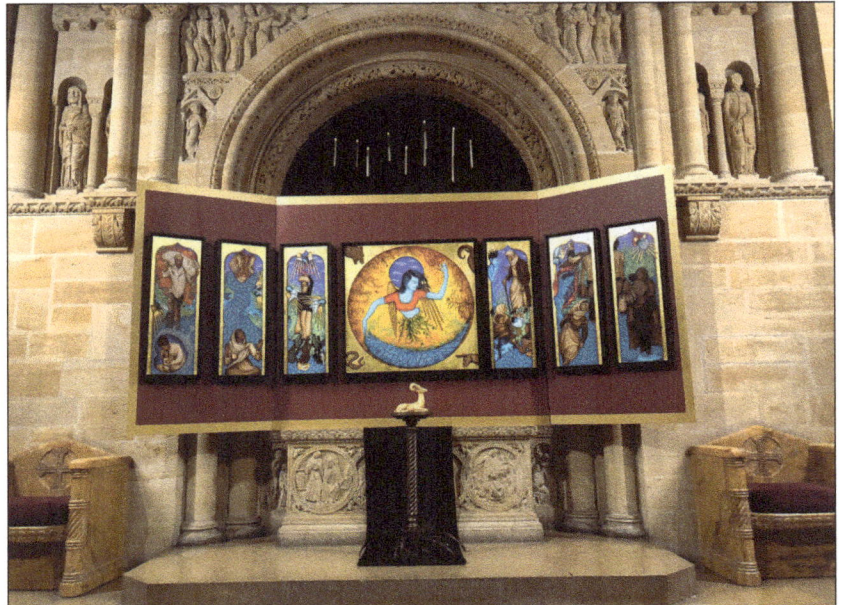

Figure 9.1

Closely following the conflict in Syria through the news, Benjamin has assiduously gathered clippings and digital images of forced migration over the past year in preparation for her new work. She began her process by isolating and focusing upon single figures in photographs, attempting to understand their pain one by one rather than *en masse*. Using drawing to identify with people who would otherwise remain anonymous,

Benjamin found herself repeating the words which later found their way into the title of this new body of work: "I see myself in you." The lines in her drawings are never merely mimetic, never simply copies of the faces captured in photographs. Through the act of drawing, she accomplishes a much more profound and complicated act of transformation, shifting gazes, postures, and gestures in ways that return to these weary figures some of the peace and tranquility that has been stolen from them. There is pain in these drawings, to be sure, but there is also a determined quietness. Even as she renders a woman crying out in anguish, for instance, she gives her the space and stillness to grieve. With palpable softness, Benjamin's pencil cradles the people she draws.

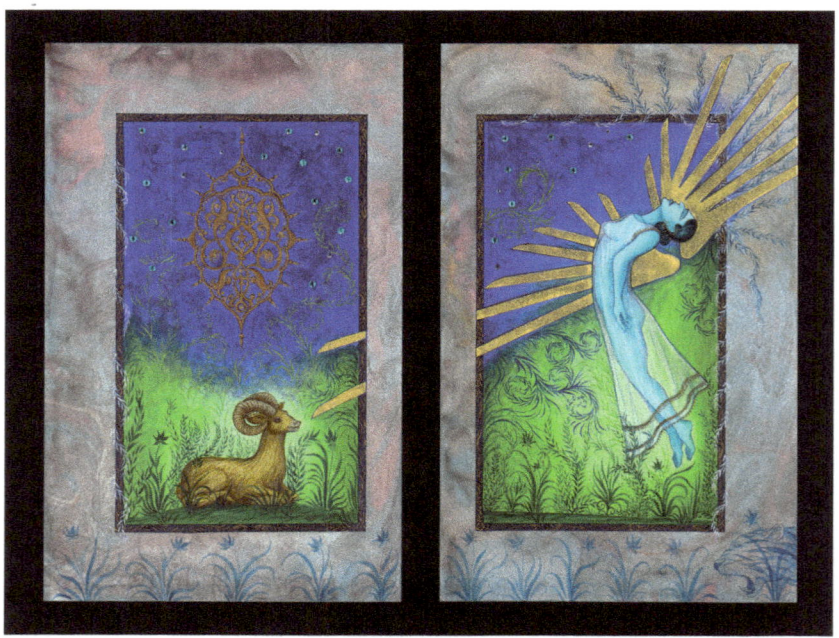

Figure 9.2

Benjamin not only brings to these figures a personal empathy but a wealth of art historical allusions and affinities. Persian and Mughal miniature paintings from the sixteenth through the eighteenth centuries have been a consistent source of inspiration for Benjamin over the past two decades. While she channeled the jewel-like precision of masters such as Bihzad (1470–1506) in her earlier work, in recent creations she has extended her engagement with this tradition in new directions (**Fig. 9.2**). Her studies of refugees recall sketches and paintings by Riza-yi `Abbasi (c. 1565–1635) and his disciple Mu'in Musavvir (active c. 1630–97), who pioneered a new direction in Islamic painting, developing single-page illustrations of characters observed from life, documenting people on the margins of society.

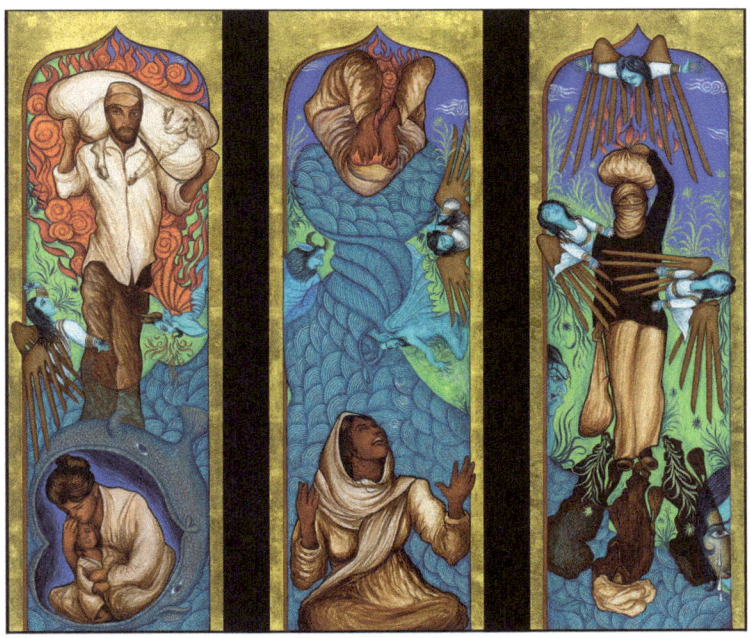

Figure 9.3

At the same time that Benjamin brings to bear on her subject a refined grasp of Islamic art, she also channels precursors from across the history of Western culture. The woman and child in her Exodus panels (**Fig. 9.3**) recall Käthe Kollwitz's haunting images of mothers mourning their children, as well as Marc Chagall's depiction of the biblical Hagar, who fears her young son Ishmael may die in the desert. The figure of the whale evokes parallels with medieval Christian illuminated manuscripts, in which Jonah's three days and nights inside the "great fish" prefigure Christ's entombment and resurrection. In Benjamin's image, the sad-eyed whale harbors mother and child like a womb. This protection is painfully undercut, however, when we remember the fate of Alan Kurdi and his mother, for whom no miraculous assistance appeared from the deep. The reference to Jonah adds yet another interpretive layer. The wayward prophet was called upon to prophesy to the city of Nineveh, which today lies in northern Iraq, near Mosul, an ISIS stronghold. Do we dare hope, Benjamin asks, that the citizens of modern Mosul will be spared like those of ancient Nineveh?

Rising up from behind the whale, emerging from the sea, Benjamin paints what is—if not an answer—a prayer. A man browned by sun and grime from a long journey carries a ram over his shoulders. The artist's source is a photograph of a refugee bearing a sack slumped against his neck. Benjamin, schooled in Jewish tradition, cannot help but render this lumpy mass as a ram. And not just any ram, I suspect, but the ram of the Akedah, the "real hero" of Genesis 22, as the poet Yehuda Amichai once called him.[11] When God stays Abraham's hand from sacrificing his son, the patriarch looks up and spies a ram caught in a thicket, which he slaughters instead. This is no random, dumb, unlucky beast, midrash tells us. This ram was created in paradise, at the beginning of time, for this one special purpose. Ever since Creation it had been running as fast as it could in order to arrive atop Mount Moriah at that very moment, that it might offer itself instead of Isaac, ensuring the future of the chosen people.[12] Maybe we have left paradise, maybe we have lost it forever. But perhaps, this story teaches us, it can still save us. This is Siona Benjamin's offering.

---

11. Amichai, "The Real Hero," 156.
12. Spiegel, *The Last Trial*, 150.

Death

10. Adel Abdessemed: The Heretic's Sacrifice

> [I]n contact with that strange man, all things reverted, as it were,
> to the roots of their existence, rebuilt their outward appearance
> anew from their metaphysical core, returned to the primary idea,
> in order to betray it at some point and to turn into the doubt-
> ful, risky, and equivocal regions which we shall call for short the
> Regions of the Great Heresy. Our Heresiarch walked meanwhile
> like a mesmerist, infecting everything with his dangerous charm.
> —BRUNO SCHULZ, "THE STREET OF CROCODILES"[1]

The concept of sacrifice has become tremendously flexible. Donald Trump,
heir to a dubiously begotten family fortune and beneficiary of five defer-
ments from Vietnam, can claim, without a whiff of irony, "I've made a lot
of sacrifices."[2] Slathering one's name across Manhattan skyscrapers and
Floridian golf courses is, apparently, the apotheosis of the Protestant work
ethic. If sacrifice can easily become diluted, it can also be dangerously concentrated. Exploiting Islamic tradition, in which acts of self-sacrifice made
during Ramadan carry special significance, Daesh has repeatedly prompted and promoted brutal terrorist attacks during this sacred period.[3] The
concept of sacrifice—already one of the most enormously overdetermined
concepts in religious and political history—has, it seems, come to mean
both too little and too much in deeply unsettling ways. In the face of such
distortions and manipulations, we need a fresh approach to discourses of
sacrifice today more than ever.

Enter the artist Adel Abdessemed. Throughout his career, Abdessemed
has honed an uncanny instinct for exposing and scrutinizing the values that
we hold most dear and most self-evident. His aim, as he formulates it, is not

---

1. Schulz, *The Street of Crocodiles*, 30. I was rereading this text when I first met the
artist, who flipped through it gleefully.

2. Turnham, "Donald Trump to Father of Fallen Soldier."

3. Withnall, "US Warns of Month of Violence."

to consolidate or concretize concepts but rather to "create oppositions, para-doxes, to put things in crisis."[4] On first blush, it would be easy to misread this antinomian impulse as simply anarchic or nihilistic. And yet this refusal to let himself—or his viewers—settle for sanctimonious truisms is itself, as we shall see, an ethically motivated endeavor. Julia Kristeva gestures in this direction in a recent epistle to Abdessemed. "You are not a moralist," she writes to him approvingly. "You don't show us the way, you have no road-map. You bring us into your laboratory—it's up to us to enjoy, to wince, to think!"[5] Egging him on, she exhorts the artist: "There's still a whole history of cults, of values, of certainties to be subverted, dear friend!"[6] And perhaps no subject is so ripe for this demystifying touch as sacrifice, in which cults, values, and certainties all converge.

Abdessemed himself has pointed to the centrality of sacrifice in our moral economies. In a 2012 conversation with the curator Pier Luigi Tazzi, he mused: "we find the notion of sacrifice in the three monotheistic reli-gions, the lamb that replaces, is put in the place of man."[7] Cryptically, and without elaborating, he adds, "It can be said that we have always lived in terror."[8] While Tazzi chose not to chase Abdessemed on this point, this sug-gestive comment constitutes a sort of Thesean thread that I would like to pick up and follow in this essay. Abdessemed places terror or violence at the very center of human existence, as a sort of primordial condition to which sacrificial rites respond. In this respect Abdessemed parallels, and perhaps even consciously echoes, the philosopher René Girard, who asserts that "violence is the heart and secret soul of the sacred."[9] For Girard, the substitutive act of sacrifice—particularly the identification of a scapegoat—constitutes a mechanism for diverting violence away from communities in conflict. True to form, however, Abdessemed is more interested in how such a system falters and fails than how it functions. If sacrifice diverts violence, according to Girard, Abdessemed reminds us that it also fuels it, feeding the very "terror" it seems to extinguish. Abdessemed makes no

---

4. Abdessemed, *Conversation with Pier Luigi Tazzi*, 15.

5. Kristeva, "Le corps d'Adel (Conversation)."

6. Kristeva, "Le corps d'Adel (Conversation)."

7. Abdessemed, *Conversation with Pier Luigi Tazzi*, 43.

8. Abdessemed, *Conversation with Pier Luigi Tazzi*, 43.

9. Girard, *Violence and the Sacred*, 32.

claims about what true sacrifice is or should be. A self-professed "detector,"[10] he is much more interested in its deceptions.

To explore this theme further, let us turn our attention to some key works by Abdessemed, beginning with *Bristow* (2016; **Fig. 10.1**). In *Bristow*, Abdessemed casts a pigeon in the unlikely role of suicide bomber. By loading this primitive messenger (carrier pigeon) with a passé detonator (the hopelessly un-hip Blackberry), and outmoded explosives (dynamite), Abdessemed lends a darkly comic touch to the work, as if we are privy to an attack planned by a comic book villain. Perched on a pillar atop the Peckham Rye Multistorey Car Park, the avian combatant twitches its neck toward central London, and the landmarks (targets?) that stud the horizon, from St. Paul's Cathedral to the Shard. The figure first appeared in *La grande parade* (2011–12), a charcoal sketch in which Abdessemed depicted an otherwise happy assembly of animals freighted with explosives. These "invisible kamikazes" are inspired—the artist tells us—by the Berber fables he grew up with and now reads to his children.[11] We might also find parallels in the classic animal tales of Jean de la Fontaine, famously illustrated by Marc Chagall.

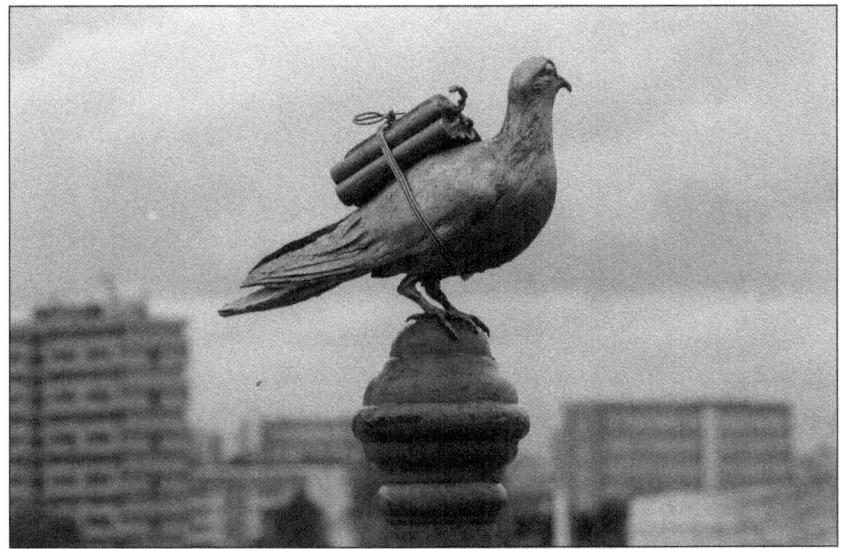

Figure 10.1

10. Abdessemed, "Adel Abdessemed in conversation with Elisabeth Lebovici," 111.

11. Abdessemed, *Conversation with Pier Luigi Tazzi*, 66.

Whereas fairy tales serve to sublimate and manage our fears, however, *Bristow* makes our collective anxieties painfully, absurdly present. In a city perpetually on edge over terrorist threats, *Bristow* satirizes our suspicions. Even the most ubiquitous, mundane, stupid presence in the metropolis—pigeons for God's sake!—might be enemy agents. Perhaps even more disconcertingly, Abdessemed raises the possibility that terrorism's unwitting or unwilling conscripts might be worthy of empathy. So long as a terrorist chooses the path of "martyrdom," he remains safely, self-evidently condemnable. But what about the individual offered up on the altar of someone else's ideology, for the sake of someone else's God? Is it possible, Abdessemed asks, that such an individual might be as blameless as *Bristow*? In another world, *Bristow* could have borne happy tidings, carrying an olive branch instead of a bomb, like the dove dispatched by Noah (Genesis 8.8–12).

In the face of violence, we routinely insist that God could never, would never, sanction the shedding of innocent blood. And yet Scripture itself denies us such certainty. On the contrary, Judaism, Christianity, and Islam each exalt the willingness of their common ancestor, Abraham, to sacrifice his son—whether Isaac or Ishmael—at God's request. That the Angel of the Lord ultimately stays the patriarch's blade, providing a ram for the offering instead, dampens but does not undo the damage of God's command. In both Jewish and Islamic tradition, the devil actually attempts a humanitarian intervention, arguing—as Immanuel Kant would later do—that such a monstrous request transgresses moral law, and must therefore be rejected. Like Jacques Derrida, we may want to believe "that it would be most improbable for the sacrifice of Isaac to be repeated in our day," that it would be impossible to "imagine a father taking his son to be sacrificed on the top of the hill at Montmartre."[12] And yet, as both Derrida and Abdessemed know, such sacrifices are all too possible, all too easy to justify. In a charcoal sketch from 2014, Abdessemed began to meditate upon and re-envision Caravaggio's *Sacrifice of Isaac* (c. 1603) from the Uffizi Gallery. By pasting a surgical blade onto his drawing, Abdessemed implies that the story of Abraham's sacrifice slices into itself, paring away at its own pieties. He extends this insight in a life-size sculpture, *Untitled* (2014; **Fig. 10.2**), in which his own father brandishes a knife while the artist kneels in submission. The intoxicating God-sickness of Abraham, Abdessemed suggests, is a disease that

---

12. Derrida, *The Gift of Death*, 85.

travels the generations, infecting every father and jeopardizing every son.[13] Encased in a skin of scalpel blades, there can be no embrace between this father and son. No caress that heals the wound of a zealous parent. Every touch simply whets the blade and sharpens the taste for sacrifice. Unlike Caravaggio's masterpiece, no angelic hope waits in the wings. No substitute victim emerges from the thicket to spare this Isaac-Ishmael-Adel. The artist volunteers himself as monotheism's favorite son, the promise and menace of all three faiths projected onto his bowed and terrified body. Indeed, he seems to relish this role, which he sees as a sort of birthright from his upbringing in Algeria, where the three faiths intersected in daily life. "I was born in Constantine to a Muslim mother in a Jewish house and with Christian nuns as midwives," he recalls. "On that day, I think I brought the gods of monotheism together."[14]

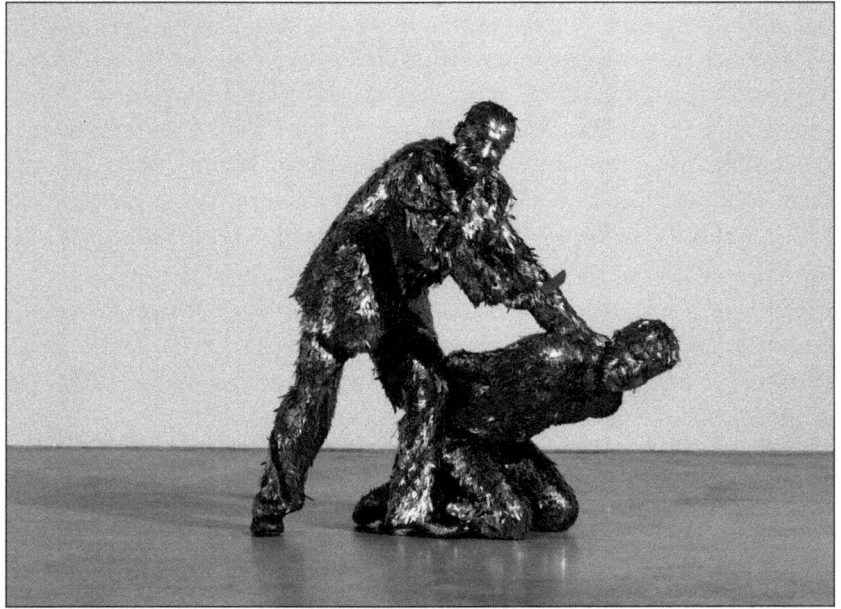

Figure 10.2

13. Abdessemed and Hélène Cixous return several times in their correspondence to the imagery of Abraham's sacrifice, and the theme of internecine struggle. See Cixous, *Insurrection de la poussiere.*

14. Abdessemed, *Conversation with Pier Luigi Tazzi*, 9.

Abdessemed is not content to problematize merely the *act* of sacrifice. Just as importantly, he disrupts the *sacrament* of sacrifice. In *Décor* (2011–12; **Fig. 10.3**), Abdessemed pays homage to the tormented, gangrenous Christ of Matthias Grünewald's *Isenheim Altarpiece* (c. 1515) in Colmar, France, to which he undertook a pilgrimage soon after arriving in the country.[15] Much like Graham Sutherland, another modern devotee of Grünewald,[16] Abdessemed is obsessed by the exaggerated spikes that comprise Jesus' crown of thorns, echoed by his bony, tetanic digits, which claw the sky. In Abdessemed's incarnation, repeated four times—as if arrogating to himself the right to speak for each of the Evangelists—Grünewald's thorns transmogrify into a distinctly modern form of torture: the razor wire of prisons and detention camps. "The thing that wounds," Abdessemed explains, thus "becomes the materials for the representation of the wounded."[17] The artist goes on to declare that his Christ is, in fact, "nothing but one huge wound"[18]—an intuition echoed by Hans Belting, who reached out to touch the sculpture in the artist's studio, like the incredulous disciple Thomas, and pricked his thumb.[19] Abdessemed's Christ may draw blood, slicing anyone who dare touch it, but—and the theological distinction is crucial—he never *provides* it. At the base of Grünewald's Crucifixion, the Lamb of God collects his precious blood in a chalice. The despicable suffering of this flayed Redeemer is not for nothing, the Lamb insists: it yields the saving blood of the Eucharist, the drink that ransoms mankind from damnation. On the contrary, *Décor*—a homonym for "décorps," or disembodiment[20]—presents us with a resolutely disincarnate Christ, bereft of flesh and blood. There is authentic anguish in Abdessemed's sculptures. But pain never translates—never *transubstantiates*—into salvation.

It is this desire to fight against the symbolic appropriation of suffering, to contest the logic of redemption at its outer limits, I think, which ultimately lies behind Abdessemed's most infamous work: *Don't Trust Me* (2007). In this video, shot on a farm in Mexico, a succession of animals—horse, pig, goat, sheep, doe, ox—are yoked to a wall and bludgeoned in

---

15. Alloa, "Portrait of the Artist as a Pagan," 140.

16. For a discussion of other modern artists who have reimagined the *Isenheim Altarpiece*, see Rosen, *Imagining Jewish Art*, 30–42.

17. Abdessemed, *Conversation with Pier Luigi Tazzi*, 71–72.

18. Abdessemed, *Conversation with Pier Luigi Tazzi*, 71.

19. Belting, "Cher Adel Abdessemed."

20. Alloa, "Portrait of the Artist as a Pagan," 139.

quick succession—"as if there was only one death for all the passengers of Noah's ark."[21] As the dull thud of an anonymous sledgehammer crushes their skulls, they crumple to the cobblestones. There is no context. No narrative. As the sun hits the brick wall behind these poor beasts there is an orange glow, faintly reminiscent of Francis Bacon's *Three Studies for Figures at the Base of a Crucifixion* (1944). But there is no mention of Crucifixion here, no allusion to the Eumenides, nor any other trace of mythic meaning left by Bacon. "In my work," Abdessemed has commented, "animals are presences, not symbols, icons, or signs. They're not there to replace something. They're really there."[22] If, as Girard asserts, the logic of sacrifice demands that "all victims, even the animal ones, bear a certain *resemblance* to the object they replace,"[23] Abdessemed's refusal of "symbols, icons, or signs" becomes crucially important. By refusing resemblance he undermines the economy of sacrifice. I think a similar intuition lies behind Patricia Falguieres's remark that "*Don't Trust Me* exposed the gap between slaughter and sacrifice, between the ritual and the minimal technical implementation of the animal's 'killability.'"[24] On the other hand, as Elisabeth de Fontenay points out, the looped format of the video connotes the "repetition of a ritual gesture," suggesting that "something of the act of sacrifice is being shown here."[25] How, then, should we make sense of this tension, the artist's simultaneous suggestion and disavowal of sacrifice? Abdessemed's cancelled gesture makes palpable—I would suggest—the absence of meaning in the act of sacrifice. Or, perhaps more accurately still, the meaning of absence.

For an artist who memorably chose the declaration *Je suis innocent* for the title of his most important exhibition, a 2012 retrospective at the Centre Pompidou, it is arguably much more important to Abdessemed, and his art, that he be found guilty. In the midst of protests and death threats over *Don't Trust Me* and other works during a 2008 exhibition in San Francisco, Abdessemed issued an unusual response. Rather than attempt to diffuse or deny accusations of animal cruelty, he simply stated: "I do not seek to feign, justify, or excuse that act of slaughter. It exists."[26] In a characteristically paradoxical manner, this statement is, of course, its

21. Cixous, *Insurrection de la poussiere.*

22. Abdessemed, *Conversation with Pier Luigi Tazzi,* 49.

23. Girard, *Violence and the Sacred,* 12; italics in original.

24. Falguieres, "State of Exception," 209.

25. de Fontenay, "Urgence d'une decreation."

26. Lee, "Animal Feeling," 171.

own form of justification. The artist cannot vindicate the work because its very nature, its very purpose, is to defy teleological expectations, to negate the logic of sacrifice. Denying the efficacy of sacrifice might make Abdessemed a heretic, but it certainly does not make him anti-religious. Heretics may invert theology, but they do not reject it. They are merely believers by another name. If Abdessemed sets flame to our pieties it is not out of cynicism, I would argue, but rather out of optimism, in order that he might burn away what is lifeless and inauthentic from our value systems, like a cleansing wildfire. So devoted is he to this enterprise, it is only on the rarest of occasions that he hints at what might be left, the epiphany in the ashes: *One life one love one god* (2008).

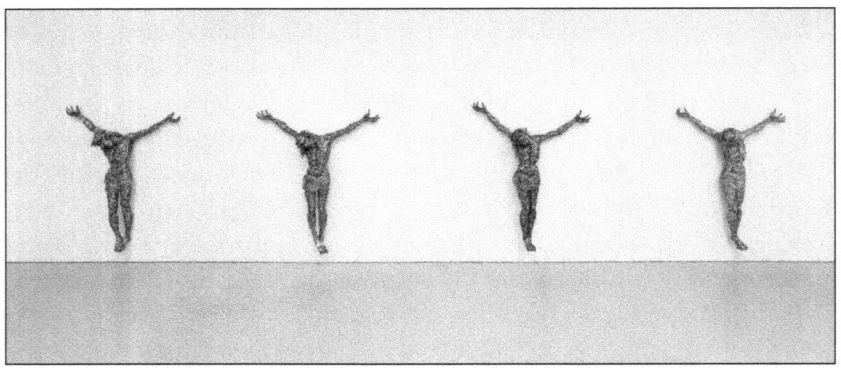

Figure 10.3

11. Art Spiegelman: Shadow Boxing

The cartoonist Art Spiegelman watched firsthand as the "glowing bones" of the World Trade Center's north tower shivered and collapsed on the morning of September 11, 2001.[27] After he and his wife retrieved their daughter from near the foot of the towers—where she had just started high school— they rushed across town to collect their son. With his family safely reunited, Spiegelman broke down into tears. Shaken as he was, and convinced more than ever that the world was ending—even now, in the preface to *No*

27. Spiegelman, *No Towers*, ii.

Towers, he only concedes that it "seems to be ending more slowly than I once thought"[28]—Spiegelman began that same day to try and draft some image of what he had witnessed. At the prompting of his wife, an editor at the *New Yorker,* he composed the cover image for the magazine's first edition after September 11. Inspired by the black-on-black paintings of Ad Reinhardt, Spiegelman's design sets the varnished silhouettes of the fallen towers against a deeper field of black. Printed just six days after the attacks, this aching image of absence inspired the cover for what is now *In the Shadow of No Towers,* Spiegelman's comic book narrative of 9/11.

A tall slab of a book—one that noses above its peers on the bookshelf as the towers themselves once presided over the New York skyline—*No Towers* reproduces a series of ten broadsheet pages composed by Spiegelman between September 2001 and August 2003. Originally serialized in *Die Zeit,* which commissioned the works, the strips also appeared in several other prominent European publications, including the *London Review of Books.* In America, however, mainstream publications such as the *New Yorker* and *New York Times* shied away from the sharp political content. Published as a book in time for the third anniversary of September 11, the work was destined for a factious reception. In America, some right-wing critics were nettled by what they saw as a deficit of patriotism from the artist. Many left-wing readers, on the other hand, saw him as a sort of comic avenger, cheering his references to "that creature in the White House,"[29] and chuckling appreciatively at his images of a trigger-happy President Bush holding an American flag in one hand and brandishing a pistol in the other. While these barbs are sometimes trite, or needlessly acerbic—Spiegelman ridicules America's red states as the place "where the 44% of Americans who don't believe in evolution tend to gather"[30]—at its best Spiegelman's political commentary is wryly incisive. His drawing of a shabby bald eagle croaking out shibboleths—"Everything's changed! Awk! . . . Go out and shop! Awk . . . Be Afraid!"—perfectly perforates the banality of much political discourse in the wake of the tragedy.[31]

Yet to evaluate *No Towers* solely as a political cartoon is to miss what makes the narrative so artistically significant, both as a work in itself and as an integral part of Spiegelman's oeuvre. Rendered in styles ranging

28. Spiegelman, *No Towers,* ii.

29. Spiegelman, *No Towers,* 7.

30. Spiegelman, *No Towers,* 7.

31. Spiegelman, *No Towers,* 2.

from traditional pen and ink to computer-generated graphics, *No Towers* employs a hectic assortment of iconography culled from early-twentieth-century comics as well as vintage trading cards, underground "comix," and contemporary advertisements. For Michiko Kakutani, writing in *The New York Times*, this scattered style accurately evokes "the chaos and cacophony of 9/11."[32] But while this is undoubtedly one effect of Spiegelman's bricolage, it lends us little specific insight into his imagery. Why is it that Spiegelman finds classic comic strips in particular such a compelling source for narrating the story of 9/11? Or, to quote a caption from *No Towers*, why is it that for Spiegelman "the blast that disintegrated those Lower Manhattan towers also disinterred the ghosts of some Sunday supplement stars born on nearby Park Row about a century earlier"?[33]

In the first instance, as Spiegelman explains in the supplement to *No Towers*, it was the apparent *irrelevance* of these comic characters that made them such appropriate protagonists. In the aftermath of the attacks, he recalls,

> my mind kept wandering. I found no solace in [poetry or] music of any kind . . . it seemed too obscenely exquisite. The only cultural artifacts that could get past my defenses to flood my eyes and brain with something other than images of burning towers were old comic strips; vital, unpretentious ephemera from the optimistic dawn of the twentieth century.[34]

Reincarnating the twin towers as the rascally Katzenjammer Kids, and recasting himself as a host of characters—from Little Nemo to Jiggs, Ignatz Mouse, and Happy Hooligan—allows Spiegelman to introduce a protective barrier between himself and the events of 9/11.

At the same time as these images attenuate the traumas of the recent past, they also combat a more distant trauma:

> Outrunning the toxic cloud that had moments before been the north tower of the World Trade Center [Spiegelman writes in his preface] left me reeling on that fault line where World History and Personal History collide—the intersection my parents, Auschwitz survivors, had warned me about . . .[35]

32. Kakutani, "Portraying 9/11 as a Katzenjammer Catastrophe."
33. Spiegelman, *No Towers*, 8.
34. Spiegelman, *No Towers*, 11.
35. Spiegelman, *No Towers*, i.

What Spiegelman must outrun, then, is not only the choking smoke of the present, but what Thane Rosenbaum, in the title of his novel, calls the "second hand smoke" of Auschwitz: the received memories of the Shoah which threaten to turn the present into the past.[36] If he is to successfully fend off these inherited traumas, Spiegelman must, in No Towers, imagine himself as something other than his parents.

To do so, Spiegelman must escape an iconography of his own design. In Maus, his two-volume opus about the Holocaust—published in 1986 and 1992, when it won the Pulitzer Prize—Spiegelman used animals to tell the story of his parents' survival in wartime Poland.[37] Alternating between fraught interviews with his father in the present and scenes from his father's memories of the past, Maus employs a deceptively simple iconography: Germans are depicted as cats, Jews as mice. While no such feline predators appear in No Towers, Spiegelman repeatedly depicts himself as mouse—or more precisely as maus—in seven of the work's ten pages. Adopting the guises of Little Nemo, Ignatz, and other characters is Spiegelman's strategy for staving off this identification, for imagining himself as something other than maus, in a time and a place other than Auschwitz. Innocuous old comics, then, are a critical bulwark against the past; a defense not against memory, but against the post-traumatic consciousness in which one trauma is allowed to seep dangerously into another, making the past predictive of the present.

And yet, already on the second page of No Towers, this defense appears to crumble. Underneath a poster for his missing brain—"last seen in Lower Manhattan, mid-September 2001"[38]—Spiegelman dozes over his drawing board. His dreams are a traumatic stew of past and present. "Equally terrorized by Al-Qaeda and by his own government"[39]—a scimitar-wielding terrorist looms to the left and a gun-toting President Bush threatens from the right. On his desk a ragtag assortment of comic strip characters stare out, disoriented, at the viewer. But while these characters pop up in later pages, often with Spiegelman assuming their identities, the very first guise which he assumes, critically, is one of his own making: maus.

By the next page this image has multiplied into a series of sixteen small grey panels in which Spiegelman, qua maus, sucks nervously away at one

---

36. Rosenbaum, Second Hand Smoke.

37. Spiegelman, The Complete Maus.

38. Spiegelman, No Towers, 2.

39. Spiegelman, No Towers, 2.

cigarette after another. What first appears to be a box of Camels, however, is a pack of "Cremo Lights,"[40] the macabre brand—its logo is the puffing chimney of a crematorium—familiar from *Maus*. Thus, rather than calming Spiegelman's anxieties about the present, smoking compounds them, symbolically piping in the traumas of the past. If, as Spiegelman put it in *Maus*, his father bled history, here Spiegelman breathes it. "I remember my father trying to describe what the smoke in Auschwitz smelled like," Spiegelman muses in the first of these panels. "The closest he got," he continues, "was telling me it was . . . 'indescribable.'"[41] Silence follows as Spiegelman exhales a series of slow swirling rings. Suddenly, struck by a realization, he blurts out: "That's exactly what the air in Lower Manhattan smelled like after Sept. 11!"[42] The commingling is darkly alluring for Spiegelman, promising to satisfy a deep epistemological fantasy, his desire to know what it was really like for his parents in Auschwitz.[43] And yet, the equivalence, even between "indescribables," is a dangerous one. While Spiegelman's traumatic associations might confuse the differences, the secondhand smoke that seeps from Ground Zero must not be mistaken for the miasma of Holocaust memory. Even if such an elision of history were acceptable—and it is not—this double asphyxiation leaves scarce if any room for living.

And so it is that, after reaching this saturation point with the past, Spiegelman turns increasingly to other comic characters. Even so, the Holocaust past stubbornly resurfaces as even the most innocent characters transmogrify into *mäuse*. On page six, Spiegelman imagines himself as Little Nemo, the adolescent hero of Winsor McCay's *Little Nemo in Slumberland*. In each episode of the classic strip, Nemo toddles around in his nightclothes enjoying the surreal adventures of Slumberland, only to awaken abruptly and find it has all been a dream. Here, in Spiegelman's homage, signed McSpiegelman, it is a "mausketeer" version of Nemo who wakes up, disoriented, on the floor. While his mother clucks reassuringly— "Hush, you fell out of bed, sweetie"—her presence is unnerving.[44] As we know from *Maus*, Spiegelman's own mother committed suicide in 1968.[45] In this image, the mother wears a menacing green gas mask. Evoking the

40. Spiegelman, *No Towers*, 3.

41. Spiegelman, *No Towers*, 3.

42. Spiegelman, *No Towers*, 3.

43. Spiegelman, *Maus*, 174–76.

44. Spiegelman, *No Towers*, 6.

45. Spiegelman, *Maus*, 201.

doubly toxic smoke that pervaded page three, the gas mask also recalls Spiegelman's admission in *Maus* that, while growing up, "sometimes I'd fantasize Zyklon B coming out of our shower instead of water."[46] As these associations make clear, Spiegelman's dreams are Jewish nightmares; a point only exacerbated by the panels above. Barking invectives at a passing Spiegelman, a homeless woman shouts: "You damn Kikes—You did it! . . . Dirty Jew! We'll hang you from the lamp posts, *one by one!*"[47]

Despite all attempts to imagine himself otherwise, in the end Spiegelman is, invariably, the man in the *maus* mask. In the final page of *No Towers*, he places himself amidst a crowd of comic characters—among them Doonesbury, Wimpy, Orphan Annie, Charlie Brown, and Hapless Hooligan—all trapped within the burning north tower of the Trade Center. Rather than assume the identities of any of these characters, Spiegelman chooses, in his final self-representation, just as in his first, to draw himself as *maus*. And, for the first time in *No Towers*, his son, daughter, and wife are also depicted as *mäuse*. On page six, commenting on the homeless woman hurling abuse at him, Spiegelman reflected that "her inner demons had broken loose and taken over our shared reality." Here, in the last panels of *No Towers*, it is Spiegelman's own demons that have broken loose, drawing his family into his Holocaust nightmare. Depicting himself frantically attempting to push his way out of the tower, he echoes the last image of his grandfather, in *Maus I*. Trapped, and awaiting imminent deportation to Auschwitz, his grandfather presses against the panes of a second-floor window. As we learn from Spiegelman's father, "On Wednesday the vans came . . . He was tearing his hair and crying . . . He was a millionaire, but even this didn't save him his life."[48]

As *No Towers* draws to a close, Spiegelman succumbs to the shades of the past. For those seeking some exportable catharsis, this conclusion will be unsatisfactory. Neither tribute nor commemoration, this dense, intensely personal work will not live up to expectations of universality. However, for those willing to wrestle seriously with the work's complexities, there is a rare satisfaction in watching Spiegelman spar with his private torments. As he tangles with the images of his own artistic past, and the classic images of his chosen art form, we get the distinct sense that we are witnessing a comics heavyweight returned to the height of his powers.

46. Spiegelman, *Maus*, 176.

47. Spiegelman, *No Towers*, 6.

48. Spiegelman, *Maus*, 117.

12. Leni Dothan: Listening for Death

The artist is omnipresent in her work. In image after image, Leni Dothan stands naked—undaunted and unafraid. These photographs have never struck me, however, as nudes. The artist's intent in such works is neither sensuous nor salacious, neither overtly enticing nor confrontational. She speaks directly to audiences about things that matter; subjects so primary and serious they can only be faced head-on, body to body, in compositions stripped bare of distractions. In a global art scene accustomed to skittishly sidestepping existential questions, Dothan's work cuts us to the quick, demanding our unflinching attention to her most basic fear: death.

Dothan bluntly announces her obsession in a marble memorial stone engraved with a simple text: *Birth & Death*. Formally, the piece feels like a riposte to On Kawara's famous date paintings, as if she has scrubbed away all referents, all history, leaving only the most basic facts behind: we live, we die. The piece serves as an interpretive keystone not only for this exhibition but for Dothan's creative practice more broadly. The early modern essayist Michel de Montaigne asserted that "to philosophize is to learn how to die."[49] For Dothan, art-making is its own exercise in mortality, requiring no less rigorous a regimen than philosophy.

Yet it would be a mistake to draw too strong a parallel with Montaigne, or with existentialists such as Albert Camus and Jean-Paul Sartre, who place death at the core of their own meditations on human freedom. The death that Dothan habitually rehearses is not her own, or at least *not only* her own. When she builds a coffin, as she does in *Double* (2015), it is for both herself and her adolescent son Yali. To examine birth and death as the bookends of an exclusively individual quest is a luxury she does not entertain. For the artist, birth is always a *giving* birth, an action that creates an Other over and above oneself. In the giving of life, the symbolic logic of death is rewritten. Above all, it is the fear of subtraction, the eternal anxiety that the life that one gives might, at any moment, be taken away. To love, especially for a parent, is to live in the shadow of death.

Dothan's acts of preemptive mourning have an almost talismanic quality to them, as if by envisioning and preparing for her son's death she might prevent it. The primitive construction of works such as *Binded* (2015), made from crudely wrapped bandages, underscores the equally primitive fears they are intended to assuage. Like amulets, their effectiveness lies not

49. Montaigne, *Essays*, 89.

in their artifice but in the ancient forces they channel and challenge. It is not surprising that such meditations upon origins and endpoints lead Dothan into the domain of theology as much as philosophy. Her goal is not to come to terms with death but to defeat it, and this extravagant, impossible hope can only be entertained by religion not reason.

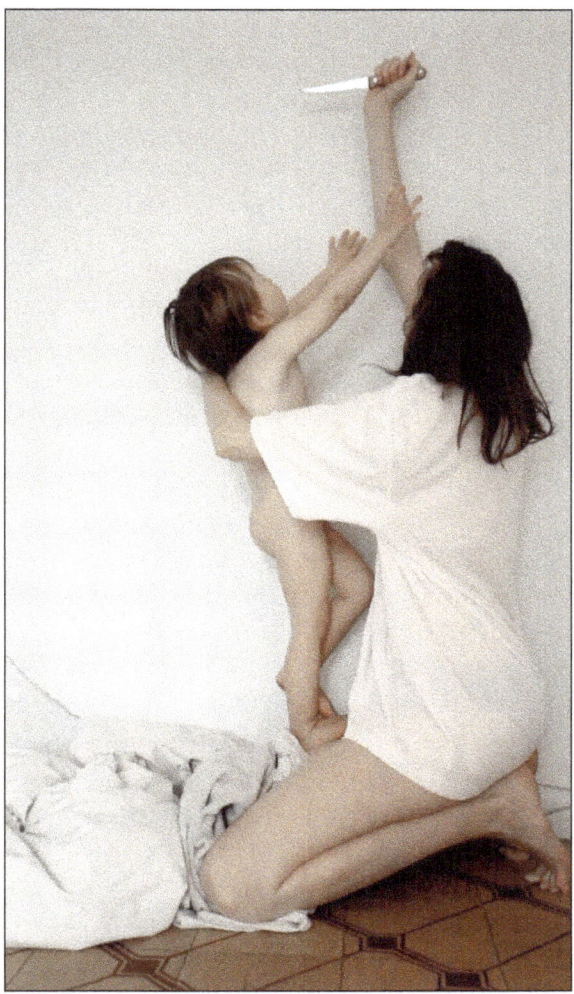

Figure 12.1

With the omnivorousness entitled to an artist, Dothan calls upon the resources of both Judaism and Christianity. In doing so, she seizes upon a motif that Jon Levenson calls "the death and resurrection of the beloved son."[50] While this paradigm is most apparent in the narrative of Christ, it has its origins—as Levenson explains—in the Hebrew Bible, which repeatedly brings its cherished sons, from Isaac to Joseph, to the very brink of death and back again. Fittingly, Dothan's own invocation of this motif, *Mine* (2012; **Fig. 12.1**), plays on loop, carrying on this ambivalent cycle *ad infinitum*. But there is a crucial difference between Dothan's video and the works of her mostly male precursors. In Dothan's rendition of the Binding of Isaac, it is not the aged Abraham who hoists a knife above his cherished offspring, but rather a young mother, clad unceremoniously in a nightshirt. There is no ram, no thicket, no mountain; only a duvet heaped in the corner. As her toddler fumbles toward her, Dothan holds a paring knife just above his grasp. There is no patriarchal test of faith, only a mother's desire to protect her child . . . even from herself.

As we explore Dothan's recent work, we see Yali grow, and the relationship between mother and son evolve. While the fear of loss never disappears, it is mitigated by a burgeoning sense of mutuality. The wooden structure of *Mother and Child in a Window* (2016; **Fig. 12.2**) suggests a Crucifixion (perhaps a reference to the *Brooklyn Crucifixion* imagined by Chaim Potok in the novel *My Name is Asher Lev*).[51] Yet instead of being pinned to the Cross, mother and child defiantly flex their arms, each determined to be strong for their other half. This is all the more true a year later in *Middle Ages/ Mother and Child* (2017; **Fig. 12.3**). With typical cunning, Dothan stages a composition that seems to look through the peep hole of Marcel Duchamp's *Étant donnés* (1946–1966) into Kasimir Malevich's *Black Square* (1915), and from there even deeper into art history, to the medieval precedents she puns upon in her title. Where most images of the Madonna and Child present the pair facing the viewer, here we look over their shoulders, joining them as they gaze towards an uncertain future. Whatever trauma lies ahead, they seem prepared to face it together. The infant cradled in Dothan's arm in *Sleeping Madonna* (2011) has become a fearless adolescent, wrapping his arm protectively around his mother's shoulder.

---

50. Levenson, *The Death and Resurrection of the Beloved Son.*
51. Potok, *My Name is Asher Lev.*

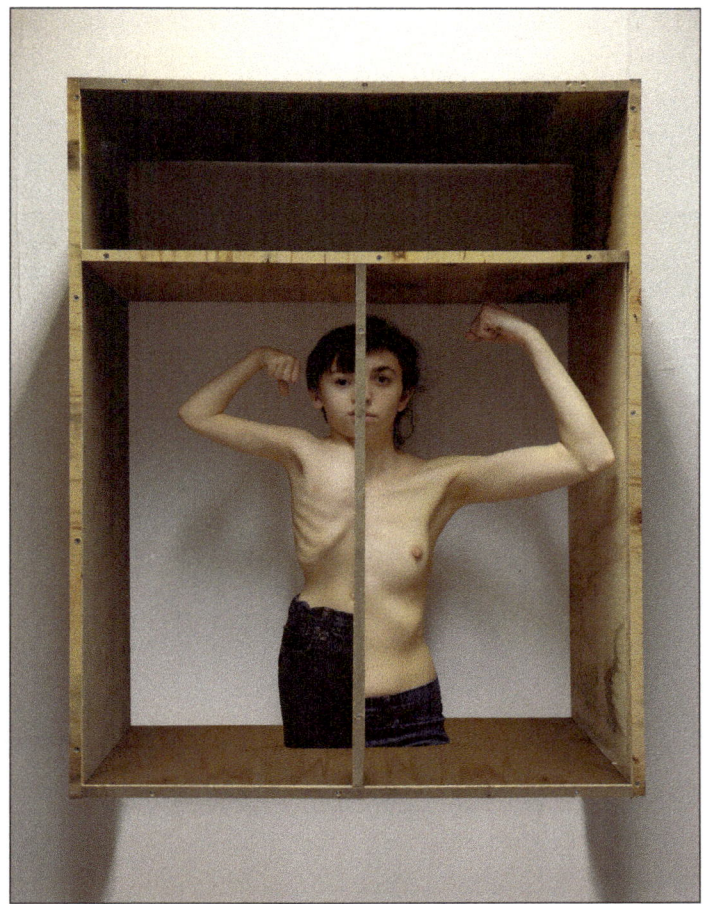

Figure 12.2

It is for just such unflinching earnestness that I turn to Dothan's works. Her private, intimate images of her gravest fears offer icons through which I find myself meditating on my own trepidations. For an artist that suffers from a congenital hearing difficulty, what makes Dothan such an impressive artist is, ironically, her uncanny ability to listen, whether to the anxious susurrations of her own unconscious or to ours. In *Young Woman with Hearing Aid* (2016), the artist portrays herself from behind, her hair swept across her neck to reveal a cumbersome hearing aid. The piece reminds me of the works of R. B. Kitaj, who often depicted his alter ego with such a device. For Kitaj, the hearing aid symbolized the Jewish condition, in which survival depends upon the ability to discern danger down the tracks, even from the faintest vibration. To Kitaj's sensitivities as a Jew and an artist, Dothan adds the auditory acuity of a mother. Amidst the clatter and commotion of contemporary life, perhaps no one listens better to the all but silent stirrings of death.

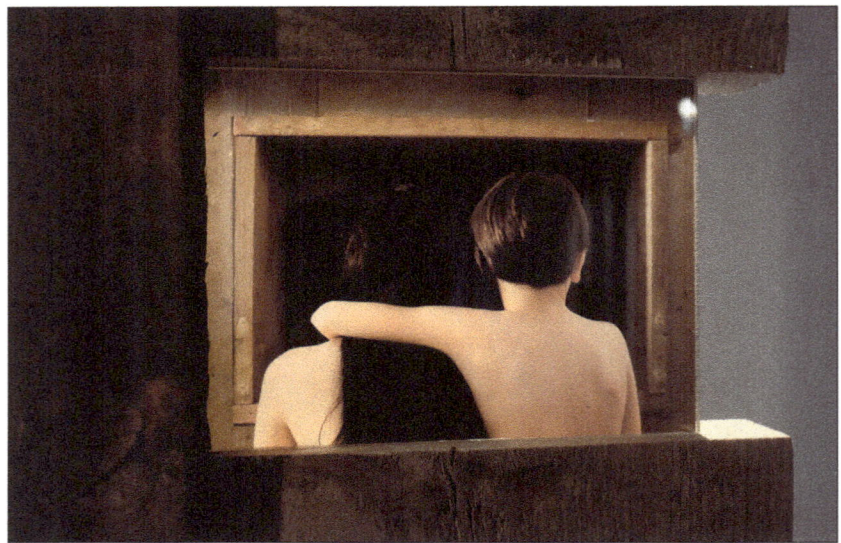

Figure 12.3

Part II

Conversations

Bodies and Senses

13. John Edmonds: Sanctifying the Black Body

Aaron: John, to me you're a really painterly photographer. Would you agree with that?

John: Absolutely. A lot of my pictures have this really classical use of *chiaroscuro*, so they're close to the kind of historical tradition of portrait painting, especially from the High Renaissance onwards.

Aaron: And of course that tradition is steeped in religion. At times you evoke that really clearly, like in your work for the *Family Pictures* exhibition on right now at the Columbus Museum of Art. There it seems like you intentionally hung your works to resemble a polyptych behind an altar. Could you talk a bit about where your religious interests come from and how they began to percolate in your art?

John: For me, my relationship to art began with my relationship to religion. And a lot of this has to do with growing up in a city like Washington, D. C., where the art institutions are fairly conservative. When I would go to museums like the National Gallery of Art, the first paintings I was able to recognize and identify were those with religious or biblical themes. I knew exactly what an Annunciation painting looked like, for example, or how light is used to communicate divinity. So, I think that those things never really left me. And even in the beginning, making pictures on my own, light became a big part of my visual language. So, in a lot of ways, I came to think about photography and imaging through religious painting.

Aaron: On the one hand, we often think about art as a kind of a missionizing tool in Christian history, where art draws people into Christianity. But what's really interesting about what you're saying is that in some ways Christianity taught you about art. It gave you a language that's really lacking for many people today, who can't really decipher many paintings of the past because they don't have the religious vocabulary. The other thing I wonder about is how we might connect up the theme of light, which you mentioned, to color. You're a young, successful African American photographer, and you often deal with questions around race, but as we've talked about before, you don't see your work as encapsulated by that discourse. Does the concept of light help frame the conversation about your work in a more open-ended way? Light is intimately connected to color, but it situates color in relation to multiple discourses, whether scientific, cultural, or religious.

John: Yeah, I think it's so interesting to think about light as a psychological and social construct, and connect that to how we understand color. So much has to do with perception. To me what's especially interesting is that at the same time historically when people were thinking about the pictorial plane, or engaging with new ideas around sense perception and aesthetics, there were also questions about how different sorts of bodies inhabit space. To me there's a holy trinity, which would be time, light, and space.

Aaron: When I look at how you use light in relation to bodies, it's interesting that it seems to hide as much as it discloses. Individuals are illuminated but at the same time not a lot of information is delivered. In your early images, ages are indeterminate, and sometimes even genders. That sense of obscurity, the unfathomable nature of the person right in front of you, is where I really feel a theological sensitivity in your work. I've also been thinking about your image inspired by Caravaggio's *Calling of St Matthew*. In Caravaggio, the light is searching out the figure. It's behaving almost like a camera seeking a focus point. Your photograph picks up on that dimension and explores it. And in a larger sense, it seems like you're always questioning where you stand in relation to your subject.

John: With the students in my "Photography as Language" course I've been discussing how so much of how we see and understand is based on who's doing the looking. I'm always interested in who's looking, and my own positionality with the camera. Photography

84

to me is this insistent asking of the viewer to place themselves in my position. It's very interesting when there are obstacles, when figures are partially obscured, sometimes by light. And this brings up a play of both perception and perspective.

Aaron: It's difficult, because in a sense you're inviting the viewer to occupy the space where you were when you took the photo, and yet in many ways that space is undefined or ambiguous, with very few markers, especially in your *Hood* or *Du-rag* works (**Fig. 13.1**). Then in recent works, like your *Tribe* series (**Figs. 13.2, 13.3**), there's a screen behind the models, and it feels like you're calling attention to the staging of your images.

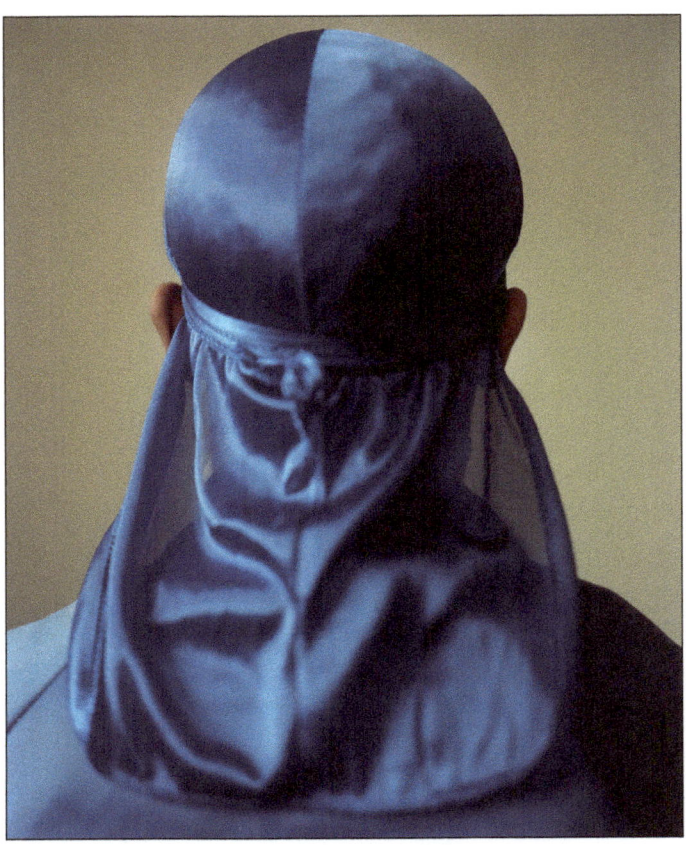

Figure 13.1

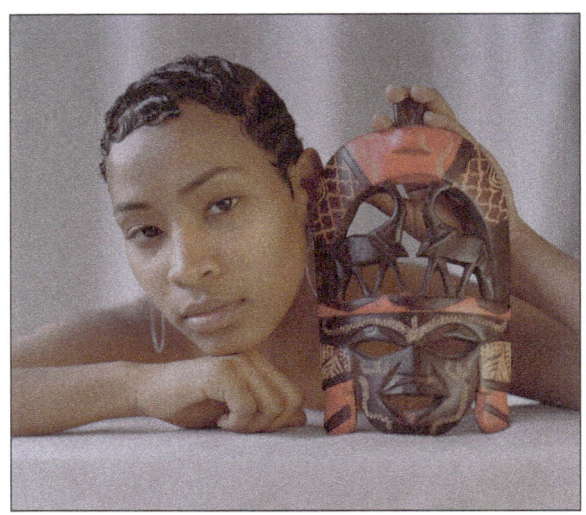

Figure 13.2

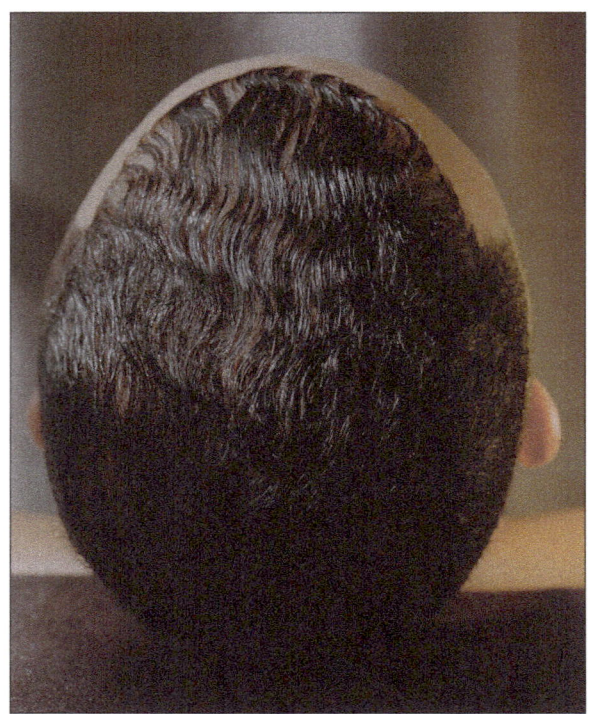

Figure 13.3

John: Right. In the *Tribe* series I wanted to depict the studio as a con-
          structed space, a place for work, with models modeling, and
          labor getting exchanged. To me one of the most inherent truths
          in photography, specifically within portraiture, is that it's about
          transaction. So in making the *Tribe* series I was really interested in
          something that was a labor of love, as well as sacrifice by the sitters.

Aaron: And there's the difficulty of the power dynamic within that trans-
          action. In the history of art, of course, those power plays were
          usually predicated on gender dynamics, with a male telling a
          woman what to do. And then in many cases there was a racial dy-
          namic, with bodies of color posed and painted by predominantly
          white artists. But as your series reveals, even when there's a male
          photographer and male subject, with an African American pho-
          tographing a black model, it doesn't mean that a transaction isn't
          still taking place.

John: And when power is a part of the exchange, there are moments
          when one party is in a position of privilege, and I've always be-
          lieved that ultimately being an artist is a very, very privileged
          space to occupy. So when I'm making my pictures, I ask how
          do I give both myself and the sitter a form of agency. And a lot
          of that I think comes from time. My shoots can take hours and
          hours, not just because of the technical aspects but because of
          the care and labor that goes into the construction of the pic-
          tures. I like to say "making pictures" because I don't like the
          language that's typically used with photography. "Taking photo-
          graphs" seems violent in a way. To me, when you make a picture
          with the four-by-five camera there are so many variables and
          it's this very decisive act, similar to painting. I think that like a
          lot of photographers, I wrestle with how photography is misun-
          derstood or underappreciated as an art form. But I've come to
          understand that when photography is deceptively simple, that's
          when it's most powerful.

Aaron: Well, I suppose a theological response might be to say that por-
          traiture is always a thing of the imagination, always the product
          of inspiration. I think it's telling that the greatest portraitist ac-
          cording to Christian tradition is St. Luke the Evangelist, who is
          often shown drawing or painting the Virgin and Child. And yet,

even according to the tradition itself he never actually met either of them! So the most accurate portraitist had to trust his inner vision. I wonder if we could talk a little more about how it is that religion perhaps opens up different ways, or different dimensions of seeing.

John: Well, when I think about religious modes of viewing, what comes to my mind is the feeling of being so small in the presence of something overwhelming, of not being worthy. That aspect of the numinous is certainly a part of my thinking. I put my installation *Holy Family* together like an altar at the Columbus Museum. I think a lot about the sense of offering in my practice. The models have to offer themselves; they have to be open to being seen. In the Columbus installation, it feels like they are asking for you to see them, and there's this radical presence that I think comes from that. And that's heightened through the arrangement of photographs as well as their palette. The figures are all dressed entirely in black, subverting the expectation that divinity should be white. I wanted to mess around with ideas regarding presentation, and clothing as a sort of second skin. At the same time, each person is their own, honored figure within the body of pictures. That's the line I feel like I'm always encountering: being subversive without getting to the point where it feels slapstick or campy.

Aaron: I think in some sense, what you're describing is a feeling of communion. There's a communion between the different figures in the photographs, who seem to find one another across channels of space in your installation. There's something akin to Giotto's Scrovegni Chapel, with all those intricate relations taking place between the paintings. We could speak about a communion of figures in religious art, but also the way that images set the stage for the *act* of communion. You mentioned transactional relationships earlier, and the importance of "offering" in your practice. In a chapel, all these different forms of offering come together. The Eucharist is *offered* to congregants, commemorating Jesus' *offering* of his body, and art *offers* context for this experience.

John: It's interesting in that liturgical context that the whole event, even the experience of the art, requires one's presence. One of my favorite painters is Mark Rothko. What I love in his work is the idea that something really quite spectacular can happen in the presence of an artwork when you really make yourself available and present to it.

Aaron: Rothko's such an interesting case, especially in his chapel in Houston. His painterly idiom is quintessentially modern, but at the same time he deeply respected traditional religious modes of looking. It wasn't just a formal decision to hang his chapel works in triptychs. He wanted people to bring the same expectation of transformation that they would to an altarpiece to his own works. Do you see yourself playing more with these ideas of presence and transformation in your future work?

John: I feel as though I've explored the idea of innocence and the divine pretty thoroughly. So now I'm really interested in the inverse or shadow of the sacred in the profane. I'm also really interested in thinking more about the symbolic function of photographs in visual culture. In some ways, there is still a lot to work through from some of my earliest photographs. When I made *Marcus with the Sacred Heart* I was just starting to become really interested in the *colors* of the black body. I went to a predominantly black high school and I remember an art teacher who talked with us about depicting ourselves, and all the different colors in our skin. I hadn't thought until that point about how the black body is also gold and red, for example. There are all these different colors in our skin that really make us beautiful. I never forgot that and remembered that when I took that picture of Marcus. He's first generation from Togo, and I met him on a bus in Washington, D. C., right down the street from where my family lives. The blue is so vivid, just like the seats on the public buses. For me that picture is just loaded with so much personal history and memory, but also a kind of iconographic power as well, which still interests me.

Aaron: His Superman tattoo is amazing. It's this symbol of invincibility—and also this powerful claim of assimilation—and yet he's so vulnerable. Actually, there's even another paradox: Superman's symbol is stitched into his uniform. He could never have a tattoo because he is impervious to needles (not to mention bullets!). So

89

in every way it's like Marcus is unconsciously inverting the very symbol he's claiming.

John: Yeah, I thought to myself that there was something so contradictory about this young man with a Superman tattoo on his chest, with this incredibly androgynous, really quite feminine look. It's almost as if the image says, "I'm strong enough to be weak." I put that image up on my wall to get me through difficult times.

Aaron: Whether in those mass-produced cards of the Sacred Heart, or Matthias Grunewald's *Isenheim Altarpiece*, one could make the argument, I think, that being "strong enough to be weak," as you put it, is a theme that runs throughout Christian art. Maybe we could even say that about art more widely, including yours. The best art doesn't simply deny our weakness or frailty, it ennobles it.

14. Eva Petrič: Materializing Absence

Aaron: We've been talking a lot recently about your projects in churches, and also about your interests in biology, especially your *Collective Heart* project (**Fig. 14.1**). Have you ever thought about the church, especially a large cathedral, like a body? Walking through St. John the Divine in New York the other day, it struck me how much the aisles felt like arteries running out from the transept.

Eva: Well, the first thing that comes to mind when talking about the heart of the church is the confession box. In a way, a confession box is a type of open-heart surgery where people open their hearts to themselves and to others.

Aaron: There is really such a spectrum when it comes to confession, from communal modes to private confessions. I suppose every denomination has different machinery for expurgating things that are dark or undesirable from the social body or from the individual.

Eva: Personally, and probably also because I do not belong to one particular religion, I like to think about and focus especially on collective human trauma, and how religion, on a general basis, might either provide resources or hindrances to people through confession.

Aaron: Oddly enough, I wonder if there's an analogy to be made to the gallery experience. To what extent can a gallery be a place of unburdening? What does the visitor leave behind emotionally? I always felt something like this in the Sainsbury Wing in the National Gallery in London. People like me come in just to look at their favorite painting (for me it's Paulo Uccello's *Battle of San Romano*). Person after person sits in front of the same work, and I can't help but think there's something confessional happening, and that there's some sort of spiritual residue that gets left behind.

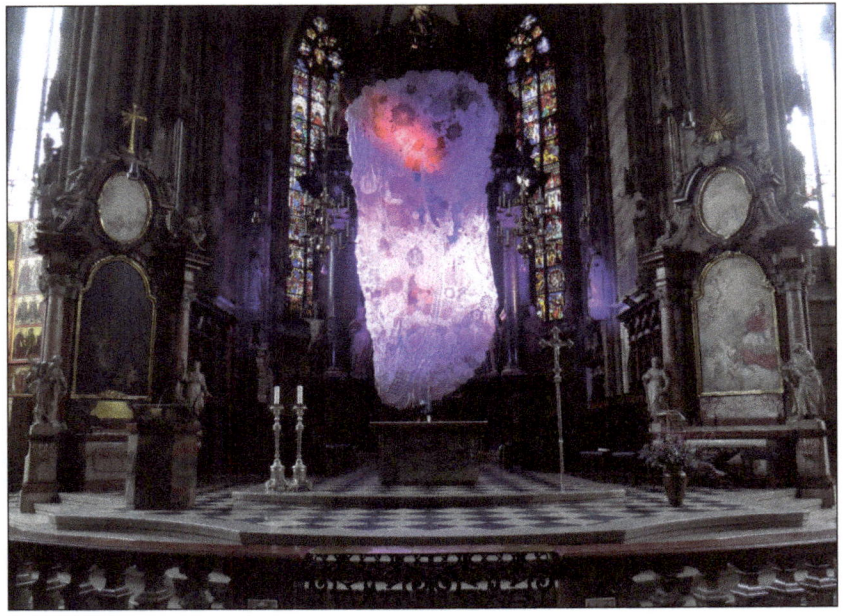

Figure 14.1

Eva: That is very true, and in my opinion a very important function of art. What I find interesting, but also troubling, is that in our current time there's often an aversion to art functioning in this manner, cathartically; there's suspicion of it enabling a purging and purification, which Aristotle spoke of as art's mission. To-day, there's little appetite for the artist being an open book for viewers. And yet for people receiving the artwork, the emphasis is, "How is this affecting me, and how is it going to take me on a journey? Will it transform me, will it speak to me?" I feel that there's a prejudice amongst a lot of younger curators in terms of how much they think an artist should open up, how much their art should be allowed to touch its viewers. It's interesting to explore what the right balance would be with the so-called universal. I believe that as an artist one needs to get really personal or subjective in order to connect to universal or archetypal emotions in people.

Aaron: And what do you think the role of the body is when it comes to this act of sharing between the artist and the viewer? On the one hand, the body can be a symbol of openness, or even a device for accomplishing it. I think about the sheer, naked openness of Jesus upon the cross, not only within art but perhaps even as art. But then again, in contemporary art I wonder whether we've gotten to a point where the body is offered as a sort of shortcut, whereby the exposed body becomes a substitute for offering something even deeper; as if the stripped body truly and completely means the artist is offering their full self, that the transaction is complete. Does that make sense?

Eva: Yeah, definitely. Intuitively, I would say the body can be offered both as presence but also as absence. There's a tension between being here and not being here. Also, in existential terms, the body as an artwork can be everlasting, existing in the particular status quo that the artist has subjected it to, enabling it to exist within. In this way the body becomes something that's not going to change. But also the sheer subject of the body is at the same time the very symbol of passing and change and mortality. This creates a persisting tension. So art gives the body a sense of immortality, but at the same time through the subject of the body, speaks mortality . . .

Aaron: That's really interesting—I like what you said about the body being something that can be an absence as well as presence. It problematizes the very notion of a gift when what's offered is fleeting. It becomes: "Am I here enough to give this to you?" "Are you there enough to receive this?" "And what is "this" that's really being tendered?"

Eva: I feel there's a painfulness to this. There's a longing for ultimate presence and unification that you cannot have in the frailty of a human body. There is the aspect of time that is always acting as a sort of diluting agent to this feeling of completeness and unification. It's kind of like what Piaget said about the child looking in the mirror and realizing that they're not one with everything. There is one and the other, and you can't fully unify them. There's absence.

Aaron: The recognition of the self always comes with the price of a recognition that the self is not consubstantial with everything. I've been thinking about that a lot recently with my wife Carolyn being pregnant. She said at one point, "I'm already sad for the time when Arthur [the baby] and I won't be one person anymore." And from Arthur's perspective, he of course has no idea what it would be not to be that singular entity. It's not even that he has a relationship with his mother, it's that he has a relationship with the whole world that happens, from our perspective, to be his mother. Coming back to that dynamic of absence and presence, I suppose birth is not just the beginning of presence, but really the first absence, the first time the baby is separated from the Everything.

Eva: Really, it's a traumatic event, though we don't really think of it in this way. At a microscopic level, it's also interesting to look at cell formation, and how one entity breaks off from another and becomes its own replication. One could say this dynamic is a part of the whole process of life, from the very beginning till the very end with various possible mutations taking place within each of our lives. In some ways, the work I did called *Hematoma* (2012; **Fig. 14.2**) brings up these issues.

Aaron: This brings us into territory I wanted us to talk more about, which is the intersection between biology and theology. Where do you think this link is most palpable? Since you brought up hematomas, it made me think that perhaps the connection is most present in the phenomenon of the wound. Not to turn you into St. Thomas, but does that put a finger on it?

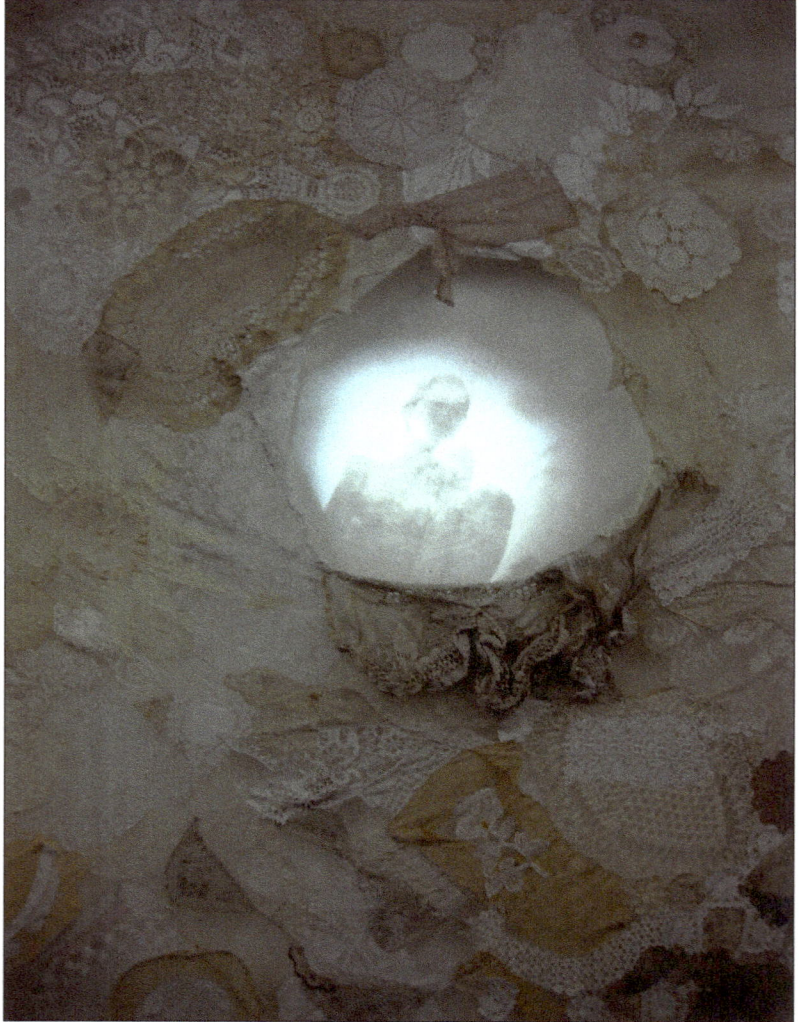

Figure 14.2

Eva: I see the wound as the sign of the body's inability to sustain us for more than a given amount of time; in other words, its mortality. I suppose passing away is kind of the ultimate wound. For me, the symbol of this physical body and existence is the skin, and I process it this way, in terms of biology. But for me it's always a kind of inner-outer dialogue. Death takes place in the inner world of our bodies that we can't really see. Everyone has their own internal psychological, spiritual, as well as biological existence. We might believe people are how we perceive them from the outside, but we can't really know what's inside other people, spiritually, psychologically, biologically. We can just assume. That's also for me the spiritual side of life, the not knowing, not seeing our own selves and others precisely, but just having a sort of blurred view through our feelings (**Fig. 14.3**). The wound, which records the passage of time, the effect of life upon our bodies, is somehow the connection between this inside and outside existence spiritually, psychologically, and biologically. Each of these three dimensions influence each other, and define our perception of life.

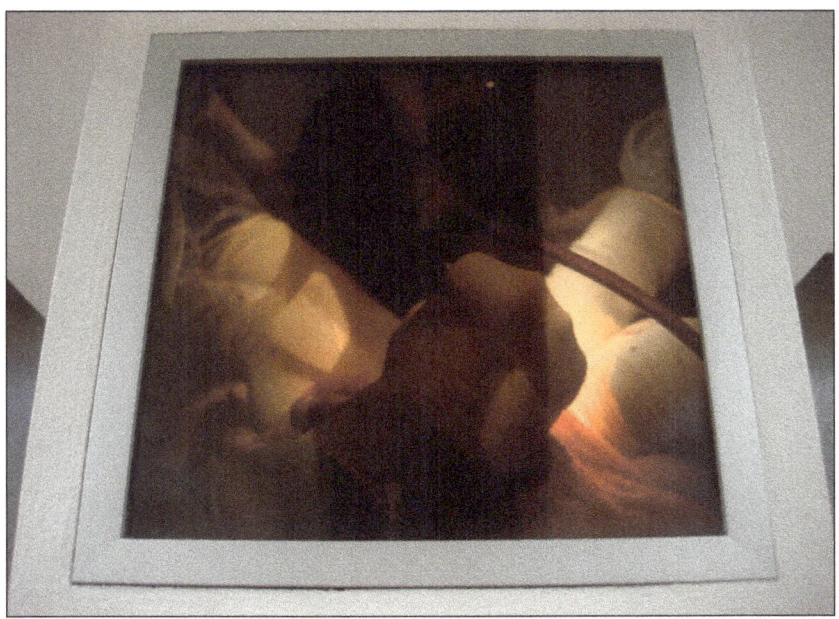

Figure 14.3

Aaron: So it's not so much that you go in search of archetypes, but that the archetypal is deeply resonant within bodily experience. The moment you start dealing with sensory experience, and especially with the skin, you're already touching upon the most profound human questions and experiences. In that sense we already have, through our bodies, the language to speak to one another, to empathize, to understand our own limited nature, or our own creative fecundity. Then the question really becomes: Can we inhabit our own bodies profoundly enough? Can we comprehend the language our bodies already seem to understand?

Eva: That's well put. I like that. And I think with food, for example, as a most basic and universal example, if you really listen to your body you can tell what you need. The body really has its language, its dialogue with us on a biological level that we seem to forget or not understand.

Aaron: And then there's the question of spiritual nourishment. There are of course debates about whether people who believe in God have a certain biological propensity for faith.

Eva: In a way, art is like that. It's not necessarily something everyone does or feels an innate connection to. Most artists hardly finish one project and they're already on to another project. It's like a constant craving or addiction. Where does this impulse, this need come from? Is there a deficiency that makes you seek something, or is it more a protection from the overabundance of the world within one's self, which needs to be released through constant creation, materialization, or reflection of the outside world?

Aaron: It reminds me of the inner-outer dialectic you were mentioning. Do artists have a need to receive something or a need to put something out into the world? Kandinsky called it "inner need."[1] Picasso always strikes me as someone who created not from a lack or sense of incompletion, but out of a need to put something *into* the world, to populate it. He wanted to turn the world Picassoid. It's like he was seeking to replicate himself through his artworks, in an almost cellular way.

Eva: I think it is a combination of both. Artists must take into themselves a lot, they must be constantly observing the world around them, and taking it into themselves and digesting it in order to be able to bring out new views, manifestations, and materializations. But I think it is the giving, sharing, producing, and materializing that takes the lead. The need of an artist to create is

---

1. Kandinsky, *Concerning the Spiritual in Art*, 32–35.

greater than that of interpreting or reflecting, as would be the case, for example, with an art historian.

Aaron: In Cormac McCarthy's *The Road*, he writes that maybe the world is slowly dying, but maybe in its unbecoming it will reveal the secrets of its creation.[2] Maybe death, that withdrawal of breath, might be the only moment that tells us something about what it means to be creative, to breathe the world into existence like God does in Genesis. But the nature of things, of course, is that in dying we don't know—or at least can't tell anyone—if we've received that secret or not.

Eva: This makes me think of Nietzsche. I remember reading how it is against nature to perceive certain secrets, and that in the event you do, nature will punish you. And he connected that to art because he claimed that, through experiencing art, one is perceiving something of nature's secrecy and mystery that one is not supposed to. And as a result one is filled with grief.

Aaron: It becomes radioactive. You can reach out and touch this knowledge. But it makes you not long for this world. It comes back to a point that Arthur Danto makes in terms of the power of art, which our philosophical traditions attempt to neutralize.[3] And of course in many religious traditions, too, there's this implicit awareness that the artist is powerful, maybe too powerful. But I want to come back to the idea of the secret. You have a project right now where you're working with terminally ill people, right? Are there things you're learning, or that they're revealing that are surprising to you?

Eva: I'm exploring perception of time in terminally ill people and through conversations with them, "marking" so to say by their presence of voice specific soundscape works. I am learning how they perceive time differently. I think we can learn a lot from their experience.

Aaron: It must be very interesting thinking about making art out of such experiences. My friend Tobi Kahn has done a lot of artwork for

2. McCarthy, *The Road*, 274.

3. Danto, *Beyond the Brillo Box*, 186.

people in hospitals and convalescent homes. Very few people think about how important art can be in such contexts. And in a sense, people who are terminally ill, for example, might have a sense of time uniquely suited to engaging with art.

Eva: Exactly. This is something I wish to explore. What have they not had time to do, which they would like to, and does art fit into this? What kind of trace, if any, would they like to leave behind? I want to help them leave behind traces. I want to help them be present in their absence. I plan to utilize the idea of a spider web to present the intersection of different lives and their connections, reinforcing each other's presence through memory, and the trace which the art leaves inside the viewer's perception.

Aaron: You were talking about confession earlier, and it seems like in this project you as the artist receive their secret hopes or memories.

Eva: Hopefully . . . I feel very grateful to them for their trust.

Aaron: That's a lot of responsibility!

Eva: Honestly, I'm a bit scared of the project. But that's what makes me want to pursue it, similar to my transplant project. I can remember how nervous I was, but also thinking: I will never again have a chance like this to experience presence and absence, so I must take it! Being an artist, I believe that we must digest as many experiences as possible and of course also reflect upon them. An artist should strive to materialize that which is not material!

Aaron: I like what you're saying in terms of the tremulousness of the experience, and paying attention to that reaction in yourself. It's an interesting barometer for an artist, that when you feel afraid of something, perhaps that means it's most worth doing. Ancient cultures, I think, were far better at understanding and respecting the sense of what it meant to touch the numinous, and the sacred charge of responsibility that might entail.

Eva: Again, I think it's related in a sense to the opposite of presence— the absence; the possibility of absences within life. And the question is how to see yourself in that situation. How to be in the now, even when it seems impossible.

15. Sam Winston: Darkness Visible

Aaron: Sam, you just returned from Norway, where I know you're thinking of doing a project. Given your interest in light, I imagine that
was quite an interesting place with how radically light changes
there during the year.

Sam: Well, one of the things I'm thinking about at the moment is
liminal light, not just creating a body of work in liminal light,
but also taking viewers to the smudge itself, to experience how
different luminosities change the nature of the work (**Fig. 15.1**).

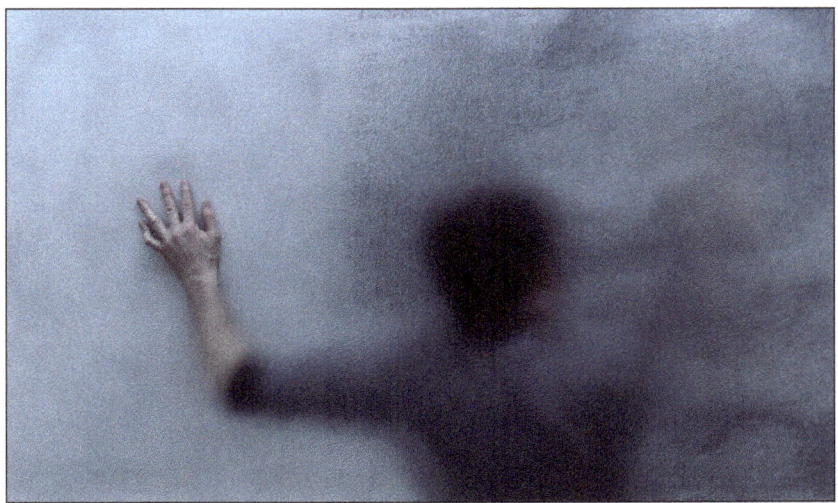

Figure 15.1

Aaron: At the moment, though, you're very much immersed in doing
dark works, right?

Sam: Right, I set up a dark space in the National Poetry Library [South-
bank Centre, London]. I thought it would be really interesting
to navigate spaces with your eyes shut, with a combination of
vulnerability and sensitivity. We've had a really strong response.
I think we had over a thousand hours' worth of people standing
in the dark. The hardest things to work with are the preconceived
ideas about darkness being a place of evil, fear, torture, or mental

illness. But from the 170 or so remarks in the comments book, about 80 to 90 percent of them all referenced it being deeply restorative, deeply restful, un-scary, but also at times very transcendent. And three or four people said, "I felt like a kid again." A lot of people had quite an out-of-body experience. There wasn't an average. It was kind of marmite, it split people: either it was intense and they couldn't do it, or it was quite moving.

Aaron: Those reactions really seem to reveal the supremacy we give to vision among our senses. A lot of recent scholarship has explored how we've hierarchized our senses in various ways at different times and in different places. But certainly now, in the West, we place an immense empirical value on sight. When that's taken off the table, it's interesting to think about how we might validate our existence in different ways. When people say they have an out-of-body experience in your dark space it's interesting because of course the body's still there. So where is it that we think we exist when we aren't using sight to verify our experience?

Sam: I think the most threatening but also most appealing questions are who am I and what am I? What happens when we can't lean on the predominant visual cue to have a "sight body"? Using a "touch body" or a "sound body," you begin to learn the new language of this space. For a while, people thought this was a project about blindness. For me it's about exploring this liminal transition between one sensory form and another, between sight and touch, or sight and sound. It's about trying to cope using different strategies in a completely different landscape, where you only have your ears to look. People going into the space might have five minutes of near panic, realizing they're in a completely dark space, which is different than turning the lights out or having the curtain closed. Your eye is desperately looking for any frame of reference. And when it's not successful, the payoff is a new freedom: you get out of the mode that you're existing in, and suddenly you have a new framework.

Aaron: It reminds me of pre-modern ideas about sight as a sort of extramission, that sight isn't so much received as sent out. In this case, it's like people in darkness send out their gaze but it can't latch onto anything. And you have to let that sense recognize its failure. But it's not blindness so much as the other senses being forced to "do sight" in a different way. We aren't somehow instantly endowed with super-senses like superheroes. Our other senses try to create a totality of experience, and what constitutes a total experience gets reconceptualized.

Sam: That's a perfect description. Another way of exploring it is visual acuity. I've been looking into the developmental stages that we have no conscious recollection of, the very early stages of sight. You are born at a stage in life where vision isn't up and running, so your first experience of the world is whilst vision itself is being built. And it seems like different stages of consciousness can be marked by how infants are able to discern between black and white and then between facial features and so on. It's a really beautiful primary language of shape and color that is based around the visual acuity test. And that's what I'm exploring at the moment, whether viewers—consciously or unconsciously— can return to early vision, of say a week old. When you look at abstraction, is that part of what's going on? Can we trigger some of the first types of seeing that you ever did? So a part of this journey has led me into really thinking about the history of sight from a developmental perspective.

Aaron: That's so interesting. A mentor of mine, Doug Adams, used to talk about the process of learning to look at Abstract Expressionist paintings. For a lot of those painters, especially Rothko and Newman, who played a lot with latitude, the goal was to absorb you, to enclose you in the world of their painting. And if that entailed a lack of focus—akin to the sight of an infant—that actually meant getting it right. Maybe it's not incidental that Rothko was interested early in his career in childhood development. Another thing that interests me, especially as we're about to have a child, is how much we do for babies that's predicated on our own sensory experiences as adults. When we decorate a nursery, for example, we map our sensory experience onto babies, rather than trying to come closer to what it is that they are able to experience at a certain age.

Sam: I suppose you just resign yourself to the idea that basically you are passing on an inheritance that you received at a stage where you didn't have discretion either. When new people appear they have this massive download of information with very little filter. The issue of preconceptions ties back into the dark works. As I mentioned, I make a distinction between saying blind drawing (**Fig. 15.2**), which I've also done, and dark drawing, which is a different experience. In blind drawing, you are visiting for a certain amount of time and whilst you're doing without sight, there's less of an altered state that happens. Whereas if you do a prolonged period in the dark, your consciousness and how you actually perceive and think is fundamentally different. Things like lucid dreaming become very prevalent. You're in a hypnagogic state; a dream space that you don't really get unless you start losing a sense of time after a couple days. I think there's an interesting connection in those experiences to early developmental stages of vision. I think it's not a coincidence that visitors said they were reminded of childhood. Not being a psychoanalyst, I can't quite say how that works, but it does seem that prolonged lucid dreaming brings up very early imagery, which is exactly why I'm interested in drawing from that space, which takes me back to a really early time (**Fig. 15.3**).

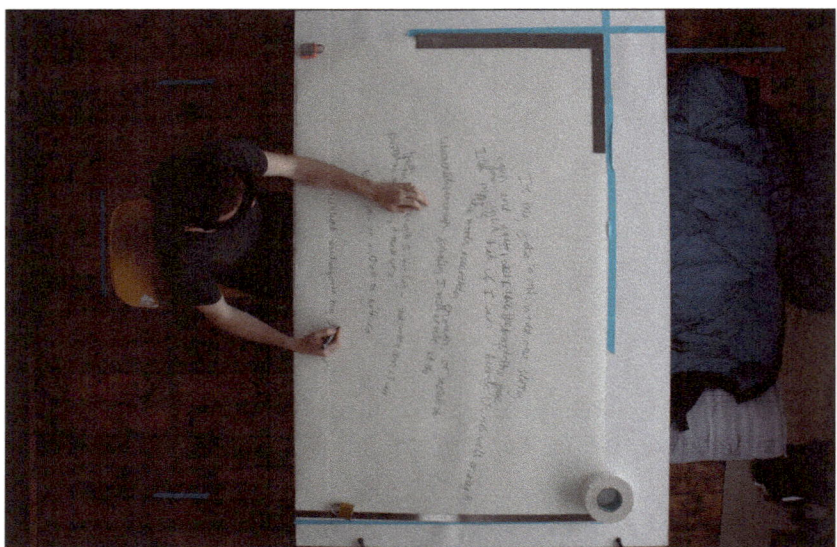

Figure 15.2

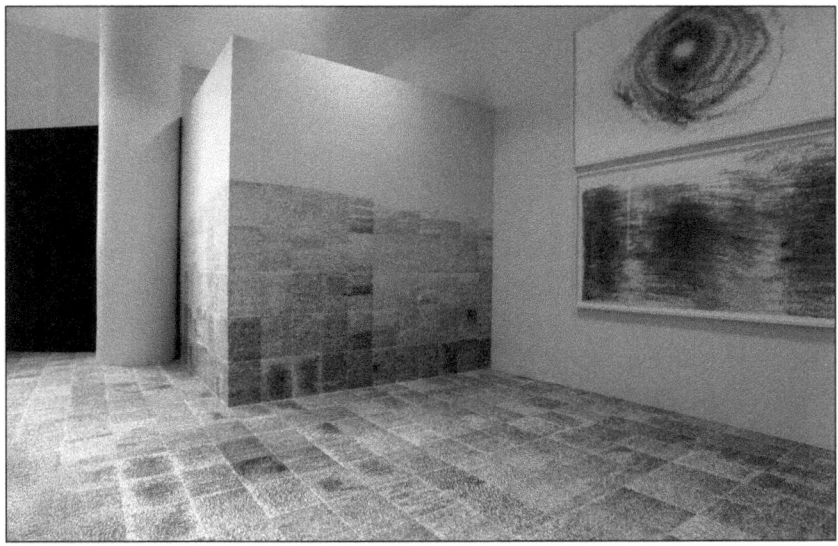

Figure 15.3

Aaron: And maybe when people say they felt like children, that's simply because that's as far back as they can reach because of childhood amnesia, where we lose our early memories. So maybe when people are in the dark, what they're really tapping into are those experiences *behind* their memories.

Sam: But then there are also questions on the cultural level: how do you prepare people to go into a space that is fundamentally below consciousness? When we were doing the darkness exhibition at Whitechapel Gallery, most of our resources and time were spent building a useful narrative for audiences to explore the dark, and a comfort with the kinds of thoughts and emotions they might have. It's amazing how much energy was spent creating a story—that the dark is a very rich and fruitful place—which is completely true.

Aaron: What you're describing is a classic hermeneutic circle. I'm reminded of Heidegger and Gadamer insisting on acknowledging the value and force of the pre-understandings we bring to any act of interpretation. Your process acknowledges that people may not have a meaningful experience in the dark unless they're prepared to find it. I imagine one of the biggest challenges is to try and distill everything you've learned and try to give people an opportunity to have similar experiences, but without the luxury of spending a full week in utter darkness!

Sam: A lot of what I want to help visitors experience comes through my own process. At the moment I've been developing a series of drawings that involve looking at someone else, which in itself is quite hard. I think this also connects to early development. Children stare unabashedly for vast amounts of time because they're taking in this massive data set. But culturally we eventually start to find this embarrassing. In the workshop we're developing, you draw the face blind, relying on your mind to pull up features in the right place. And then once the face is finished, you "turn on" the eyes and create a replica of the blind drawing that you've done. In theory, this is all just looking, but each of those stages is a vastly different experience. It goes back to a really simple thing, which is looking at looking.

Aaron: In some ways, that workshop seems like a metaphor for your process more broadly. By analyzing all of these different types of looking, you're trying to say something about the essence of looking. You're taking snapshots to get to a bigger picture.

Sam: Yeah, the work for me is always intuitive at first, then seeing where culture surfaces and how much of that experience you can translate, and what is acceptable to people. What I'm learning is that conversations with the health and safety and ticketing departments—convincing them that it's okay to let a thousand or two thousand people into a dark room without fire exit lighting—is also part of arts practice. There are norms in a public institution that say, "This is what you need to do in a given situation." But if you're trying to create a new experience, you have to take away some of the normative behaviors.

Aaron: Thinking about cultural and bureaucratic norms, I'm reminded of how much the social history of London is marked by evolving technologies of light. Gas streetlamps in the early nineteenth century completely changed public safety and discourses about criminality and poverty, while electrification in the late nineteenth and early twentieth centuries meant huge changes in commerce for places like Electric Avenue in Brixton. And now there's a big push for LED lights, which are meant to be more environmentally friendly since they use less energy. So there's this teleology of luminosity. Yet what you're doing is actually telling a story about *de*-illumination, about returning to the dark. How those stories intersect is fascinating. I'm also interested in how you see this project in relation to cultures with potentially different ideas about light and darkness.

Sam: In my research I'm definitely borrowing from various cultures. My friend who is a Tibetan monk does dark retreats and I know that there are a lot of indigenous practices like Native American sweat lodges, which focus on inwardness and darkness. Overall, there's a positive lexicon of light because we're all attracted to it, but the discourse of darkness tends to be about avoidance, aversion, and distraction. People want to disturb the darkness with light. Part of what I'm doing is counterintuitive, because we live in an attention economy and a screen economy that's saturation rich.

Aaron: Emptiness and darkness often seem to be used pejoratively in our culture, constructed as qualities to eradicate. But illumination can also represent a type of loss. It's interesting that we're having this conversation on Earth Day, when we're being encouraged to turn off our lights. Not only does electric light use energy, of course, but light pollution obscures the stars and also alters animal migration. So, in a way, our desire for illumination can have damaging effects on our planet.

Sam: And of course it's not only affecting other species, we're reshaping our own behaviors. At a personal level, I've noticed how I use my eyes has changed over the last two decades. Especially with handheld devices, we're now constantly drifting between the screen and the natural landscape. For me, I still haven't got over the book, which induces its own kind of augmented reality! But now we're shifting into a world like that of Alice in Wonderland, in which you can go within the phone, within Instagram, within someone's feed, and then even go within that. There's this mysterious sense of depth and distance at the same time, which is becoming intuitive in its own way.

Aaron: So given all of these systemic challenges, how is it that you pre-pare people to step into a different type of space and experience, at odds with what they might be doing right before?

Sam: I realized I had to build up a series of strategies that I initially got from meditative practices. I realized you can't deal with the void by just saying, "I'm going to pop into nothing." You have to pro-vide something for your body to do, an apparatus for certain types of thoughts. It's a very delicate balance where you're providing enough so you don't end up in a traumatic state, but not so much that you create just another routine. We have this amazing habit of turning our experience into what we were doing before.

Aaron: One of the things that strikes me as central to your practice is duration. On the one hand, you had to remain in the darkness for a certain amount of time to enable certain realizations, but you also had to know to go looking for that experience. So there's the durational arc of your creative practice as well.

Sam: I tend to put the whole narrative of a project's creation—with the time and the effort and the sacrifice involved—into the final thing. I've spent a couple of decades being a visual artist and to spend a week without being able to reference what I'm doing and to look at it meant that it was probably the hardest project I've ever done. Relinquishing sight meant a loss of the visual story. When you're doing the work in complete darkness, there's a real pronounced longing to see something, and you build up quite an elaborate narrative about what the thing looks like. You know that there's a thing there and it exists and it has a whole, and the question is how to get the audience to experience that.

Aaron: The sense of longing that you're talking about is so powerful. Do you think consciously of that having a theological dimension? I know you're quite literate in a number of different religious and cultural contexts. Do you find theological analogies useful, or do you find yourself fighting that kind of language?

Sam: Well, I continue learning. I'm literate in that language, as you say, and I've been able to access religious experience in differ-ent traditions. Over time I developed this sense of what I'm aiming towards in different contexts. I was doing a talk for the

MA at Wimbledon College of Arts recently and someone asked me, "Are you a monk?" I've never framed my work in that way because it explains it in far too simplistic a term. I don't fight it, but I try not to give frameworks that people are already going to assume about the work, which is hard because generally people won't do something until they've been told what the thing is. Even just saying something is an art exhibition means people pull up fifty art exhibitions they've been to before. If I find myself in a particularly religious setting, then I feel very much drawn to questioning the institutional side of art. But within the art context, I find myself pushing against the norms of the art world, looking for a way to experience the transcendent, or something without form.

Aaron: So it sounds like ironically there's more latitude for you to open the door to theology when you're in a museum or gallery context because there's no risk that it will be the totalizing frame by which people see their experience.

Sam: Yeah, in some ways, that's because of the age of this form. Art—in the way we understand it presently—is a baby in comparison to spiritual life. I do think at one point it will be studied and considered in a similar way one would do theology now. But I'm well aware that I'm walking very much around your territory here.

Aaron: It's okay, I'll give you a day pass into the divinity faculty . . .

Communities

16. Nicola Green: Visualizing Difference

Aaron: As we're talking by video, you're in your studio and there's a life-size picture of Archbishop Desmond Tutu. Could you talk a little about that image, which is literally looking over your shoulder?

Nicola: Well, there is a literal answer and a longer answer. The literal answer is that I took the image seconds after he received the Templeton Prize. My husband [David Lammy, MP] had met him quite a few times. I have South African heritage; my family is from South Africa. My husband's paternal line also originally came from South Africa. So, our kids have black and white South African heritage. When we got married thirteen years ago, ours was the first interracial marriage in St Margaret's Church, Westminster Abbey. Desmond Tutu sent a prayer especially for us, for our wedding. It was an Ubuntu prayer. As you know, the whole theory of Ubuntu—"a person is a person, only through other persons"[1]—really underpins my *Encounters* project (**Fig. 16.1**). Tutu took forth what Martin Luther King, Jr. and others had started in terms of different religious leaders coming together to work on a cause that transcended their differences. So, the picture of Desmond Tutu is very personal for me.

My projects *In Seven Days . . .* and *Encounters* come from my personal experience of having an interracial, multicultural, mixed-heritage family. That daily lived experience, and all the difficulties that come with it, motivates my work—the exploration of difference, of how as human beings we understand each other. So, for me, Desmond Tutu has been a starting point in many ways: from personal South African connections, to the philosophy of Ubuntu, to the story of interfaith dialogue.

1. Tutu, "Who We Are."

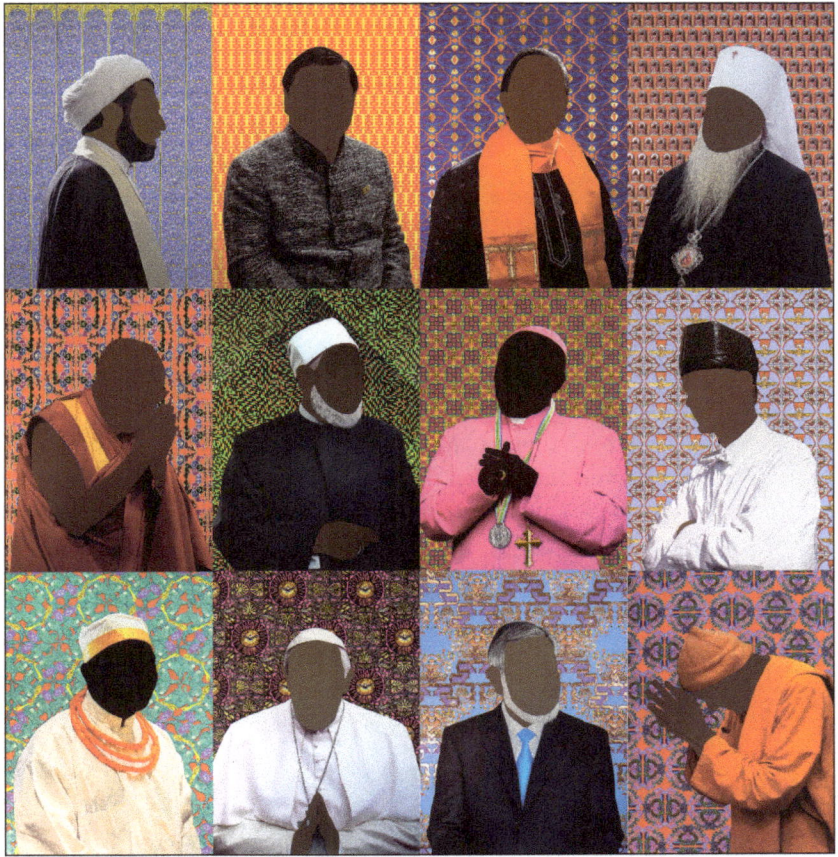

Figure 16.1

Aaron: He almost seems like a gatekeeper, blessing the proceedings of your studio. I think as writers and artists we often discover that what we've been doing in our work is self-exegesis, whether we see it at the time or not. Your reflection about genealogy gives a lot of context to what you're doing in the *Encounters* series about meetings between global faith leaders.[2] You set interfaith dialogue within an intercultural dialogue, which is part of your history and your family's daily experience. *Encounters* touches on wide-ranging geopolitical issues, but it also has quite an intimate genesis.

2. Rosen, ed., *Encounters*.

Nicola: When I was pregnant with my children, I was very focused on being a white mother of black children, whom the world would see differently and who would experience the world very differently from me, in ways that I have never experienced or would ever be able to fully appreciate or understand. I wanted to go on a journey as a mother to try and at least think about it as much as I possibly could.

Recently, I've been thinking a lot about my heritage. Some of my paternal family were originally Ashkenazi Jews that went to South Africa. My maternal grandmother was a refugee. She and her mother were the only survivors of their White Russian family that were otherwise all murdered in the Revolution, and they were Orthodox. My husband's family were Catholics in Guyana, and then when they came over to the UK in the 1950s, there were no Catholic churches that would accept black people in Tottenham, so they ended up in an Anglo-Catholic church. Originally his mother's ancestors came from Niger, so were probably Muslim. Furthermore, his great-grandmother was Indian, an indentured worker from Calcutta who went to Guyana. So, our boys have an immense amount of religious, cultural, and geographic diversity in their heritage.

Aaron: There's a presumption that if one is a Christian then it's because everyone before one was Christian. But what we forget is that people pick up religions and lose religions like baggage as they travel, and sometimes you leave something behind . . .

Nicola: Sometimes out of survival!

Aaron: And there's no Ancestry.com for testing religious heritage. It takes research, as well as a certain self-conception, to go looking for this heritage. One has to see one's own religious identity not as diluted but enhanced by discovering diversity.

Nicola: Yes, exactly, and I think it's incredibly important. I think one of the most important new developments in interfaith dialogue is that religious leaders are holding on to their absolute faith but exploring how to be brothers and sisters at the same time. Actually, that's what happens with interreligious, intercultural, interracial families. You have to navigate how to hold on to what is true to you and where you come from and still live in harmony.

Aaron: Right, and when sameness becomes the ideal model it usually involves an act of erasure.

Nicola: Or denial.

Aaron: We have an interesting reflection from former Archbishop of Canterbury Rowan Williams in the foreword to our *Encounters* book. He talks about the strange dynamic of having one's own body read as representative of a tradition, in his case the Anglican Communion. But, actually, everyone has some experience of that, to a greater or lesser extent. You mentioned your children, who can't help but be read by people as representing a particular history.

Nicola: I'm really aware of that: if the children are seen with me, people read something different than if they are seen with my husband, and they make assumptions.

Aaron: Religious difference is interesting in relation to ethnic difference, since it can be altered. I've been thinking about this recently in relation to the March for Our Lives protests in the US against gun violence. When I protest, I have a desire to be seen as a Jew. Often times you hear people interviewed saying, "I can't speak for everyone." But I suppose I want to present myself in a way that will be taken as representative; to suggest that I'm something larger (or nobler?) than myself. When researching your *Encounters* series, did you notice a similar sense of self-consciousness in religious leaders in interfaith settings?

Nicola: Well, at first I didn't know what was happening. If you spoke to any of the religious leaders themselves, they would hardly have been able to articulate it ten years ago either. Things were initially quite *ad hoc*. I think that because of the hard, considered work of many religious leaders, including former Chief Rabbi Jonathan Sacks, former Archbishops of Canterbury George Carey and Rowan Williams, former Archbishop of Westminster Cardinal Cormac Murphy-O'Connor, former Grand Mufti of Egypt Ali Gomaa, and many others around the world, we are now in a slightly new era. Because of their hard work, Pope Francis, Archbishop Justin Welby, and other current religious leaders across the world have a greater platform for this kind of dialogue. We may take this for granted, but people have become more familiar with religious leaders being imaged and imagined together. So, I would say that it took quite some time before faith leaders started to work out how they could speak about this subject, but I have witnessed them beginning to publicly articulate their respect for other faiths, without undermining the absolute truth of their own.

Aaron: It's interesting that in some cases they were already speaking just by being visible. Their iconicity generates discourse and participates within it. It's not something that's a separate act.

Nicola: They were often quite cautious about what they said in public until very recently.

Aaron: It's interesting to consider the optics of social change. I'm really interested now in how young people represent themselves in social justice movements. Sometimes informality is its own statement. I thought one of the most powerful points in the March for Our Lives protest was not only Emma González's silence but also her style, which seemed to say: "I'm a powerful young woman, and I can dress like a revolutionary with fatigues, patches, and ripped jeans. This is who I am. This is what youth looks like." In that moment she was redefining what it looks like to be socially active in this generation, and to completely own one's self-image. It will be interesting to see how a generation that is increasingly conscious of their optics—a "selfie" generation used to taking and uploading thousands of photos of themselves—will operate with different visual benchmarks as they enter political, cultural, and religious dialogues.

Nicola: I totally agree. I used to do a lot of teaching, mentoring young people from nontraditional backgrounds and children with learning difficulties and special educational needs. The workshops I led were really about why visual language is just as important as learning English or mathematics. And the school system is not set up for that. Art is usually seen as this extracurricular playtime.

Aaron: It's interesting that at the very age when young people are learning how to un-puzzle and explore their own identities, we dismiss the importance of visually presenting and interpreting identity.

Nicola: I really see the *Encounters* and *In Seven Days . . .* projects as explorations of the importance of visual language today.

Aaron: The question of vision and difference is something I see as an arc running through your work as a whole. At a personal level, you've spoken about your family history as one of intersecting diasporas, indeed diasporas upon diasporas. How does this come out in your work?

Nicola: Well, for *In Seven Days . . .* (**Fig. 16.2**) I spent lots of time in America, on Obama's 2008 presidential campaign, and became focused on questions of race and identity. Obama's story is so multi-faceted, so the nuances of his mixed-heritage identity are not fully explored in my work. After finishing that work I was left with a desire to explore mixed heritage in more depth. My series *Dance of Colour* really came out of that desire (**Fig. 16.3**). Brazil is one of the most ethnically diverse countries in the world, and 43 percent of citizens identify as mixed race. When I first went to *Carnaval* in Rio I thought it was just going to be my starting point for this project. But that changed when I started really researching the history of *Carnaval*. It started with European colonists in the New World, who already had a tradition of masked balls. But Mardi Gras was also one of the only days off permitted for slaves. For slaves and indigenous people, it wasn't just a party, it was— on the deepest level—an exploration of identity, belonging, and heritage. They'd lost everything. They'd been ripped from their homelands, their culture, and their families. So it was the only moment they got to explore that experience and think about it and share it with each other. So, I really started thinking about that unspeakable pain.

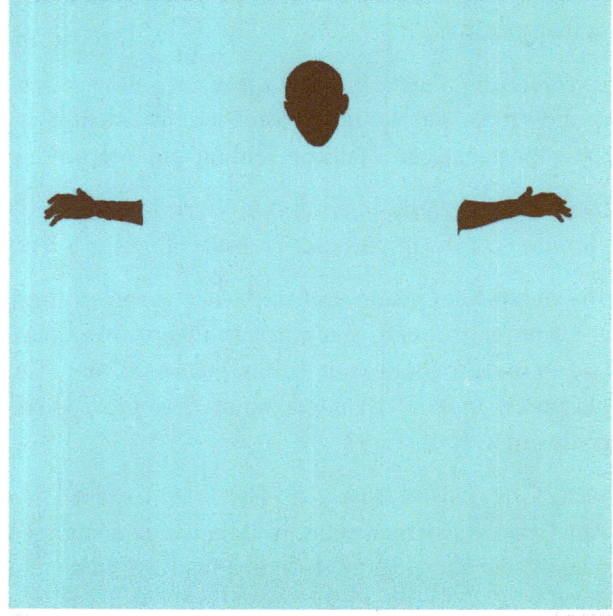

Figure 16.2

Aaron: There's that liberating element—dancing prophetically into the future—but also reaching back to the past. For people that were ripped away from West Africa, rhythms were surely some of the only things they could retain and perpetuate.

Nicola: Absolutely right. Then, the white Europeans joined everyone else on the street. The European tradition of the masked ball joined up with traditions of mask-making in Africa and indigenous cultures in South America—creating a space for hiding, sharing, and exploring identity. There are no visible hierarchies during *Carnaval*. All the normal vestiges of power and hierarchy are lost in those couple of days. Everyone can explore what they aren't, what they want to be, and where they come from—and that goes for power, gender, and sexuality, as well as race and heritage.

    Dance of Colour led me to the *Bate Bola* works. We're talking about religion and ritual, and the tradition of Bate Bola is passed down through generations. They're just amazing. They're peculiar to Rio. No one knows where and when they're going to be; they're like mystical fairies. The costume traditions have arisen over a couple of hundred years, and the Bate Bola gangs spend a whole year making new ones. Even though their full costumes are amazing, I decided to shoot them like mug shots, to focus on our perception of people and how we judge them.

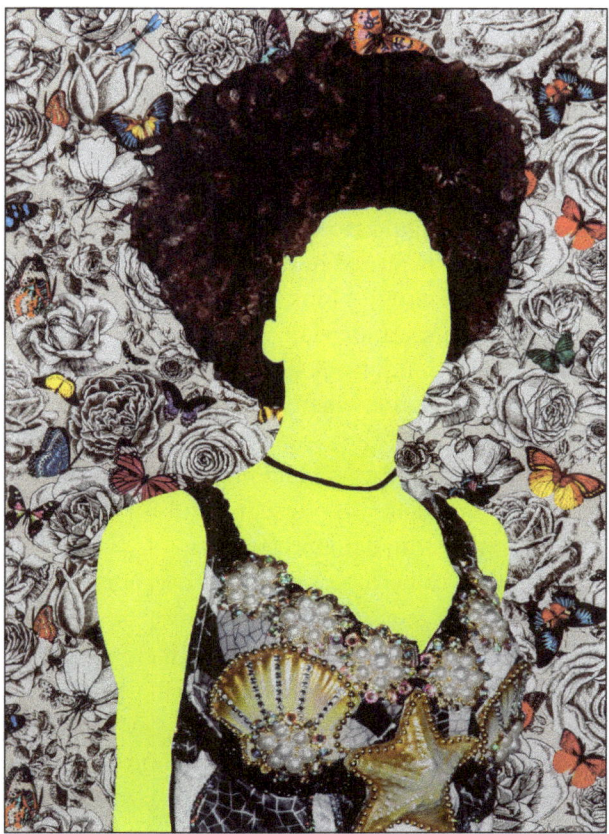

Figure 16.3

Aaron: In a sense, these works, which are all about pageantry and role-playing, seem to have given you permission to see the more performative dimensions of the religious gatherings you photographed. This adds another element to what we were talking about: how these figures signify their traditions, and their roles within them.

115

Nicola: Yes, absolutely. Now that I'm talking to you, the depth of understanding of difference and identity in *Carnaval*, and where it comes from, has more to say in this interfaith story then it might have seemed at first.

Aaron: In addition to your work as an artist, you've also explored diasporic identities as a mentor and a curator. Do you want to talk about that?

Nicola: After I got married, by virtue of my husband's job, and the workshops I was running, I began mentoring young people in my local community here in Tottenham, North London. A lot of young, ethnic minority artists want to study creative subjects, but lack the support and guidance they need to do so. Many of the young people I have mentored have been from first-generation immigrant families and they look around at the art world in London, and despite London's diversity, do not see anybody that looks like them or who comes from where they do. That profoundly contributes to a situation where everything is stacked against them. After my experiences teaching people with all sorts of issues, as well as teaching my own children, I was in a position to be able to make a difference. My husband and I have really focused on helping young ethnic minority artists.

This all came together in the Diaspora Pavilion which I co-founded. In 2015, when Okwui Enwezor was the first BAME (black, Asian, and minority ethnic) director of the Venice Biennale, I developed an initiative delivering networking, mentoring, and professional development for BAME emerging artists. I found funding to bring four artists whom I'd mentored to that 2015 Venice Biennale. Khadija Saye—who died in the Grenfell Tower fire in 2017—was one of them. Khadija found her way to me because I'd curated an exhibition at the Mall Galleries in London focused on young ethnic minority artists making work that was exploring identity. She came to my studio and ended up working for me. In fact, she worked on all of the *Bate Bola* pieces. The 2015 Diaspora initiative was so successful that we got Arts Council funding for a whole Diaspora Pavilion of young artists, with ten mentor artists also working on the theme of diaspora. I was adamant that that relationship between the mentor artists and the younger artists was really established in practice. It's a part of success that isn't talked about a lot. People from privileged families and backgrounds just take all kinds of mentorship for granted. They don't really think about the help and guidance they're getting on a daily basis from parents, friends, colleagues, and indeed their whole community. It's like an exclusive privilege that people don't really want to acknowledge.

Aaron: In a way it's a story that connects with various diasporic experiences. I think of the first generations of modern Jewish artists in the late nineteenth and early twentieth centuries, who had to struggle not only with external legitimacy but internal expectations in their families and communities, who often felt doing art was a waste of talent or resources. So there needed to be forerunners to prove that success in art was attainable.

Nicola: Yes, completely! And I think that people talk a lot about financial privilege, but actually it's much deeper than that. People around you that lift you up and tell you the secrets of the world and how to make the most of your predispositions, which is kind of the ultimate privilege. I think that if you're a first-generation immigrant family struggling, you're going to have much less ability to do that. It doesn't mean that you can't, or that some don't, it just makes things a lot harder. Khadija Saye was an amazing human being, but when I met her she didn't really think that she could possibly become a successful artist. But she worked incredibly hard at school and she joined IntoUniversity, which provides mentorship and opportunities, which helped her get a scholarship to Rugby boarding school. At that school, they helped her to apply to the University for the Creative Arts at Farnham to study photography. I met her when she left university and had gone back to live with her mum in Grenfell Tower. She was working as a care worker. I'd curated her first exhibition and she was incredibly excited, but she said to me, "I can't see how I can actually pursue this." In the Diaspora Pavilion, most of the other emerging artists had some track record already. She was the youngest, but I was adamant that there should be an artist on the programme with little track record, that we believed in and supported and helped. There were so many well-known artists in the Pavilion, including Yinka Shonibare and Isaac Julien, but Khadija ended up with the most press coverage and reviews of her work.

Aaron: It's interesting that we're beginning to see a more open art world in some respects, but there are still many forms of privilege. Even when there is diversity, there's often a preference for artists who tell their narrative according to certain established conventions, or work in certain media. There are expectations that artists arrive as fully formed participants in the international art world. So the discussion of diversity at every level—whether religious, ethnic, or socioeconomic—has a long way to go from the ground level to some of the more luminous success stories.

Nicola: Some people, for whatever reason, have something powerful to say at a very young age that everybody wants to hear. That's the exception, yet we count them as the road map to success. Most people need mentoring and opportunities, and there needs to be a kind of synchronicity to these things. I'm really passionate because it took until I got towards my forties for me to fully understand my work myself. I never forget the opportunities I had and the people that helped me, because I know perfectly well that I wasn't fully formed after art college. I was not one of those exceptional artists or human beings. It's been a very long journey for me. Lots of the young artists that I mentor are not at all fully formed. Khadija was far from that when I met her and that's one of the many, many reasons that I loved her and her work. She was just so up for the fight and pain of pushing through that.

Aaron: As Stuart Hall says, identity is itself never fully formed. It's a process.[3] The challenge seems to be how to find the intersection between the process of identity formation and artistic formation. And when they do join up, there needs to be a platform—like the Diaspora Pavilion—to share that experience.

3. Hall, "Cultural Identity and Diaspora," 21.

17. Güler Ates: Absorbing Histories

Aaron: Güler, things seem very challenging in Turkey right now. You must worry a lot about family and friends.

Güler: I've always thought things were going to get worse. Thousands of people have left in the past five years. They knew something was going to happen. The UK media generally portrayed something more positive and people saw art and culture flourishing in Turkey. This of course was very exciting, but misleading.

Aaron: And you left Turkey much earlier, right?

Güler: I was interested in exploring a new culture and learning English. I wanted to rediscover my own identity by being an outsider to my own culture. I had first come to the UK in 1998. My friend and I were employed to pick strawberries at a farm in Norwich. During this work placement they took us to the National Gallery. I thought I would faint when I saw real paintings at the National Gallery. It was a mind-blowing experience! I had only seen these paintings from illustrations in books, and that was it. I had to study art in the UK. I came back to the UK in 1999 and it was a long and difficult journey to be able to study in the UK, but I was very lucky to get some support and encouragement from people whom I met during this journey.

When I was studying in Istanbul, I didn't believe I would make it and become a practicing artist. Sometimes I felt unwelcome in certain artist groups because I couldn't blend in culturally and financially. I was born in a rural village in Eastern Turkey and culturally it is different to Western Turkey. I learnt Turkish when I was seven. My mother tongue is Zazaca.

Aaron: In what ways was that difference apparent to people in Turkey?

Güler: Well, when I was studying at the University of Marmara, I made a piece of artwork about women from Eastern Turkey. My tutor, who was going to mark it, looked at my work and she said, "This is so old fashioned, you need to be more modern, you need to look at Western art." And I thought, well, you told us we should do something about ourselves, and my heritage is from eastern Turkey. And then she gave me a grade that I was not expecting.

Her senior professor was present when I was collecting this work from their shared office. He asked me why I did this work, and I explained it. He seemed very excited about this work and they had an intense discussion and he took this work and asked my tutor to give me a higher grade and said this work should be included in the group exhibition that was organized by the department. I was really touched by this positive intervention. I was also very encouraged by one of my favorite tutors, Nevhiz Tanyeli. She was a fantastic teacher.

Aaron: So the assignment was "tell us about yourself," but there was a predetermined idea of what they wanted you to be. It reminds me a bit of the experience of an artist we both know from Pakistan, Dua Abbas. It seems like a lot of places in the Middle East and Central Asia have art academies, often with colonial foundations, that feel this extreme pressure to demonstrate how modern they are, based on perceived Western norms. But ironically, by training artists they see as not engaging with regional or cultural issues, they're actually *less* contemporary because they're working off an outdated idea of modernism.

Güler: Exactly.

Aaron: How did you find it when you came to the UK as a student? I imagine there were new issues of identity to explore based on that experience.

Güler: I always felt very welcomed in the UK and I found most people very open and easy to speak to. I did a one-year foundation course first at Lewisham College in London and that was an excellent course and had fantastic tutors. Then I did a BA in painting at Wimbledon School of Art. When I started, I couldn't speak very good English and they generously offered me extra support with my speaking and writing. And I didn't understand many things including the British class system—which was good in a way! In my second year, I got a lot of help from my tutors. Jennet Thomas and Alison Turnbull were very critical in a constructive way and yet were very sensitive to my needs. I started to look at artists who dealt with similar subject matter or concerns as me, like Mona Hatoum, Shirin Neshat, and Zineb Sedira.

Aaron: Your work really started to transition in the middle of your degree, right?

Güler: In my second year at Wimbledon I started to use text in Turkish as a layer in my paintings. During a group crit I was actually questioned by one of the tutors why it was in Turkish instead of English. I was surprised and I said, "I want to use a word that has a deeper meaning to me." And then he carried on saying that he thought writing in Turkish wasn't very sensible for the English-speaking spectator and I should consider my viewer. My peers were very supportive, but for the first time I began to question why I was doing art and if I should carry on.

I changed my aesthetic direction. I wanted to stop using paint but still work on the canvas. A couple of tutors were unhappy with these big changes in a very short time. They were concerned for me and gave me an unsatisfactory mark in my report. I went to see the artist George Blacklock, who was the head of fine art. I was so mad I had fire coming from my ears. We had this very intense, honest conversation, and I said, "I'm going to do what I want, not what other people like." And he was amazing. He said, "You do what you like and I'm going to support you." Jennet and Alison also gave me more support and it was the best decision for me. Since that time, I've worked with everything.

Aaron: Does painting still play a role in your practice?

Güler: Not directly. Wimbledon trained me technically how to paint, which was fantastic, and I really enjoyed the painting course. I struggled to capture feeling in a painting as it has such a long history, and to add something new to it is very difficult. I now try to capture the possibilities of painting through my camera lens. I find this more exciting.

Aaron: You mentioned you took inspiration from Shirin Neshat. I can see that influence in the frontality and textuality of some of your early works. Then you started doing work that's much more mysterious. Rather than wanting to declare things, it seems like you started to cloak them. When did you start playing with that approach?

Güler: I did a three-month residency at the Cité Internationale des Arts in Paris. I got this wonderful award in 2007 from the Royal College of Art in London, where I did my MA. I had time to think and question my practice. I knew that I didn't want to paint anymore. During the residency I realized that I wanted to do performance and work with the idea of cultural displacement in a different way. I bought fabrics in Parisian markets, I think from an Algerian seller. I combined this with Western style wall fabric and made my first handmade costume. Cité des Arts was a perfect setting to start to work with fabrics in colonial architectural settings. The site-responsiveness merged Eastern and Western sensibilities.

Aaron: Was architecture ever part of your training?

Güler: I used to work doing technical drawing in an architecture office in Turkey and I planned to study architecture, which fortunately didn't happen, although I enjoyed learning about the history of the buildings.

Aaron: It's interesting how painting and architecture both eventually found their way into your later work in subtle ways.

Güler: Working at the National Gallery in London was a big inspiration for me. I was a gallery assistant for fourteen years, beginning when I was studying painting at Wimbledon. Those paintings I saw at the National Gallery must have gone inside me. So painting definitely came back into my work in another form, through my camera lens.

Aaron: The way you describe it, it sounds like it wasn't so much that you were looking at the paintings. You were absorbing them.

Güler: Most colors in my work are inspired by those paintings. In Eastern Turkey, women are also very expressive with their dress colors, which are often very rich.

Aaron: And that really follows historic trade routes as well. When we think about Venetian painting in the early modern period, many of the rich colors and patterns in the fabrics they depicted came from trading with the Ottoman Empire. It's really fascinating to me that Turkey comes back into your work directly but also indirectly, by way of the Western art history that was seeping into your head in the National Gallery. You just had to find your own way to integrate all these different sources.

Güler: That took me a while to realize. At the National, I learned so much about the history of art. *Bellini and the East* (2006) was a very interesting exhibition in that respect. For the first time, I saw the portraits of Mehmet II painted by Gentile Bellini, who traveled from Venice to Constantinople to work for the sultan. I loved being in the National and surrounded by paintings. Sometimes I worked twelve hours a day and I started to dream about some of these paintings. I got to know which room a painting was in, the frame, the corners, and the details; how they changed in morning or afternoon light, or depending on the weather. For me, the light was one of the most intriguing parts. I didn't have to see a work the same way every day. The dark paintings, especially, change so much. Sometimes you can't see anything; it's as if they're all gone, all concealed by the light. Especially the Dutch paintings. It's a form of concealing and exposure at the same time. Before studying in the UK, I didn't know which artists to look at, and who I needed to read. For example, it took me a long time to find Edward Said. I think I found him in 2003 when I was writing my dissertation at Wimbledon. That discovery changed my work.

Aaron: I like that just as you were establishing your relationship with the Old Masters, you also had to find and develop this kind of personal approach to a theorist, someone who could help you articulate what your sense of being both interior and exterior to a tradition looked like.

Güler: Unfortunately, he died in 2003. I would have loved to hear him speak and meet him. At that time, he was the only theorist I could relate to my subject matter or find personally interesting. His books helped me to find a place for myself in the history of art.

Aaron: Turkey has such a hybrid history. Thinking about Orientalism, the fact that Turkey was so close geographically to the West, ironically seems like it made it a crucial place to define as non-Western.

Güler: This hybrid history definitely shaped my identity. The Western ideology of Orientalism defines the "Orient" as weak and inferior. I think such constructed weakness sometimes creates a confused identity for Turkish people.

Aaron: Do you find that your sense of self or belonging in British society has changed over the years? Your time in the UK, like mine, coincides with a massive transition in the society.

Güler: After 2008, things started going the wrong way for artists. We lost the spaces, the galleries, the funding, and there was not much to protect artists. And then after Brexit, I felt like I lost someone I love so much, like a close family member. For days and days, I wanted to cry.

Aaron: As these political events have unfolded, have you noticed people start to interpret your work differently?

Güler: Only once. I had an exhibition a couple years ago in London, where the curators asked me if I was concerned to exhibit my work, or what would happen if people were offended, or there was a threat of some type. At the time, I thought they were just being over sensitive.

Aaron: On the one hand, there are always people who have a strong visceral reaction to something they think is offensive or polemical. But what's interesting to me is that sometimes what people find offensive is actually ambiguity regarding something they feel should be set in stone. I wonder whether some people might actually be threatened by the lack of ideology in your work!

Güler: I like openness, and for people to find something for themselves. In my work, I provide commentary on the Western notion of Orientalism, and the effect of the cross-pollination of cultures on female identity (**Fig. 17.1**).

Aaron: It definitely seems like the art market encourages people now to accentuate their cultural identity in some ways. But is there also a negative side to that embrace? Rather than the Orientalism of exclusion, is there an Orientalism of exoticism at play?

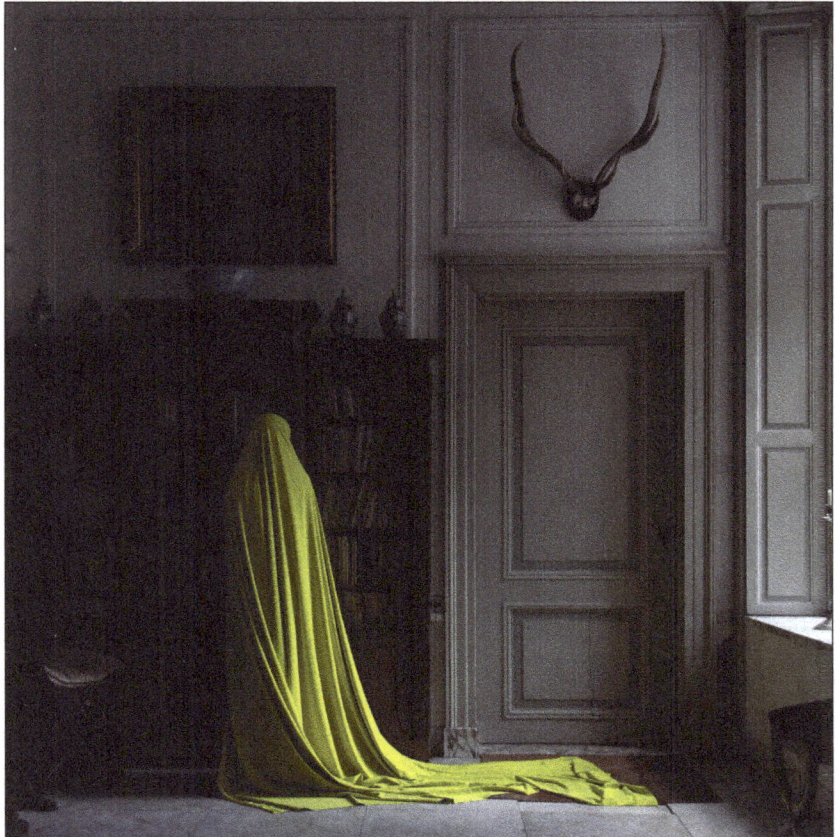

Figure 17.1

Güler: It's a problematic marketing strategy. I think there is an element of exoticism, which still may be in demand. I believe the artist should do what he or she wants to do without being controlled or influenced by the art market. It's very unhealthy. Gallerists often want to know who you are before they have your work!

Aaron: The perfect pre-packaged narrative . . .

Güler: It's a selling point if the artist experiences some sort of pain or suffering, or can be labeled as exotic due to their background. The art market, media, and public also love such stories.

Aaron: To what extent do you think people read your work biographically? It seems to me that you intentionally hold back a lot of information in your work. Do people often ask you, "Is that you in this image?" or "Who's behind that veil?"

Güler: In my first photographic work in Paris I did the performing. I asked a friend to take the photographs. It was difficult to be in front of and behind the camera. The outcome of four days was only three photographs. So then I decided: maybe I should work with someone who can feel what I'm trying to do. People do often ask me who is behind the veil. I always invite my performance artist to join me during openings and talks so she can speak for her own experiences. The performance artist, whom I mostly work with, is a practicing artist herself.

Aaron: I think a lot of people would be surprised to understand how collaborative your process is. Have you had moments when your model has done something you really didn't expect?

Güler: There's a lot that you don't see, which is interesting. My model moves continuously, but she has to make little movements. The idea is that I give her one character for each room where I work. She has to do it so subtly, sensitively, like a snake almost. As part of the performance, the model unfolds a story drawn from the history of the site.

Aaron: And her movement leaves a kind of trace behind. It's almost as if we see the subject stirring the air, the molecules slowing shifting in her wake.

Güler: She moves very, very slowly, and that's actually harder for her.

Aaron: Right, I think about models in life drawing classes, and how challenging it is to be still. You have to practice to be able to be still. One of the impressions that you get in looking at your work is this kind of undulating, languid sensibility. But I think it's really revealing that this softness is a product of so much control and difficulty and exertion.

Güler: Yes, when we work together, she often has to come with a kit for her muscles and backaches!

Aaron: So there are all these things that are hidden in the experience of the model and in your process as well; things that need to happen to create something that appears so slow and contemplative. We also mentioned architecture. What's your process like behind the scenes when deciding where to shoot?

Güler: Mostly, I've contacted places I want to work, like Leighton House Museum and the Victoria and Albert Museum in London. Other places like Eton College have approached me (**Fig. 17.2**). I'm especially interested in places with an interesting colonial history, like the V&A and the Museum Van Loon in Amsterdam. I look for visible marks of the past. I usually don't find them immediately but I feel them from the aesthetic. I want to unfold my subject matter through the history of the architecture. I am interested in layering in the performances (**Fig. 17.3**).

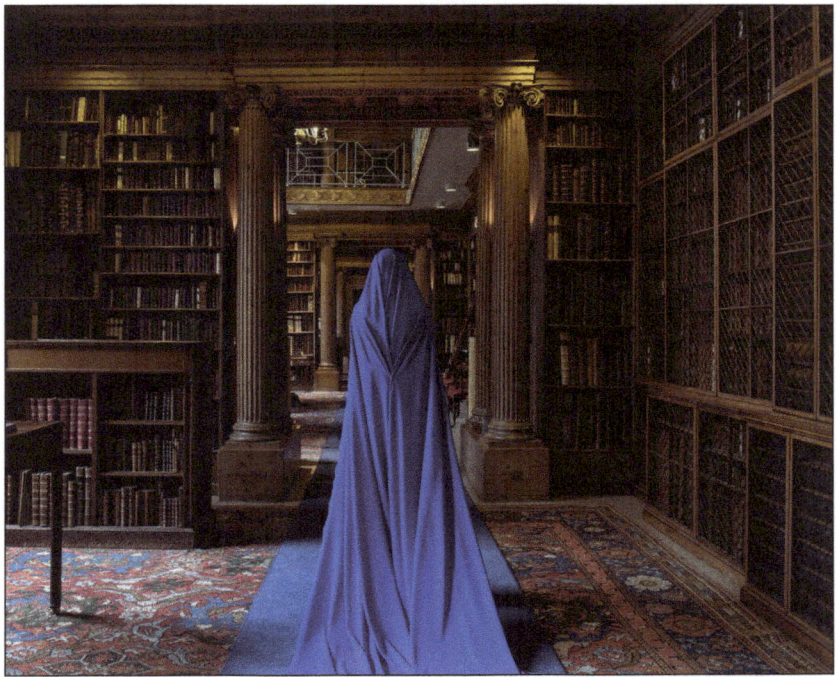

Figure 17.2

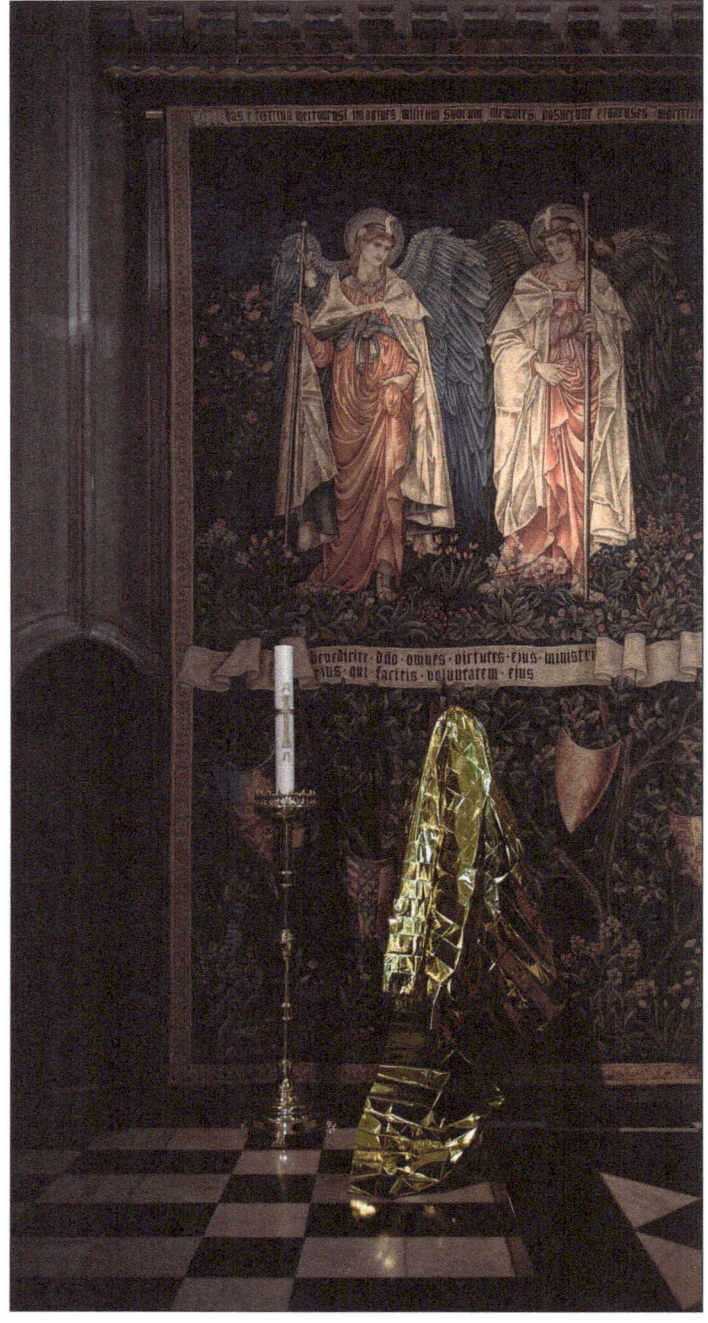

Figure 17.3

Aaron: There's an interesting dimension of host and guest in those kind of interactions. It's almost like you're dusting for fingerprints of the past. And what you discover has the potential to be unsettling for institutions if they don't want to reckon with certain histories. On the other hand, it might be seen as a gift.

Güler: It depends which country we are in. In the UK, generally it's easier to get access. Often institutions welcome such proposals. But in India and Brazil it wasn't easy to get permission. In 2014, I went to Rio de Janeiro. I visited many historic buildings built by the Portuguese, but I didn't connect to the historic sites that I visited. I've been invited to make work in other locations, to which I've said no; nice, peaceful houses with lots of artifacts. But if it doesn't feel right, I don't do it.

Aaron: I imagine that there's a risk of people assuming that one has some "native" gift for identifying with all postcolonial contexts, as if all forms of difference are the same, or interchangeable.

Güler: Yes, that's correct. In Rio, it didn't feel right, maybe because I saw the class system, which still has colonial resonances. When I went to visit art galleries and museums there, I mostly saw certain types of visitors, which bothered me. So I decided I wanted to make live performances outside the gallery space, for people—and with people—who may not feel welcome in galleries themselves.

Aaron: Speaking of working outside with people, I remember how powerful your *Sea of Color* (London, 2016) piece was, about the experience of Syrian refugees. A bunch of us helped carry your tapestry back and forth across the Millennium Bridge. It was so serendipitous the way the fabric caught the wind and rippled, and some of the pieces of children's clothing flew out into the Thames. And it was moving watching strangers stop and even help. The whole process really made me think so much more about the kind of curator I want to be, and how to create spaces where unexpected, transformative experiences might happen.

Güler: It was an important realization. The journey we took across the Millennium Bridge was a very small reflection of the experience of modern-day refugees, who take extraordinary risks to reach a safer home. It was meaningful to work with many people and their contribution remains in this work. In *Sea of Color*, I realized how much I wanted to speak from my heart, about things that are close to me.

18. Bently Spang: "Indian of the Future"

Aaron: I've found it really interesting moving to Montana and hearing how non-Native people talk about Native people. On the one hand there's this familiarity that you don't get in a lot of the country, but then there's also this really unnerving level of prejudice, too.

Bently: In this country it's just that big old broom, let's sweep Native history under the rug again. When Native people speak out at a national level, I think it triggers some unresolved guilt about the genocide committed against Native people in this country and that can limit dialogue because institutions are wary of stirring up that guilt. There's a reluctance to encourage that discussion and I'm sure there's worry about patrons staying away. It's a difficult, complex history but the fact is it's what happened.

But, I've found that at a grassroots level people want change, they don't want things to go on this way. They want to hear what really happened in the past—not the sanitized version in the mainstream—and how we're doing today. When I lecture about my work, I get a terrific response from people, with lots of questions and curiosity. But there can be a disconnect between the grassroots and institutional levels. Thankfully, some institutions *are* open to change, and I've been lucky to find them in my career. I think once you have a place to talk about what really happened, then you start to see connections to the present, like the situation with immigrant children being separated from their families on the Mexican border.

Aaron: Right, we've been talking about how that relates in pretty eerie ways to the history of Native American "boarding schools."

Bently: To me, this supposed education was just another form of geno-cide, an attempt to eradicate our cultures. I was just up at the Fort Shaw Government Industrial Indian School site. They placed a monument there a couple years ago to the 1904 World Champion Ft. Shaw all-Indian girls' basketball team. They only lost one game ever and were amazing ball players. My great grandmother, Gertrude Parker, was the mascot with the team—that's what the team called her—and the girls on the team took good care of her. She said they were like mothers to her and I'll always be grateful to them for that. She was nine years old at the time and one of the entertainers who performed in Native regalia at halftime. She did the Lord's Prayer in Indian Sign Language. There's a monument there with a picture of my grandmother, and it really triggered some stuff in me. It really made me think about what her experience was in that boarding school. You were punished, often beaten, for doing anything cultural—speaking the language, especially—and there was sexual and psychological abuse in these schools. Kids tried to run away all the time and they would drag them back. Some died in those schools. I'm sure there's a graveyard next to every boarding school. My mom said there's one at Ft. Shaw and I know there's one at Carlisle. It was a real dark time in Native history in this country. My grandma Gertie was there at Ft. Shaw from five years old to sixteen. All those years away from her family in those conditions, it breaks my heart. A lot of kids were taken from their families with total disregard. They apparently didn't think Native families cared about their kids.

Aaron: If you think about all the different ways in which you can challenge someone else's humanity, denying that someone would care about their own children is maybe the most destructive thing you could say about them. And there's something quite demonic about buttressing it with the idea that one's saving the souls of the children one's stealing! I'm reminded of examples of people stealing children from Jewish families and rushing to baptize them so they couldn't go back to Jewish parents who might "corrupt" them. And then there's the example of Trump officials taking away children under the fiction that their parents, desperately seeking a better life for their kids, are human traffickers.

Bently: In the case of the boarding schools, for us, when it's acknowl-
          edged at all it's usually a really sanitized version, making it seem
          like separating families was actually a good thing. That hap-
          pened to three generations in my family: my mother Sandy, her
          mom Stella, and her mom Gertrude. My mom says they weren't
          educating you as much as they were creating these exotic young
          Native servants for white families. My grandma Stella went to
          Flandreau Indian School and they taught her to cook and clean,
          then hired her out to local white families. She said the families
          would bring around groups of white folks while she worked to
          show off their "Indian maid." It was very dehumanizing for her.

Aaron: It sounds more like de-education, making sure young people had
          only certain horizons, and no kinship network to go back to.

Bently: In the late 1800s, Capt. Richard Pratt, the founder of Carlisle
          Indian School, gave that famous "Kill the Indian, and Save the
          Man" speech, which was basically the motto for a lot of the
          boarding schools. It was really about eradication of identity and
          assimilating them into society.

Aaron: I think that's something that resonates painfully for a lot of mi-
          norities: the idea that integration is possible, but it basically has
          to be purchased at the price of losing, denying, or forgetting your
          cultural identity. It basically assumes you can scrape people's his-
          tories out of them like a gourd. But if you take away language,
          history, religion, and family, what is there to "save"?

Bently: And what do you have generationally down the road? I think that
          has to do with some of what we're dealing with in our commu-
          nity today. Some of the challenges started there in the boarding
          schools with that forced separation and this societal wound that
          was created. On my reservation, there's a little community called
          Rabbit Town. It came into existence, my mom said, because
          people moved to that area and started camping there to be close
          to their kids who were taken to the St. Labre Catholic School on
          the eastern edge of the reservation. So parents moved across the
          reservation so they could at least see their kids through a fence.
          She said there was one man who put his tipi on a hill right next
          to the school, where the graveyard is now, and made sure he was

standing outside the tipi for his kids to see him every morning. Good father. I'm always trying to understand the motivation behind efforts like the boarding schools; this intense desire to break up people.

Aaron: I would guess that not that many of the people involved in setting up the schools had a systematic vision of what they were doing. But in retrospect, the institutional logic of community destruction is really clear. When you think about the British in India, for example, that's a recurring refrain of colonialism: break communities apart, take away traditions, replace them with something else that makes no sense in a given context, and complain that people aren't embracing the values they've been "given"!

Bently: Right, and then if you don't get it, then it must be because of the weakness of your culture. That's the history that I see, a subjective version that supports the dominant culture's viewpoint. That's why it's important to tell people's history in the words of those that lived it. Let us tell it for a change, not some non-Indian, Indian expert.

Aaron: Denying people's memories is another part of the colonial strategy.

Bently: When I talk about people in the past, I call them "my relatives in the past" and try not to use "ancestors." That word disconnects me from them. Those relatives in the 1800s and earlier were my uncles, aunts, grandparents, and cousins, and we're still connected. When someone else, like historians or ethnographers, define you, that's often the only definition that you get in the mainstream. Then if we don't fit their definition that focuses on only the 1800s—if we're not living in tipis and we're not wearing buckskin every day—we're not real Indians. That's what I struggle with all the time when it comes to people's perceptions of us: separation.

So, I try to put little markers in place to help people understand that we're the same group of people from the 1800s, not two different groups as they sometimes define us. It's because there's a time period that's missing in the public consciousness, the reservation period, which for Northern Cheyennes was from about 1886 forward. Filling in those blanks has been a real challenge, but it's been rewarding because once you start, you also begin to fill in the blanks of society in general, not just for Native people but other cultural groups. There were moments of conflict for my people, but also positive interactions with non-Native people, despite the propaganda the powers that be at the time created so that people would dislike us.

Aaron: It's hard to get people to listen to complicated stories. I can imagine it's extremely difficult to open people's eyes to the trauma of that past on the one hand, and on the other hand show the resistance to that history.

Bently: Well, if it's all negative then there's no point where someone can enter into it, so it means talking about what really happened—both the good and the bad—then creating spaces where resolution can take place. It wasn't all conflict in the past. We had a powerful, intellectual culture and strong communities. We wouldn't still be here if we didn't. We still do. Contemporary Native artists talk about those things in the context of the art exhibition all the time so that's definitely a space for resolution.

Aaron: I've seen that problem of "empathy fatigue" come up in different contexts. Ernst van Alphen writes about being over-exposed as a child to the story of Anne Frank, and that it's challenging sometimes to teach people about the Holocaust because they feel their moral positions are all predetermined for them.[4] But in America maybe we haven't even got to that point, because there's still so little knowledge about Native history.

Bently: As an artist, there are so many different layers of responsibility. Sometimes it feels overwhelming to try to negotiate that space. One thing I do is look back as much as I can at the artwork that came before me by my relatives and think about what they were trying to say. I go into museum collections and see my relatives' work a lot and I ask myself how I can continue that way of "saying" in today's world with the materials and forms of expression available to us today. They created a gift for my generation of

4. van Alphen, *Caught by History*, 2–3.

how they met their challenges and it's in the artwork. How can I do the same for future generations?

Aaron: What kind of work do you most respond to?

Bently: Well, I really look to the bead and quill work, but also to the context of these objects that we were wearing, using, and interacting with. They were created to honor people in different ways, to celebrate their accomplishments and moments in their lives, and to keep track of history. These are really complex, multi-layered, and intense pieces; the level of detail and the amount of sweat and action that went into them give them a heavy presence. I did a Smithsonian Community Scholar Fellowship after my undergraduate degree and I designed my own research program to study the beadwork designs of my people and our allies, to try to understand what we were trying to say and how we influenced each other and collaborated. I discovered that there wasn't a lot of information. The curators admitted they didn't know what a lot of the designs meant and that the meanings were in the minds of the makers. We didn't sign our work back then either, so that information is really only around in families that owned certain designs still used today. My elders gave me things to do to prepare myself to go into these contexts, to be around these works and respect them. But there wasn't anyone in the museums there teaching me, saying "here's what this or that means." For me, just being in the presence of the pieces helped. And that's one of the things that I came away with: how much we need to be in the presence of this work as Native people. Part of what we're up against in our community is that we don't have this work in our community to reference, for our kids to see growing up, to say "this is how we felt about each other in the past, and these are the lengths we were willing to go to show love to each other, to show respect for each other." To create these complex masterworks and then give them to each other to honor someone, those are the actions of a healthy, loving community. So all this information came at me as I was looking at the collections in the Smithsonian museums in DC and in New York. It was one of the most pivotal moments in my life as an artist. It just taught me so much and I learn more each time I see that work.

Aaron: And then I imagine there's an opportunity to take that knowledge back to the community, if not the objects.

Bently: We're still making those kinds of outfits for everyday use in powwows and celebrations back home. Mothers, aunts, and grandmas, grandpas, uncles, and dads are making them for the kids out of love to represent the family in powwows so we still have that knowledge and there are still ceremonies going on, but it's true we've been disconnected from those historical objects. Many of them were designed to go back to the earth, but some would have made it to today.

Aaron: The debate around authenticity, preservation, and use is interesting. There's the tendency to think that locking objects up, calibrating the perfect humidity levels, etc. guarantees the survival of objects in their "original" state. But that completely neglects the importance of preserving culture itself. And sometimes it's not even literally true that objects do better in museum conditions. I think about how some historic Japanese ceramics actually suffer when they aren't used. So the tradition of the tea ceremony actually protects the objects themselves.

Bently: The whole issue of our patrimony in museums is a complex one. The work is there from multiple sources: taken from battlefields and massacres, stolen from graves, sold to museums by hobbyists, etc. Our human remains are in museums as well for cranial studies, etc. but, thankfully, they're being returned along with some artwork through the Native American Graves Protection and Repatriation Act. One of my elders, Bill Tallbull, started that whole NAGPRA process years ago. It's an incredibly complex situation.

Speaking of Japanese ceramics, though, when I was developing my practice early on, I was really drawn to Isamu Noguchi, and I found myself gravitating towards ways of thinking from the Pacific Rim about materials having a life force, a sort of personality. And I thought: that's how we feel about our materials. Seeing similarities across cultures helped me understand the importance of material choices, kind of negotiating with those materials in order to hear what they wanted to say, to become a sort of facilitator. But it's always tricky, too, because as a Native artist I learned early on to respect the power of certain realms, and so I don't talk about that much in my work because I'm not a medicine person. I'm always deciding: how far do I go?

Aaron: Then again, you're also part of another genealogy, of Western art. A lot of modern artists, like Kandinsky, Klee, or Beuys, saw themselves almost like prophets or shamans. What do you do with that history, and those problematic claims?

Bently: Yeah it's tricky because I love all those artists' work but I also want artists to acknowledge their influences, in homage, and also understand the issue of cultural appropriation and question if they're doing that. A lot of artists have been drawn to my relatives' work because the power of it is undeniable. But appropriation is not the answer. Why would you want to speak in someone else's visual language about your own life?

We need to have more of these discussions in the art world today. Just look at what happened at the Walker Art Center recently.[5] Cultural appropriation is happening right now across the country. I see it in my own state all the time. Our lives and histories are not just fodder for non-Native artists to build careers on, which takes opportunities away from Native people, and misses the opportunity to hear truth from people that are living it.

Artistically, there's a long history of exploitation of the "mystical" part of us. And I don't want to be a part of that. But I know that within my creative process there's a power that I'm tapping into that draws me back constantly. It's a healing process that gives back to me, that sustains me, that feeds me in a lot of ways. I can't explain. It just does. And there's a power there. Our relatives in the past knew that. But I'm not a medicine person and I respect what they do so I steer clear of defining myself in those ways.

Aaron: So on the one hand there's that shamanistic trope to avoid (which at times explicitly appropriated Native culture). And then there's the risk of trespassing boundaries within your tradition. But it

5. For information on protests following the exhibition of Sam Durant's *Scaffold* (2017), see Sheets, "Emmett Till's Coffin, a Hangman's Scaffold and a Debate Over Cultural Appropriation."

sounds like keeping it personal, speaking to your own experience of the power of art, allows you to avoid those pitfalls.

Bently: The other piece of it is knowing that you're part of a community. My family were, and are, bead workers. They're everywhere in my family on both sides. On my dad's side my great grandmother Artie Wolfchief was a great beadworker and her daughter, my grandma Jenny Wilfred Spang, and my grandpa, were both well-known hide tanners. People would come from all over the country to get their pure white buckskins. They even published a book called *Cheyenne Way of Tanning*. My mom drew and painted and instilled a love for art in me too. So I was immersed in art growing up. We grew up on and off the reservation but always found Native people and artists wherever we went so there was Native art all around me even when we weren't on the rez.

For me it's just this constant process of placing myself in this continuum of creating and trying to understand this Tsitsistas/Suhtai [Northern Cheyenne] stream that I am in the center of that's separate from Western European art. They're two different streams but they converge at different moments (**Fig. 18.1**).

It's a challenging place to be. But when it all comes together, it's kind of mind-blowing. I could have easily decided not to talk about my experience as a Tsitsistas/Suhtai. And there were junctures where I had to decide: am I going to go this way or am I going to go that way? It became clear to me early on that I would be denying my personal truth not to express my experience as a Native person in my work and that I really had no choice.

I remember one of my professors in undergrad said, "You want to be careful with the direction you choose for your work because if you do express your culture, it's going to close some doors for you." At the time, I thought, why is he warning me about this? And then I realized later on that he was right, it did close some doors. But, you know, it opened others.

Aaron: It seems like there's an increasing appetite in the art world for talking about identity, which is good. But there can be a lot of expectations about what it means for an artist to be "authentic," and there's a risk of mapping preconceptions about artists' cultures onto their work.

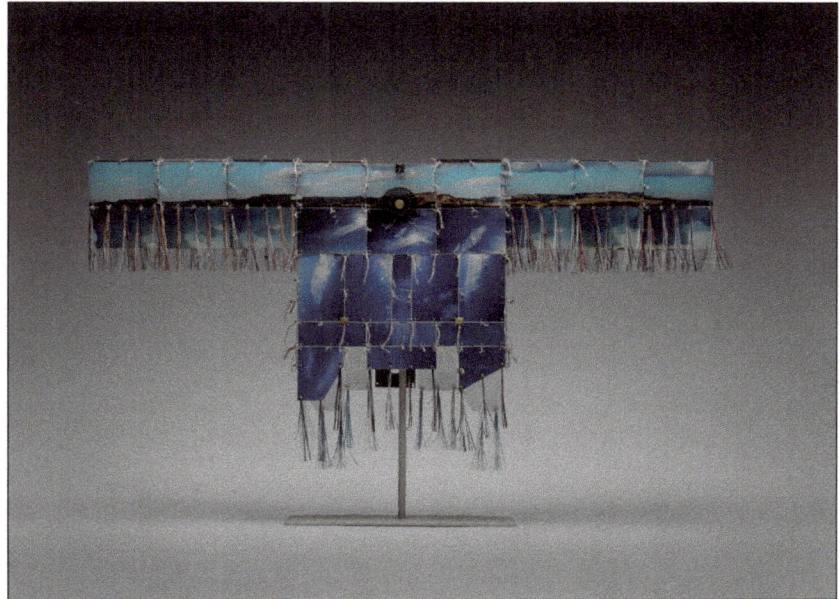

Figure 18.1

Bently: Well, that's the thing. When I was in grad school, I had a couple of epiphany moments when I got a chance to look at the broader picture of art and the history of certain voices. We studied movements like feminist art, the Harlem Renaissance, and Native art, which opened my eyes to where I was at as a young Native artist trying to negotiate this territory. I wrote a paper talking about taking back how we define ourselves, which Melanie Herzog and Ronald Neperud helped get published.[6] It's still important for me to express myself through writing and to be a part of the dialogue. I started to understand that you can have both a physical and written practice, which both move the work forward.

Aaron: I imagine that was complicated, because on the one hand you want to be shaping how that debate is taking place, and yet there are still outdated conventions about what the role of the artist should be.

6. Spang, "The Process of Self Definition."

Bently: Part of it, for me, comes from understanding the multifunctional aspect of the art of my relatives. It was not just utilitarian or conceptual or aesthetic. It was all those things, plus it had a community dimension built into it. It was also there to acknowledge and honor people. So there was potentially a personal or political or spiritual aspect, or a combination of them all, depending on the role of the artwork in the community. Artists back then were doing a little bit of everything: dancing, creating regalia, painting, sculpting, beading. They were like the ultimate multidisciplinary artists (**Fig. 18.2**).

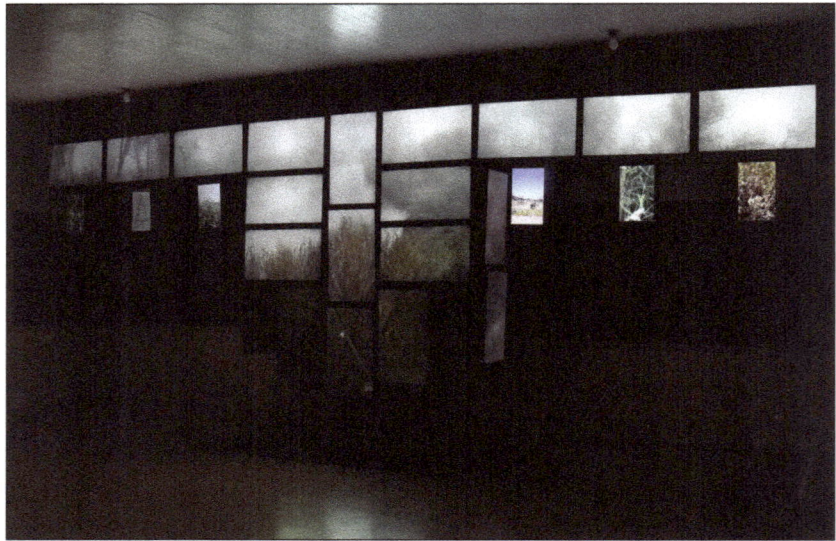

Figure 18.2

Aaron: It's funny how long it takes us sometimes to rediscover these fundamental insights, which were there in practice for centuries.

Bently: That's really what helped me to understand my place as an artist. I realized I have to express myself in multiple realms, multiple media. I feel required to do that to carry on the Tsitsistas/Suhtai way of creating. And suddenly, in this time period, it's more acceptable than ever in the Western art world. But I still feel some constraints. Even though *multidisciplinary* is a common term, there are still expectations that you should stay within a certain framework, or contextual space. Early on, I took my portfolio to galleries, in a city that will remain nameless, and I remember almost every single one said, "Oh, you know, there's a Native gallery or Native museum over there, I can give you their information." That's changing, there's more inclusion going on, but it's a slow process.

Aaron: I imagine it's damaging to have people assume that your work is somehow only relevant to certain people. It takes away the chance for the work to speak in various registers, and of course runs the risk of fetishizing or exoticizing Native culture.

Bently: It keeps us in the box, the one created by the Indian experts that fuels misconceptions of us and limits our voice. Otherwise we might get out and change history. The stereotypes that result from "the box" are a real concern to me, and that's why I've always tried to understand historically how images of Native people have been produced, like mascots. They were propaganda initially, designed to control public sentiment about us and justify taking the land at all costs. Then they morphed into sports mascots and humiliating representations in media that are still with us today. They're slowly being dismantled now thanks to Native people speaking up, but it still exists, which is disconcerting. The damage to the Native psyche, especially for kids, is very high. We have the highest rates of suicide for youth in the country. It's an odd thing, where people think they're honoring you as warriors, for example, with these mascots. But nobody ever asked us how we want to be honored.

Aaron: Right, once you turn people into these imaginary entities they can function symbolically however you want them to.

Bently: There's definitely that dehumanization in terms of language, whether before or after persecution.

Aaron: Americans are really gifted at forgetting. We pretty much demand it of immigrants. How quickly you can forget where you're from is basically the gold standard of assimilation! I look at my relatives, who fled persecution. Aside from one Talmud tractate we have no physical objects, and only a faint sense that our relatives came from somewhere near Odessa.

141

Bently: I did a performative video installation years ago called *The House of Tsitsistas or . . . I'm Not Your Daddy's Indian Anymore*, and my performance character is this sort of over the top guy in a silver cowboy hat and sunglasses, silver pants, red painted face and shirtless with body paint who restores some of the missing dimensions—stylish, sexy, and funny—that the mainstream excludes. He showed up in another piece called *Boutique of the Damned*, in the video in that installation I called him "the Indian of your wildest dreams." Nowadays he wears a gold lamé jumpsuit, silver hat, platform shoes, and blue face, and I call him the "Indian of the Future," aka the Blue Guy. He is the emcee of my *Tekcno Powwow* series performances where I bring together break dancers and powwow dancers and DJs and powwow drums. He goes against that mystical, stoic representation we always get in the movies and he rankles the know-it-alls about Indians to no end. I heard someone in Montana say once, "Oh, that's not how *our* Indians act." I've always felt like there's this odd sense of ownership of our identity by non-Natives in this country. In my article, I created a scenario where I was sitting in a lecture by Native experts that aren't Native, which has happened too many times, and I had a sensation of having my tongue cut out. I coined a term for that sensation: cultural dismemberment.

Aaron: What's the way out of those situations, or into different ones?

Bently: Well, on a grassroots level, when I show up as a Native person in a teaching or museum context I think there's a certain attraction for the public. They want to sit down and talk with you about your experience. They want to know the truth and are ready for it. For the majority of people in this country, that just doesn't happen. They don't get a chance to talk to a living Native person, ever. There's never been a lot of demand institutionally for that type of engagement because there's the idea that "we've already studied them." We've already been defined. Add to it that fear of stirring up the unresolved guilt and suddenly you have institutional silence. But, if the institutions don't provide the opportunity, where does the public get to hear from us? I would challenge the institutions to be more fearless and come to us and ask us what we want to say. Make our work a regular part of the offering of the museum, not just something to feature once every ten or twenty years when a historical moment comes up or you need to showcase your historical Native collection. Don't be afraid of something you can't predict, or "capitalize" on. Personally, I think it's beautiful to hear how people from different groups express themselves. It really makes you hungry to know more about the artists and be in the presence of that work and have a connection to it. Then you start to understand the real history of this country, and the history of this world.

Destruction

19. Julian Bell and Aithan Shapira: Who by Fire, Who by Water

Aaron: Julian and Aithan, I'm really glad to be able to introduce you across the world, with me in Montana, Aithan on a train to Boston, and Julian in England! The reason I wanted to bring you both together is to talk about the deeply personal experience of losing artwork, and how that changes your experience as an artist, how you get back into creating, and even how it alters your self-perception. Julian, would you like to begin by talking about your experience?

Julian: Well, my entire work, my studio, everything went up in smoke one evening four years ago, on March 29, 2014. I had actually just got all my work back together in the studio from galleries. And that was the moment that the accident struck due to a faulty chimney and a fire spread. No one was hurt. It was a spectacular sight. I arrived about ten minutes after the fire started, and there were glorious, fast tongues of flame leaping up into the evening sky. The sight was actually very beautiful. If I had come earlier, I would have tried to run up the stairs and get my paintings. And I often think about what I'd have got first, what I'd try to save. But it was my fate to turn up too late. I actually just fell down to the ground and bowed my head and said, "Okay, you've taken it all away" (**Fig. 19.1**)

Aaron: So in some sense there was nothing to do but surrender to the experience. When you said, "You've taken it all away," was there a clear sense of who or what had done the taking?

Julian: Of course! It was very personal—me and the boss. It was a problem between me and God and we needed to sort the problem out.

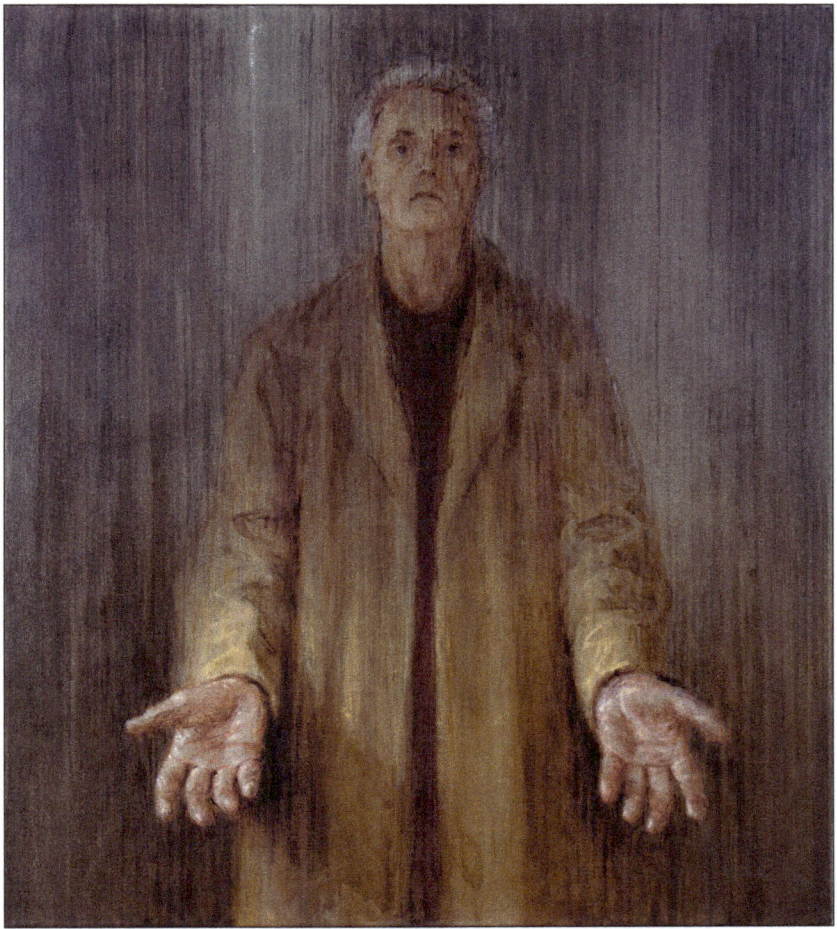

Figure 19.1

Aaron: How do you begin to make sense of this? It almost feels like it was a kind of biblical burnt offering. In fact, you've done a painting of Noah offering a sacrifice after the flood (**Fig. 19.2**). I couldn't help but think of your studio in that piece.

Julian: Absolutely. That was painted afterwards. Noah's face is turned towards the heavens, very much with a challenging look of "Here you are—will this satisfy you?"

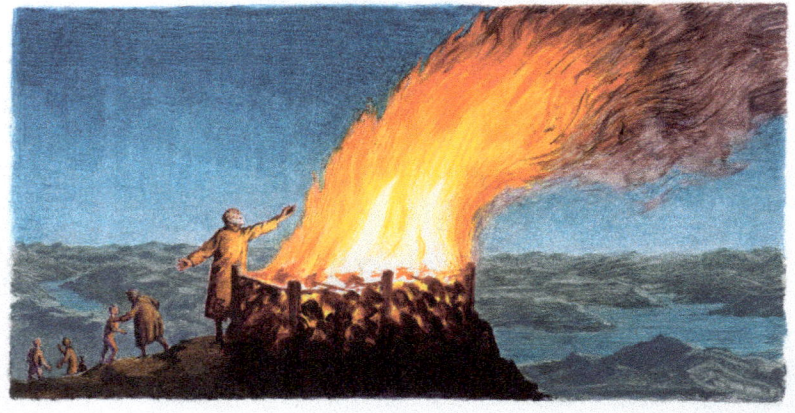

Figure 19.2

Aaron: It's especially interesting because Noah is sacrificing some of the very animals that God has told him to preserve! So God's appetite for death continues even after the flood.

Julian: He wants this sweet smell—a "sweet savor."

Aaron: So do you think that your works provided a sweet savor?

Julian: Well, in my good moments I think that to have seen them go like that was an experience given to me to learn from, but of course I talk about my good moments, not my bad moments.

Aaron: With the amount that you lost, you must feel you carry so many pictures within yourself now.

Julian: The strange thing is, 96 percent of the stuff that went up in smoke is dispensable. It's a shame about the 4 percent. It was wonderful. For some reason, there were a few paintings that were better than I could do, but I did them.

Aaron: And that's presumably where you felt the divine most palpably, in the works that felt as if they'd come from somewhere beyond yourself.

Julian: Making them is certainly a matter of learning and—occasionally, yes—the learning results in miracles. Aithan, tell me if you will, about these haunting photographs you sent us today (**Fig. 19.3**).

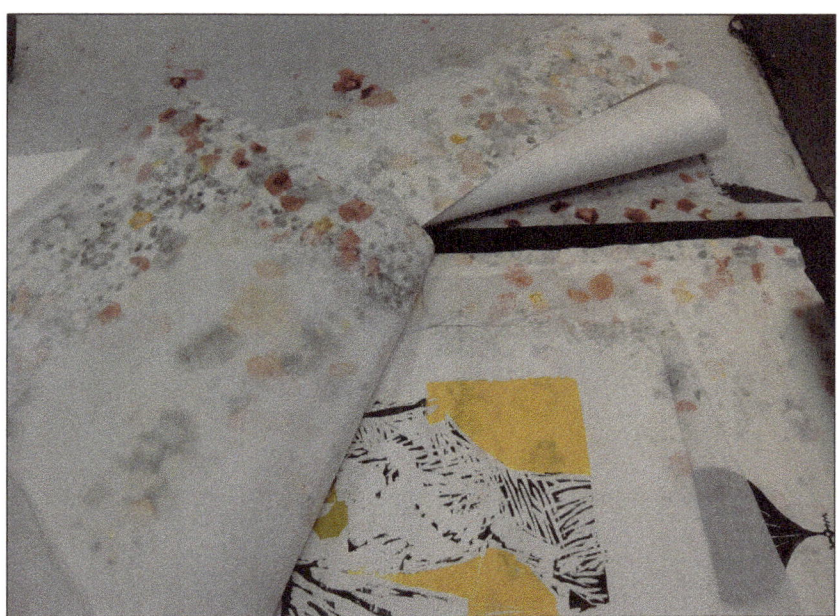

Figure 19.3

Aithan: Well, there was a flood in my studio after a radiator pipe burst and hundred-year-old, moldy hot water sprayed all over my studio for several days. I've never shared those photos of the ruined studio with anyone other than my wife, actually. Aaron, when I talked about what happened with you a while back it was the first time I'd ever mentioned it to anyone really besides my wife, family, and people involved because I feel comfortable with you and our friendship. So I don't quite know how to talk about the whole experience. But to answer your question, Julian, they were taken on the days after I came back and saw my studio for the first time, after everything was destroyed.

It was helpful to hear what you're saying, Julian. For me it was devastating that the artwork got destroyed, but I think, on reflection, that the thing that was truly destroyed was my identity. That's the thing I feel was taken away from me, and I don't think I'm ever going to get that back—it's just changed. It's different now.

Maybe another bit of detail to share is that I trained under one of the greatest artists alive, John Walker. Following John, being an artist to me meant that you're in your studio working, you don't leave. I mean, you bring what you need to survive and step away when that's what it takes. And for fifteen years, six days per week, doing ten- to twelve-hour days, that was my life. That's what it meant to be an artist. And when this happened, it was really the first time that I had left the studio for such a period of time—it was six days.

Julian: How far are you away from that experience?

Aithan: That was in 2011.

Aaron: And it was a long time before you could paint again, right?

Aithan: Yeah, I kind of disappeared for three years before I could do anything. Anything. My whole identity was lost. It vanished. I realize now that as an artist I was practiced at destroying what I'd made—destroying myself in order to learn. I think creation is really about destroying first. But I had never *been destroyed*. I didn't have anything to do with this. I just showed up and it was all in ruins.

Aaron: You'd trained yourself in this act of rigorous self-criticism, learning to break down and continually build back up. But it sounds like what happened when your studio was destroyed almost felt like a deep, profound sort of art criticism, but one without any capacity or desire to build you back up. In some ways, it seems like you're saying that every painting you'd kept had somehow helped build your identity as an artist. But when you lost all these works it was if your fortifications had been swept away. So it was hard to paint again from nothing, without a foundation of work.

Aithan: I was in the business of making things and then everything that I had ever made was gone. So it wasn't just disorienting, I had begun a freefall into an abyss. Being an artist wasn't just something I was doing, it was what I was. But once that was taken away, there was nothing. It was bizarre looking back and trying to grasp who I was, what mattered. There was so much sadness in that, and shame and disgust, and relatively quickly all of those became emptiness.

Julian: I'm looking at these photographs of your studio, and is there not some strange beauty there—at least in a couple of them?

Aithan: You know, there are images that I didn't send. I think those are more in that category. At least for right now, these are the ones I can look at, particularly the images of the books and other tools I had for teaching and learning. I had studied at the Royal College of Art in London, where I devoted two years to just printmaking. And when I came back to painting after that, I just saw painting differently. Anyway, at the time I had made many, many prints on a historic press that was given to the Queen in the 1850s. I was using all of those prints as tools for both students and myself. I was painting from them and referencing them in different ways. And when I walked into my studio after it flooded, the prints were there in pulp form—not just pulp, but yellow, blue, white, and black puss. There was mold in the fibers of all of it.

It hasn't been enough time to entirely process. I think I'm slow. I think about Isaac Luria, the sixteenth-century Jewish mystic. He describes how the world was created in a breath, blown into existence with one big exhale. What Luria then discusses is the inhale that must exist before the exhale into existence. And I think right now I'm still on the inhale. I still might be at zero.

Aaron: I like that sense that you withdraw and then you breathe—that there is, hopefully, a cycle. In Jewish mysticism, as you mentioned, it's called *Tsimtsum* when God withdraws in order to create. In Christianity, there's the concept of *Kenosis*, of God emptying himself. I think this takes us into an interesting discussion about what creation means. You've both described something of what it is to experience emptiness, and then trying to figure out what comes next. Aithan, it's interesting that you took photographs of your ruined studio, that you felt you needed a record, and that you used a visual means to do so. Even before you were ready to internalize it, you still took photos of what had happened. It's as if you knew these images might be necessary for some later catharsis you weren't yet prepared to have. Now, Julian, did you take photos in that same moment? How did you first start to make sense of that feeling of "My God, my God, why have you forsaken me?"

Julian: It happened that shortly before the fire I had been given the idea of painting a sequence based on the book of Genesis. And so, as soon as I could afterwards—very soon—I picked up a pencil. The idea had only been just a seed, but in the context it was perfect. I started thinking about the story of Adam naming the creatures (**Fig. 19.4**). But, Aithan, this disaster happened to me when I was sixty-one and so I'm kind of too old or stupid to change my ways at this stage! It was only after I'd finished painting thirty-seven little paintings of Genesis that I stopped, and then I felt kind of a large hole in myself. But it wasn't quite in the way that you're speaking of as a complete obliteration of identity. It's too late to alter my identity, such as it is. It was perhaps a shallower destruction.

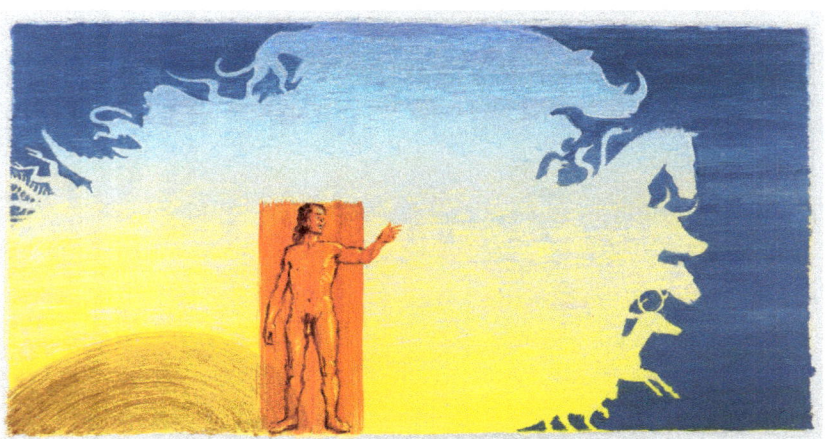

Figure 19.4

Aaron: It's really interesting to compare these experiences as a younger man and an older man, and what makes the crisis different. Julian, it sounds like in some ways you found it was a resource to find yourself not able to change, or past seismic change. You describe yourself in a sort of curmudgeonly fashion, but at its core it seems that your habituated practice sort of pushed or pulled you back into creative work. But also, I think that there's a sense of grace in your account, when you describe having had an idea before the fire, which outlasted the fire: to paint Genesis. Genesis leads to regeneration.

Julian: I just picked up the book of Genesis a couple of months before the fire and started reading it. And I started *seeing it*.

Aaron: There's a short story by the science fiction writer Arthur C. Clarke, in which he describes a space voyage in which a crew from Earth find a distant, glorious civilization that was suddenly destroyed.[1] They research it and find out that the date at which it was destroyed by a supernova aligns exactly with the time when the night sky in Bethlehem would've been illuminated for the shepherds, announcing the birth of Christ. It was that star that flamed out in a distant galaxy that brightened the sky on Earth. It's quite a beautiful evocation of the link between destruction and creation. But of course it's not necessarily clear we know where to find the creation or where to find the destruction.

Julian: I have a slight reservation. I've never felt very easy about the word *creation* as a description of what I do. Maybe because it's sacrilegious. Maybe because I know how an awful lot of my things are cobbled together. Sometimes it's better than that, but it ain't my own creation if so. It's definitely *making*, but *creation* sounds too grand a word to me. It lays claim to a kind of divine license.

Aaron: That sentiment definitely runs through the Abrahamic religions. I think about Islam, and the idea that painters will be called to account at the end of time for attempting to arrogate to themselves the power to create. Perhaps we're too grand in how we usually speak about Creation. God's great work of performance art, as we talked about earlier, began with breath, exhaling across the face of the waters. God does everything right and declares that it's good and he is pleased. But still everything goes pear-shaped, and then a new world has to be formed from the muddy earth following the flood. Maybe there's a parable there:

1. Clarke, "The Star."

there are two creations, and we're living in the flawed, imperfect one. A soggy, moldy world filled with ancient radiator fluid, like Aithan's studio!

Julian: I'm really interested in Luria's ideas, which Aithan mentioned.

Aaron: It's interesting, Julian, that in searching for metaphors, you used the language of Genesis, as seen from a Christian perspective. And Aithan, what you're describing is Genesis seen through the prism of Jewish mysticism. So both of you come back to ideas that are particular to a tradition and to an identity.

Aithan: Julian, I just want to say right now, I just am so thankful to hear you speak about this, and Aaron I'm so thankful for you connecting us in this way. As we're talking, I realize that in some ways when I say I lost my identity that I ended up kind of doing it myself. I left the university. I left my gallery. I left making art. I left the city. I just contracted from all of it. I disappeared for three years. Maybe I wanted to lose my identity when I lost my art.

Something else that's really coming up for me when we're talking about Genesis is that the big questions are really: What is the role of an artist? What's my role? What is it really that we're doing when we make art? It's funny how the beginner questions are the same as the advanced questions. I started thinking that what art was to me—what art still is to me—is holding a mirror to the world. Without judgment. It's just showing: Isn't this what this is? What we are? Isn't it?

Julian: You're right, you're right.

Aaron: In fact, Julian wrote a book called *Mirror of the World*![2]

Aithan: There we have it! A few years before everything was destroyed, I was in London. There was a life preserver on Hungerford Bridge that I would go back and forth across almost every day. Years later, it's still there. It's an abandoned life preserver on a pillar of the bridge that no one can reach. I was drawing it for a couple of years, and then it was in my paintings (**Fig. 19.5**). I was asking what the symbol of our time was. 2008 happened and I said, goodness, this is really it. Our world is this abandoned life preserver. It was

---

2. Bell, *Mirror of the World*.

making sense. It seemed like the mirror of our world. It was a universal symbol. Anyway, when I came back to making art in 2015, this life preserver was the piece that was available to me. The one thing that survived in a way was the life preserver. It started as this mirror of the world. And then I realized that this symbol of the world was actually a reflection of myself. It was the only thing that was floating, in a way, after my studio flooded (**Fig. 19.6**). It's my symbol now. I keep thinking about Matisse at the end of his life. He made that chapel in Vence, France, and he was asked, "So Henri, do you believe in God?" First there was this big pause—I always wonder what that hesitation was—and then his response, "When I paint, I believe in God."

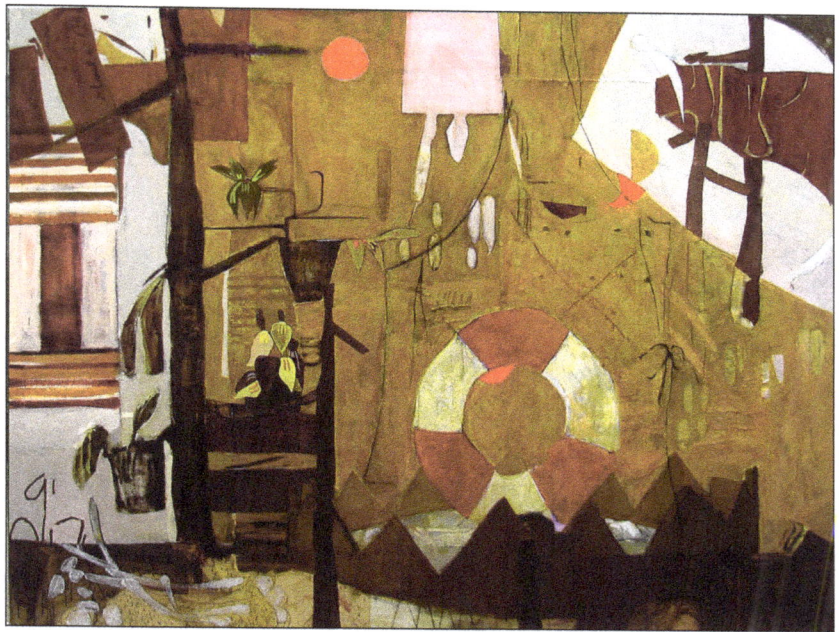

Figure 19.5

Julian: It's beautiful, what you say. I suppose my gloss would be that you paint what there is, what you believe *exists*, and it's a way of affirming that there is something. And with that there are affirmations that the world stacks up. All these things are bound up in this thing I was refusing to call "creation."

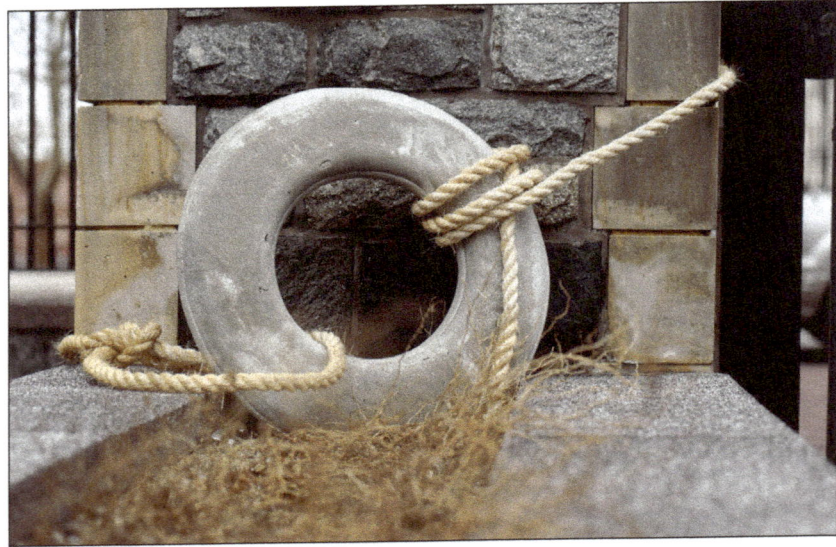

Figure 19.6

Aaron: The logic would be: if I'm painting, then there must be a something that I am painting. And there must be something that exists for which I am creating this thing. So it's proving something to yourself. So Julian, you began your Genesis series in your mind before the fire, and Aithan you found your life preserver before the cataclysm. Each of you had fashioned for yourself a form of continuity before you knew you needed it. As T. S. Eliot would put it, "These fragments I have shored against my ruins . . ."[3] That says to me something very profound about the artistic act, that there's a kind of a presentiment of what to create in order to survive. That's a terrifyingly grand purpose for art, but also quite humbling: artists are trying to create the things that we may need for the future. But we have no idea what those are, or when we might need them.

Aithan: It reminds me of Philip Guston, when he says, Rembrandt comes into my studio, we have a conversation, and then he leaves. Then Velázquez enters my studio, we have a conversation, and then he

3. T. S. Eliot, "The Waste Land," 41 (line 430).

leaves. And Giotto, and Piero, and so on, and one by one they all leave. And eventually, on a really good day, I leave too.

Aaron: In some ways, there's this sort of paper-thin division between self-creation and self-dissolution. And there seems to be something to be learned, as we've discussed, from erasure. Even— maybe especially—when it's painful or unexpected.

Aithan: I'm much more aware of these moments in the studio now. I am actively practicing for death. These moments need—even deserve—grieving, like the Jewish ritual of *shiva*. This might sound miserable or tortured or something, but it's not that way to me. Practicing death is practicing life. Making art is about choosing life. The loss of my studio, all my work, my identity, is still something I keep present, knowing it will in some sense happen again. I notice more dimension on the canvas now. If there's sadness, it's for how much I love life.

20. Alfonse Borysewicz: Broken Icons

Aaron: You've been doing some interesting new paintings involving wires, which you're calling "Riza Cages." They're in a show called *Backdoor to Easter* at the Sheen Center (**Fig. 20.1**). Can you tell me a bit about how these came together?

Alfonse: They sort of happened by accident, but I'm running with it. A composer friend and his wife who has a dance company commissioned me to do a wire piece for one of their performances a year and a half ago. I liked it so much, I did one for myself, but then I felt like something had to go inside it. I couldn't figure out what. Then almost a year later, right before this show, I had this eureka moment and I just cut the back open—quite dramatically but not self-consciously, instinctual almost, making that incision suddenly into something I so laboriously knitted together over weeks, even drawing scratches of blood on my arms from opening it up and placing the painting inside and sewing it back up.

It was sort of a reversal of the birth process. I did this now with three pieces—*Mary*, *Gabriel* (**Fig. 20.2**), and *Pantocrator* (**Fig. 20.3**)—with varying differences. These protective shells are very well made, strong, and yet, soft and silent, like little sculptural chapels (the armatures are made of tomato plant cages, so there is also that garden motif going on as well).

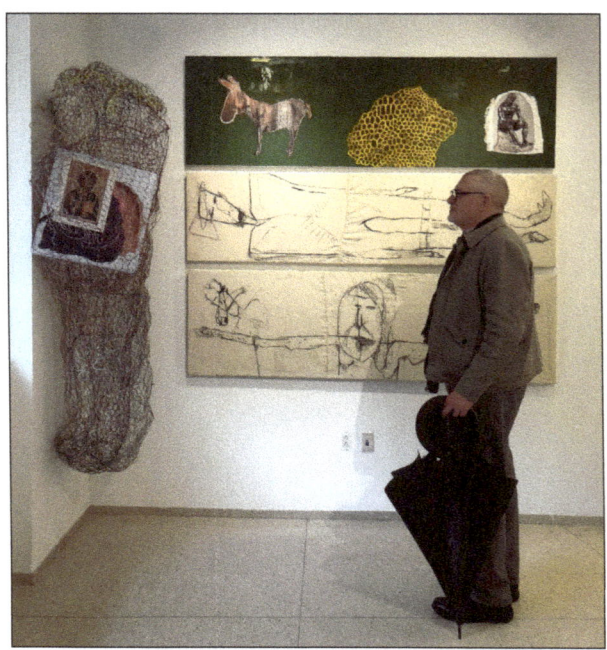

Figure 20.1

Aaron: The twisting wire reminds me of the honeycombs in your paintings. There's something chrysalis-like as well, which suggests transformation or even resurrection, but without being too celebratory. It still has something fragile about it.

Alfonse: It's funny because right before you called I had to go to the hardware store to get some more lamp wire. It must be my twelfth trip buying yards and they keep asking me, "What are you doing?" I like the symbolism of it. To me it's like Dan Flavin has the lights and I have the wires.

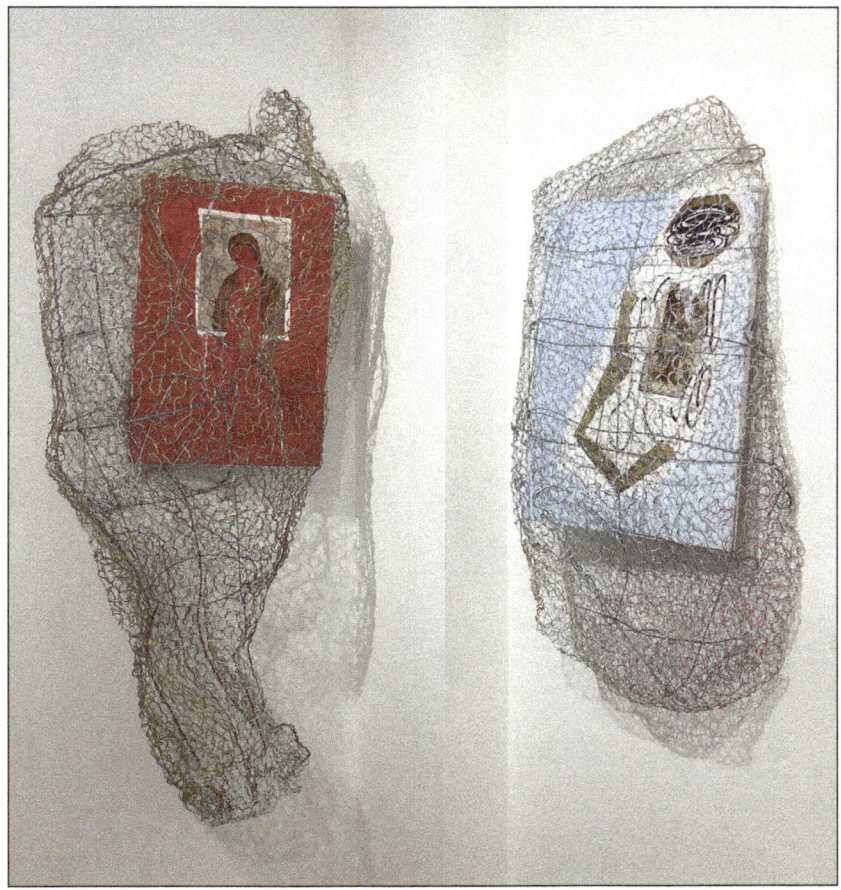

Figure 20.2

Aaron: I'm also reminded of Andy Warhol's *Last Supper* paintings where
he used the General Electric logo to suggest Jesus bringing "good
things to life" as the slogan goes. Formally, the wire forms are
an intriguing way to pull paintings into the third dimension, to
remind us that they are objects. And it creates a new relationship
with viewers. The wire reaches out to them, but also encloses the
painting, allowing it to be itself.

Alfonse: I'm also using icon segments in a collage. So it's very traditional,
but the wire brings it into dialogue with current art happenings. It
holds that tension between the traditional and the contemporary.

157

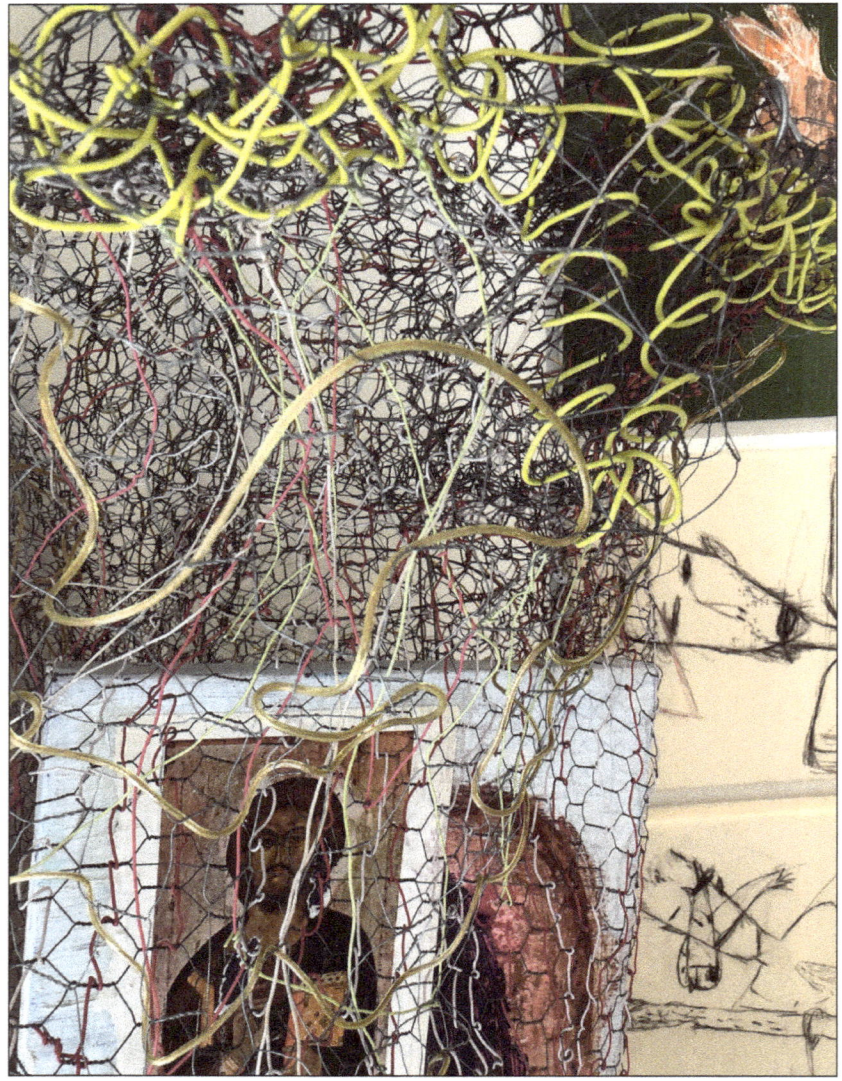

Figure 20.3

Aaron: Actually, can you talk a little bit more about that dynamic?

Alfonse: Well, there was an art critic once who told me that he loved my work, but he thought I was torn between trying to do two things: being a contemporary artist and engaging in long-gone religious traditions. He thought I should just do "real" icons. And I love

158

icons, but at the same time I'm a person in the modern era and I feel like I have to be in dialogue with that.

Aaron: There are some artists today who do more traditional style icons with contemporary imagery, like Regan O'Callaghan or Mark Dukes. But it's interesting to live in the productive tension you describe, asking whether it's possible to make a "real" icon today. I think about someone like Philip Guston, who was obsessed with Renaissance painting but felt that in 1970 it simply wasn't possible to paint like it was the *quattrocento*. One couldn't act as though there's an unbroken continuity with the past. So he felt like he had to paint previous traditions "badly," as he put it; showing his admiration for the past, as well as his inability to inherit it directly.[4]

Alfonse: I guess that's the frustration I have. I would love to paint like the icon painters of the past, but without giving up all the forces that have shaped me.

Aaron: From a Jewish perspective, I think about how the great scholar of mysticism, Gershom Scholem, explored how the breakdown of tradition could still represent a perpetuation of that tradition. As a modernist, it doesn't mean that you're necessarily broken off from tradition like an iceberg. Coming back to your work, when you make an altarpiece, it feels cobbled together, like you've been forced to scavenge from resources to hand, however damaged. There seems to be both a theological implication to that process, as well as a formal one. How do you see yourself navigating that relationship?

Alfonse: My panel paintings set up in a row so they're sort of fragmented, but still cohesive, like a liturgical setting. You could even rearrange the panels if you wanted to. I had my *Dormition* (2011) up at a church in Brooklyn for the month of August (Dormition, along with Mary's Assumption, is celebrated that month) and the contemporary art people loved it except they didn't like the little Jesus figure hanging out there in the middle! And the church people didn't like the way Mary was so abstract, and seemingly just floating there. I actually did another *Dormition* earlier in the

4. Guston, "Philip Guston Talking," 50.

1990s. It was completely minimal. General Electric bought it, but I had a sense they had no idea what the title meant! Paradoxically, that pushed me into being more representational. I realized I wanted to create a hook to pull people into a sort of religiosity, and—at the same time—the modernism.

Aaron: So you could have taken from that: oh, great, if I downplay the religious side, I can get a lot of mainstream commissions. But because people responded positively, you actually decided to go a different direction. You thought: this is the perfect opportunity to rescue myself from making money!

Alfonse: I remember this one gallery owner I had whose gripe was that I was always changing. But I have to keep interested. I mean, I'm alive. I don't like doing recipe paintings.

Aaron: On the one hand there's a real cohesiveness to the aesthetic you've built, but you also leave so much room for experimentation.

Alfonse: Like the wire piece: that lamp wire to me is the equivalent of gold leaf. I was just excited when a crossover occurred, where it becomes really traditional gold leaf.

Aaron: And in some ways, thinking about Detroit's abandoned central terminal, for example, and all of the wiring and copper tubing taken by scrappers, you realize this industrial material really is gold. It's like the last relic of a golden age.

Alfonse: Well, when I left Detroit, I came to Boston, and then I got to New York in the eighties. I felt like I was sort of back home in Brooklyn. But now Brooklyn's changed so much, and I'm in Jersey City as well (where I teach), which is somewhat like Brooklyn used to be.

Aaron: How much of your work depends on a certain roughness, do you think?

Alfonse: In my older paintings, sometimes I was accused of being too pretty. I think that was a reaction against Detroit. I wanted beauty. I found that in all of my trips to Japan, which is the antithesis of Detroit. So again there's this tension between beautiful objects and also rawness and immediacy. I keep thinking of John Chamberlain car scrap/wreck sculptures, the detritus of American manufacturing. My Riza cages are similar: the fragments of the church's visual vocabulary crumpled and discarded but now caged and protected with the promise of being made new . . .

Aaron: It's interesting that you make a connection to Japan. That reminds me of the tea ceremony, and the way it can take something that's rustic or flawed and appreciate it as a kind of unique, sacred object.

Alfonse: I went to many ceremonies. My wife's aunt was a tea ceremony teacher at the old Imperial Palace in Kyoto. To me, it was sort of like a pre-Vatican II mass, the formality of it. I also remember going with my wife to a show of flower arrangements, which were so minimal but dramatic. But then, at 5 o'clock, the bell rang, and everyone just tore them apart, put them in boxes, and it really was like this massacre.

Aaron: In terms of Japanese pottery, *ikebana*, and gardens, there's an abiding question of how much imperfection, rawness, or even wildness one should allow.

Alfonse: I find that in my paintings: a juxtaposition between a flat, waxed surface and also the very ragged painted surface. There's something Hegelian going on. I keep throwing up opposites within the work to somehow attempt to make myself cohesive, to make myself whole. The wiring has become like this. It's very labor intensive, sort of Zen. I feel like I'm knitting with wire, making a sweater of metal that just makes me feel warm and whole and cohesive. I try and offer another experience of the work of art, like it's in a capsule and you can see through it. Or it's like I put this protective shell around it, and you can't go in; you try to damage the painting, but there's somebody there to stop you if you tried.

Aaron: On the other hand, maybe you could see it as lending form to the aura which emanates out from the painting. It reminds me of my interview with Ann McCoy, where she describes having a terrible day and walking past an Orthodox Church. She went inside to see a relic there and she said she could feel its penumbra; a sort of perimeter around it.

Alfonse: Yesterday, I was coming out of Exchange Place Station, at the World Trade Center complex, and they're building a new Greek Orthodox church, which collapsed during 9/11. It looks like an igloo, all white. I kept thinking, no way would they consider one of my works for this new church, but I know what they will choose: someone who perfectly imitates the icons of the past when—actually—my work is more authentic and connected to that tradition that is being evoked.

Aaron: I felt something similar in Detroit, where it seemed that the truest vision for regeneration, especially for sacred buildings, would be to respect their trauma or degradation. There was one church surrounded by a sewage treatment plant. I thought: what better image of holiness than to be literally surrounded by shit, but somehow unbegrimed! There's a nobility to that kind of defiant survival.

Alfonse: My lament with church projects is that they're usually so focused on restoration. And they miss a great opportunity to engage in what's going on now at the same time. By the way, when I was hanging this show, they almost threw out my wire piece. They were taking it towards the garbage and I said, "What are you doing? That's my artwork!"

Aaron: Actually, I think that there's a whole history to be written of works of art that were, or were nearly, thrown out; a sort of incidental or accidental history of iconoclasm.

Alfonse: When I'm knitting with the wire, I sort of see myself in a glorified version of Joseph Beuys. Like a shaman.

Aaron: I feel the Beuys connection very strongly in your work. In so many of your works, you're finding fundamental substances somehow, and you're looking for the right way to apply them, with a sense of embalming or shrouding. All those kinds of sacred procedures are there somehow.

Alfonse: I don't want my works to seem overly precious. There's a sort of hedonism in the way some artists make something earthy and raw look too perfect.

Aaron: Well, that's the temptation, isn't it? There's also a risk of fetishiz-
           ing the raw, and claiming one's uncovered some sort of mythic
           substratum. If the qualities of tradition and innovation, or raw-
           ness and attractiveness, aren't kept in the dialectical tension you
           mentioned earlier, then the whole enterprise begins to falter. It
           needs to exist on a knife's edge.

Alfonse: Sometimes I feel so mute. But what I can't consciously express
           you . . . ?

21. Scott Hocking: State of Disrepair

Aaron: Thank you so much for taking me on a tour of Detroit when I
           visited. I don't think I've been in an American city like it. The
           whole city just felt like it had so many different strata—hope,
           hopelessness, everything—all compressed on top of one another.
           I think I'm still trying to make sense of it.

Scott: Well, it's a good sign if you're overwhelmed because it's a pretty
           overwhelming place. Part of what I like to do is just take people
           around and at least give them a little bit more information than
           they get from the most prevalent stereotypes or mythologies
           about Detroit.

Aaron: And you've lived most of your life in the city, right?

Scott: I started out in Redford township on the northwest border of
           Detroit, partly in the city and partly its own municipality. I col-
           loquially refer to it as the white trash buffer zone because it was
           basically a neighborhood of working-class white people who
           were often too poor to move away from inner city black Detroit,
           but racist enough to try and live just as far away as they could.
           My parents were separated and then divorced, so I was shuffled
           around a few different suburbs near the Detroit border. But by
           the time I was eighteen and on my own, I became a bit transient.
           I ended up living in my car and was homeless for a little while.

Eventually, I made a choice to move to Seattle and work in the fishing industry.

I prepared everything for that—quit my job, sold my car, lined up a ride—but three days before I was about to leave, I got into a car accident that derailed my plan and rerouted my life. I hit rock bottom but had some kind of clarity in that state. I decided to stay in Detroit and try to be an artist. I put together a portfolio and eventually did a BFA. Before that I had no idea what I was doing in life. I was trying to figure out who I was. The car accident was one of those catastrophic moments that leads to change. Even before the car accident I was the kind of person who looked for signs and read my gut feelings. So, when the accident happened, it really felt like the car rammed into me saying: "You're not leaving Detroit." I really took it as a sign that I was not supposed to leave. And I often make the joke now that the reason I'm still in Detroit is because I haven't had a sign equally as convincing that I should leave.

Aaron: It's almost like a magic realist story, where you have this invisible boundary that snaps you back into the city when you try and leave its precincts! It's interesting how after the fact, after such an event, retrospectively there seems to be something providential about it as you place it within a narrative.

Scott: It was unexplainable. I felt I wasn't supposed to leave, but that led to a feeling of what and why. I was stranded in this shitty neighborhood in Detroit, and now I had no car, no money, no job, and no girlfriend—no plan. I realized you never know what's going to happen in life. You could be killed at any moment, and until you just decide to say, "fuck it" and try the things that are deep down in you, you're wasting time. So, I wanted to try something I had been afraid of. The epiphany led me to believe in myself, which was the main hurdle I'd always had. I never tried being an artist or a musician or anything in those categories. Even though I was good at those things, I never really believed I could do them. I had very low self-esteem and it took a catastrophic event to let me say, "I don't care."

Aaron: Once you started creating, I wonder if your subject matter came from a similar place as your sense of self-confidence. One thing that really strikes me is how you seem to reach deep into yourself to pull out these really primary, resonant forms.

Scott: Yeah. I think I'm doing a lot of it just for myself, probably like many other artists. I'm trying to reach some kind of inner connector. I'm trying to find why certain archetypes, certain geometric shapes fascinate me, and humans in general. Why does a particular symbolic language resonate with us? Is there some kind of ancient memory in our DNA that we connect with? I'm doing introspective research, trying to examine and dig deeper and deeper into my own meaning of life and thoughts and philosophies. But I'm also really curious about how it affects other people and seeing how they react differently, for example, to an archetypal shape like a pyramid. They might have a mystical, spiritual, or philosophical connection, or make historical or political links. And then there are also people that will discover a pyramid I've created in an abandoned building and think it's funny. Everybody brings their own baggage. It's a bit like a Rorschach test.

Aaron: I think we often assume that variegated responses will be driven by the complexity of the thing that people are seeing, but maybe the opposite is equally true. If you can reach a primal, generative simplicity, it can be interpreted endlessly.

Scott: In my late teens and early twenties, I was really interested in Eastern philosophy. I wasn't raised in any religious background—not even atheism. Just nothing. My mother was Polish, raised Catholic, and did slap me once for using "the Lord's name in vain" too many times, but even she was shocked at her reaction. At some point, I became a quintessential Pisces and started looking into all kinds of traditions. I found myself really jibing with eastern philosophy and it led to my frequent use, if not almost biblical passion, for the *I Ching*. I still have my copy that I was given when I was maybe nineteen. I would mostly use it when I was going through some kind of turmoil or tribulation, and I would turn to it for advice. It's the edition that Carl Jung does an introduction to. He basically says: this is not a magic book, there are no magic books, but ancient people understood that we have all the answers inside of us, and that we somehow have to believe they're coming from outside. So, when you turn to the book or an oracle, when you ask for the answers from the "other," and you believe you will get the answer, you *will* get the answer. You could throw some bones on the ground, you could look at some tea leaves, but what is essentially happening is that you believe what's coming from inside of you. You have the answers, everyone has the answers. I still believe that to this day, and the *I Ching* ended up really feeding into my work a lot. I started to really embrace chance, believing in and trusting the process. So, I'll have a gut feeling about something and I follow that. If I start working in an abandoned factory, I have to trust that it's going to lead to something. When I first started doing projects where I would build in factories, I remember thinking, "I'm like Richard Dreyfus in *Close Encounters* building the mashed potato tower; what the hell am I doing?" But I've gotten really good at trusting and believing that there is a process, and that if you go with it you'll figure it out as you go. Chance is an exciting part of it.

Aaron: What's really intriguing to me is the sort of double placebo effect at work in what you're talking about. Understanding the sociological and psychological mechanisms at play in practices like prayer doesn't make them any less effective. Or, for that matter, any less real.

Scott: And that to me is of paramount importance. I'm bothered by fanaticism in any direction. Fanatical atheists bother the hell out of me. They think they've figured everything out and proved it can all be reduced to one factor. But it doesn't really prove anything. You still come back to the reality that life is a really, really mystical, mysterious thing, and you can think you figured something out, but you really just peeled back one layer. Like a child, we can still keep saying "why?" over and over and over.

Aaron: You know, when I first started studying religion, if I'm honest with myself, I think I mostly wanted to explain to the people I grew up around how daft their beliefs were. But over time I found it was even more unsatisfying to look at the world like a Richard Dawkins or Christopher Hitchens. It seems so hubristic to deny centuries of deeply poetic thinking, and the most powerful metaphors that we've devised for understanding the human condition, based on reductive interpretations of religion.

Actually, a very good example of that kind of metaphor, which I know you reference in your sculpture, is Noah's Ark. What I love is that you explore the idea of the ark as a failure, which ironically makes it even more powerful. When you set out to build something like your *Celestial Ship of the North (Emergency Ark) aka The Barnboat* (2015; **Fig. 21.1**) do you try and build the best ark you can out of ruined materials, or do you try to build the best ruined ark? I guess I'm asking: to what extent do you aim for an aesthetic of decay, or to what extent is that the result of your process? Is brokenness something you find—or manufacture?

Scott: I'm trying to collaborate with the circumstances, with what already exists. So that might mean collaborating with a building or a site that is "in ruin." If that's the case, I'm trying to integrate somehow with the state of that building, landscape, site, so I'm completely interested in the idea that what I build will just seamlessly blend into that same cycle. It exists for a time, but then vanishes as well. It moves into the same cycle of transition and decay. In the project where I built a vessel out of a barn, that barn hadn't been used in twenty years. The work will keep decaying the same way the barn was decaying. I basically took it down and recreated it in a different shape, but it's going to continue to alter and shift and change with nature. In a circumstance like that, I'm interested in getting people to see something that's part of the mundane world around them differently; to shake up that perspective.

I like to think that work like this can sometimes act like a Zen *koan*: the idea that an enlightened monk, for example, could find the right nonsensical phrase to confuse you enough to snap you out of your reality. And if it's done properly, you might even glimpse enlightenment. Just for a moment. Just a little lightning shock of understanding. To me, that's what artworks can be. That's what the *Celestial Ship* can do. You're driving through the farmlands and suddenly something is askew that makes you do a double take and wake up out of your drone existence. Hopefully that has at least some kind of an effect on you. I'm not saying that I think that my artworks are going to lead to glimpsing enlightenment, but I'm saying that I like the idea of them snapping people out of a circumstance that has become commonplace.

That's how I felt when I would go into the factories that I've explored for years in Detroit. There was a type of sensory overload, where your senses are awakened in the same way they would be if you were in the woods or a forest that you've never been to before, where you have to be alert. You have to be aware of trees and holes in the ground and wild animals and your senses become alive in that circumstance. That's something that most people have eliminated from their daily life. We put ourselves in very predictable circumstances. I want to create sculptures that are unpredictable.

Aaron: Thinking about the idea of the *koan*, I think there's something very powerful in the fact that you're looking for something that'll be disjunctive, but doing it through familiar materials. With the *Celestial Ship of the North (Emergency Ark)*, it seems like you alter the biblical narrative in some really profound ways. Unlike Noah's, your ark doesn't hold out any promise of preservation. You use decay to help it become something different: art. Being art doesn't save it. It's still bounded by its own materiality. But I think it does experience a moment of transformation. And maybe that's salvific . . .

Scott: There are also people who will see it just as a vessel. A vessel is a very primitive image and concept full of symbolic meaning that you can interpret in various ways. And there have been people who've said to me: "that's a weird barn!" Even that perspective is really interesting. As for the biblical idea of the ark, I'm very interested in destruction mythology. I have an overarching interest in where we come from, where we're going, how things began, how things end, etc. I've always been fascinated that so many different cultures all over the earth have deluge myths, and the recurring themes of a vessel/ship/ark.

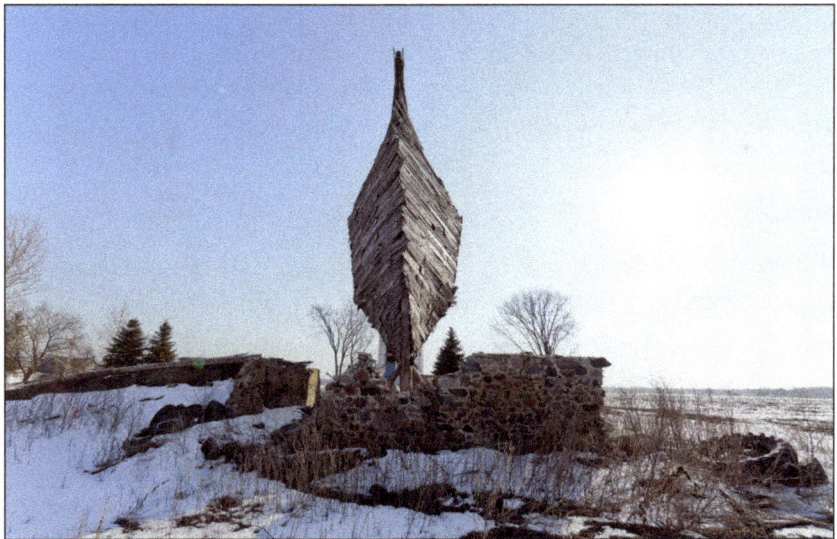

Figure 21.1

Aaron: It does seem like the fear of submersion or drowning is so primal, so ineradicable, it's shared across the world. And recent research is showing that certain civilizations may have survived not just because they were close enough to benefit from the Indus River for farming, for example, but because they learned to build just far enough away to avoid catastrophic flooding. It's a thin line between sustenance and destruction.

Scott: That's part of the reason I think that the *Emergency Ark* idea is interesting to me. I'm pretty sure tomorrow is another day that someone has prophesied the end time. There's an innate fear of the unknown, and since the dawn of time we've been trying to figure out how to predict the end and avoid it. End-of-the-world scenarios aren't based on nothing: we know there are volcanoes, earthquakes, tidal waves, forest fires, catastrophes of all kinds through history.

Aaron: And, in a sense, we're the flood, the volcano, the fire. And I think that many civilizations recognized our own destructive potential. In Genesis, humans are apparently so terrible that the only thing to do is to get rid of us, and most of the world with us. Even

169

within the more cyclical conception of time in Hinduism, there's a conviction that we're living in the *Kali Yuga*, the final epoch before things begin again. It seems like almost every religious tradition is convinced that we're near the end.

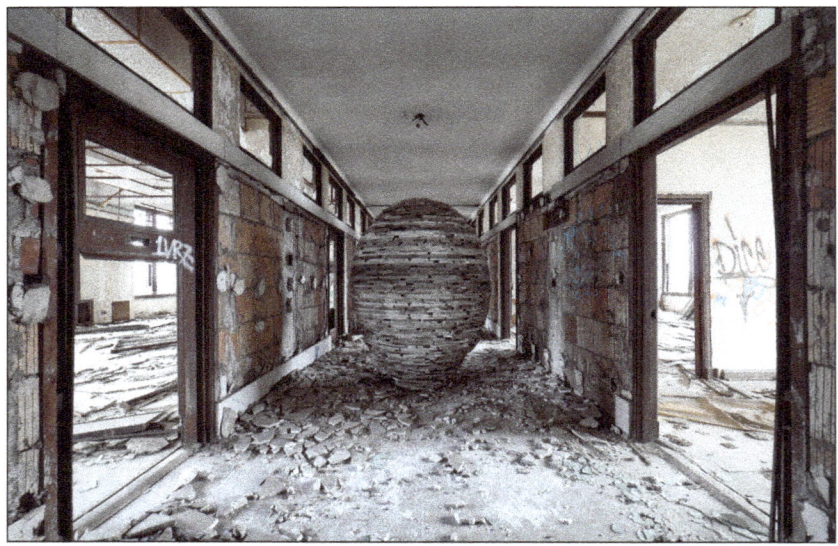

Figure 21.2

Scott: That was a big reason for my *End of the World* exhibition. I went bananas researching in every direction, from science and religion to myth and mysticism and everything in between, creating a bookshelf for the end times. It's very human to believe we live in the end times. I mean, I think we live in a really fucked up time right now. It really feels like a lot of things could happen. But I'm also aware of human history, and how we repeat this pattern over and over again, believing our time is craziest time, closest to the end time. So, I think to myself: Who the hell am I to think I'm living in the end time? And more importantly, does the world really ever "end"? I used the word *Maya* to illustrate this in the *End of the World* exhibition, referencing the so-called Mayan Calendar end-date as another theorized apocalyptic signpost, but contrasting this with the Hindu concepts of Maya, that

I interpreted to mean that this world is an illusion. So, for me, I wondered, how can the world end if it doesn't really exist?

Aaron: Speaking of disasters, it seems like writers often describe Detroit not only as post-industrial but post-apocalyptic. How connected is the city to the kind of stories you want to tell in your art (**Fig. 21.2**)?

Scott: I definitely don't feel like I have to be in Detroit, or that my projects hinge upon it, but its landscape and history have continued to be important to me. I know Detroit so well, it has been a really great place to talk about concepts I think are a lot bigger and deeper. It's a microcosm of the macrocosm. I'm interested in talking about the way humans keep doing the same dumb shit over and over again, and how we seem to be really bad at looking at things with a holistic or long-term view through human history. I really resonate with the mythological character of Sisyphus because it really does feel like not only are our lives Sisyphean, but the entire human race is Sisyphean. Right now, I'm making a giant pile of bones—my ancestry, Detroit history, Michigan history (**Fig. 21.3**). And that's basically how I feel right now. It feels like thousands of years have piled up, centuries of people just being born and dying; like human history is just a giant pile of bones.

Aaron: There's something prophetic about that in a biblical sense. But of course, usually the nature of the prophet is to be ignored, no matter how strong their cry . . .

Scott: And that's what it always comes back to for me. It's really not about whether or not people are listening. I'm constantly doing a practice, and the word *practice* is so appropriate because I'm just practicing for myself to keep making sure I'm on point and I'm learning and I'm observing. Nowadays we're so desensitized and removed from our own mortalities, and I try and make a conscious effort to focus on that. That's partly the reason that I was so interested, when I was younger, in focusing on decay, abandonment, and destruction in places that were in a transition phase, where I would be confronted by reminders of death. I was interested in how nobody wants to focus on reminders of mortality, reminders that we're all part of a natural cycle, and that just like Detroit buildings and streets, we're decaying. So, I think I'm still in my own evolution of dealing with that in new and different ways. Rediscovering it, revisiting it, refocusing on it, trying to repeatedly ask: "What the hell am I doing? What am I doing here? What is this all about?"—trusting that I have the answers, being okay with chance, change, and the unknown, and believing that I'll figure it out as I go.

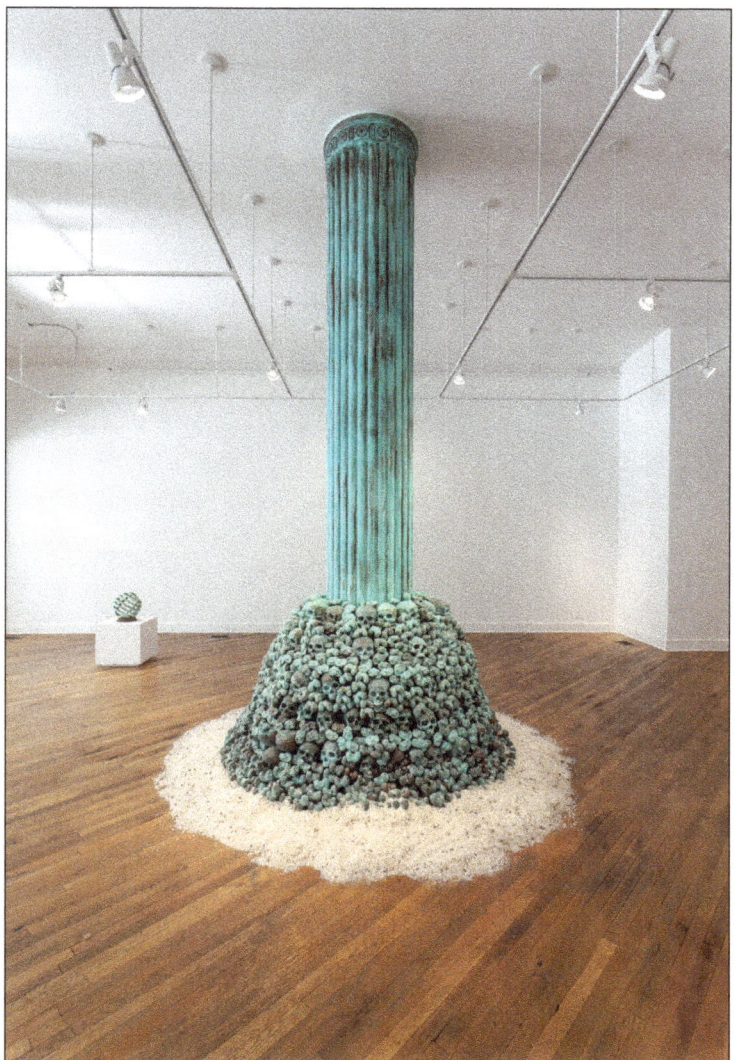

Figure 21.3

Transformation

22. Ann McCoy: Christian Alchemist

Ann: I had a strange and wonderful experience yesterday. I woke up really late. I missed two trains. It was one of those days where everything went wrong. I'd made Russian Easter eggs with icons and took them to give them to the priest and dropped them and they shattered. As I was walking home, I thought, I'm going to stop by the White Russian church on 93rd street [Manhattan] with all the great icons. Suddenly an unknown priest walks up beside me on the street and says, "You'd better hurry because they're bringing in the famous miraculous weeping icon." They were having a procession to bring the visiting icon into the church. It had a glass over the top with little droplets of water on the inside. I was feeling a willing suspension of disbelief was needed. I'd had a really bad day and I wasn't feeling like Christ was riding into Jerusalem for Palm Sunday.

Aaron: Maybe Christ was late on the train . . .

Ann: Yes, absolutely, Christ was caught on the metro. So, I went up to venerate the icon and I put my hands on either side of the glass, and put my head against it and suddenly I felt this incredible energy emanating from it. It's a special icon that they say opens the heart. I've had experiences venerating icons where I felt that I was really, like Pavel Florensky said, going in behind the image into the realm of the divine. I have a very special relationship to several Black Madonna icons, and the Black Madonna in Einsiedeln. But this was something I'd never quite experienced. And then I came home to Bushwick and there were all these tourists sitting in outdoor cafes, looking at bad graffiti murals with no idea it was Holy Week. And I just thought: am I like the last of the Old Believers? People today, in this materialistic secular society, seem so removed from the idea of a divine image, let alone experience of the sacred.

Aaron: It's interesting that you had such a deflating day before such a powerful experience. Sociologists and theologians would see it differently, but it's interesting to think about how we prepare ourselves, perhaps even unconsciously, for certain spiritual experiences. Even in a moment when you felt least predisposed to such an encounter, the icon seemed to have worked.

Ann: In a world where everything's so pseudo-rational, when you have one of these experiences it's quite amazing. I remember a trip to India where I went to see the temple at Ranakpur, one of the most beautiful Jain temples, that was first imagined in a dream. I was sitting there in this temple and I had this amazing peak religious experience when I didn't expect it. I really believe in sacred sites and these kinds of experiences from growing up in the American Southwest.

Aaron: I was thinking about some of our conversations about the West and Native American culture when I was reading Diana Eck's *Encountering God*.[1] She mostly writes about her experiences as a Christian with Hinduism, and how that's awakened profound insights. But one of the things she also mentions is Chief Seattle saying, as he signed a treaty with the United States in the 1850s—relinquishing his tribe's ancestral territory—that all of the places in these lands are awake with meaning. There's this tremendous pathos as he's signing over these spiritual resources to people who have no spiritual literacy, no way to read the sacredness of the lands they're claiming.

Ann: Dominionism was the problem. Even the supposed divine charge of manifest destiny didn't have a real sense of sacredness about the environment. Someone like Thoreau understood nature as a kind of sacred realm. But, overall, Americans had this idea that they should just dominate it, and exploit it. I think of how the buffalo was so sacred that Native Americans used every single piece of it, and how horrified they were when the men in the railroads came out with their long rifles and just slaughtered

1. Eck, *Encountering God*.

millions of buffalo and left them to rot in the sun. That to me sums up the whole American vision in a strange way—the idea of butchering the sacred for money.

Aaron: There were a few lonely figures who seemed to understand the enormity of what was being lost in the late nineteenth century. I sometimes think John Muir, climbing the mountains of the West with his staff, was the last American prophet.

Ann: In a strange way that's kind of how I felt like coming back to Bushwick the other day. In some Catholic countries like Spain or France you still have a sense of Easter, but in many places people have rejected Christianity without knowing anything about it. Now Christianity is dismissed and demonized or associated with the far right that reads the book of Revelation but not the Gospels. On the secular side, you ask somebody if they've read the Gospels and they say, "No, I hate organized religion." There's this blanket rejection of everything without any knowledge of the thing itself. In the art world dealing with Christianity in any positive way is taboo; it can only be trashed in some sensationalistic way. The art world groupthink is frightening.

Aaron: I've had a similar sort of anxiety as a Reform Jew, that a lot of the mystery of the tradition has been depleted or lost to many Jews. In the great modernizing movements in the late nineteenth century there was this really powerful vision for the future, and a sense that some things needed to be left behind to embrace the present. For those generations, that was emancipating, but what do you do three, four, five generations later when people don't have the same knowledge base, the same traditions that they can choose to accept or reject?

Ann: I remember in Switzerland when everything closed on Sunday. And it was so wonderful to have that Sabbath time. Now nothing is closed on Sunday.

Aaron: Sacred time and sacred space—both are sort of being invaded in different ways. You could argue closing on Sundays is just outdated Christocentrism, and that we should be living in a pluralistic society where we meet on neutral ground, where no time is off limits. But I suppose you could also say that living in a country where

Christians are observing a tradition gives them the potential to understand and accept religious observance from other people. So, ironically, secularism might foreclose some opportunities for dialogue. If there's not a profound model for what sacred time looks like in Christianity, for example, it might be harder to understand what it means to pray five times a day as a Muslim.

Ann: I think it's a problem of replacement. Christianity has been replaced by gross materialism in many different varieties. The Bolsheviks, who are lauded in the art world in journals like *October*, came in and killed 66,000,000 people in the gulags (or more). They destroyed thousands of churches and killed a lot of clergy, and basically replaced Christ with a portrait of Stalin or Lenin. The same thing is true in a capitalist society. Religion has been replaced by the worship of products, stressing extra time to sell merchandise. I think for me it's a problem of what we're replacing it with, including shoddy religious traditions. I can't stand the Christian far right. The "Prosperity Gospel" is replacing real religion, which requires shadow integration, reflection, and penance.

Aaron: Did you always have a strong faith yourself?

Ann: I grew up with a very vital form of pre-Vatican II Catholicism in New Mexico and Colorado. Also, the reason I was such a believer is because I was reading Platonic philosophy. Now I think about how few people are even reading Plato or the Pre-Socratics, or even think they're important. Without a meditation on darkness and the heliocentric where do you start?

Aaron: I think you'll really like Denys Turner's *The Darkness of God*. He says most of the Christian mystics don't even make sense without a deep knowledge of Platonism, and a sense of emanations. For him, Christian mysticism essentially springs from a profound marriage between Plato's cave and Moses' experience on Mount Sinai.[2]

Ann: The Harvard Norton Lectures by William Kentridge are a brilliant use of Plato's cave as a point of inquiry.[3] I also teach Luce Irigaray, who updates Plato's cave as a feminine, womb-like space of

---

2. Turner, *The Darkness of God*, 11.

3. Kentridge, *Six Drawing Lessons*.

origin. Reading Plato helped me understand that there are other dimensions of thought, also ideals. That's the piece that people are missing, this idea that the unseen may determine that which is seen (**Fig. 22.1**). I think the other missing piece is access to some larger, outside force. I think of the spiritual exercises of St. Ignatius of Loyola, where one can enter the imagination to have, say, an experience in the garden of Gethsemane with Christ. An inner imaginative experience transforms the outer experience. Or having an important, highly charged dream where you wake up the next day and your life is changed. I've had periods of intense depression where everything just seems hopeless and I went to sleep and I had some amazing dream that lifted me into another place. What frightens me is that people have lost this potential to be helped by the unconscious, to be helped by something spiritual. I look at Catholic friends and family, and sadly all of their children are now atheists and sometimes opiate addicts. It's the story of this generation.

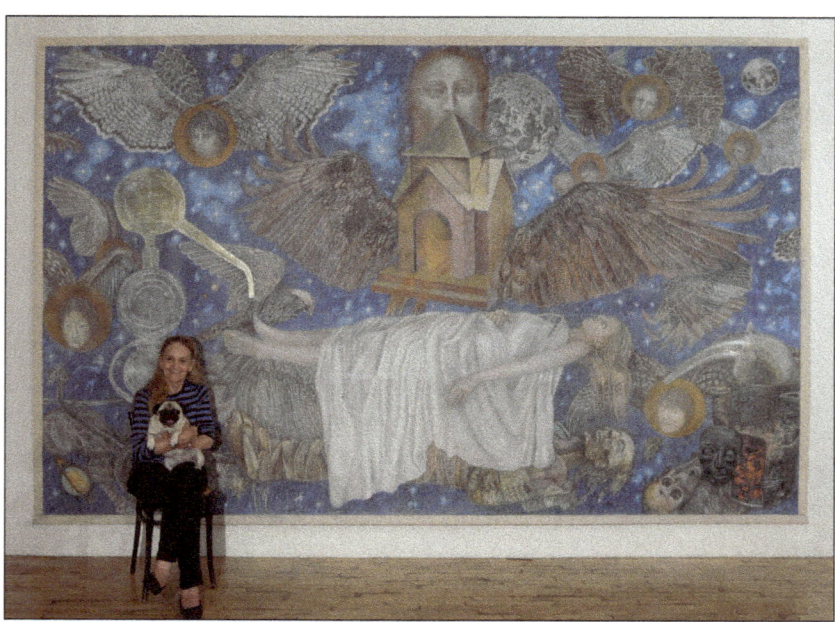

Figure 22.1

Aaron: Whether one sees the ground of selfhood in God, the collective unconscious, or in some ways both—as you're talking about it—the loss of an anchoring point seems really acute right now for people. And, paradoxically, there's an awful lot of effort put into clearing away the very resources that might most help people.

Ann: My psychiatrist was talking to me about how sad it is that she has so many people who come from rabidly atheistic backgrounds and they have no spiritual life and a very hard time accessing it. They tend to do practices like yoga, or veganism, but then find that the way it's taught in the United States just doesn't offer them much spiritually.

Aaron: Right, it's not surprising that disentangling a spiritual practice from its roots doesn't yield the same results. It'd be like praying the rosary without any Catholic education.

Ann: I wouldn't knock the power of the rosary! A Jewish friend of mine who smokes weed to get to sleep at night asked me how I get to sleep in these apocalyptic times. I said, "I say the rosary." She laughed and said: "Teach me, teach me!" I find that if I have tremendous anxiety, I can get to sleep if I say the rosary, on bad nights twice. It's not such a dead practice.

Aaron: I imagine that's at least partly because that practice has a context for you. But, thinking of your friend, it's also interesting to think about the affectivity of practices even when they're detached from that framework. The idea that there's a latent meaning or inherent connectivity in the object or practice itself, seems to me potentially positive but also maybe dangerous. The notion that the crucifix, for instance, possesses an intrinsic, apotropaic, or conversionary power over people makes me wary.

Ann: The crucifix can be frightening. We are seeing sacrifice and suffering writ large; its misuse for forced conversion was problematic. I was at an AA meeting in Rome and this gnarled man came in with eyes that were "pregnant with celestial fire."[4] You could just tell he'd had some kind of peak spiritual experience. After the meeting, I started speaking with him. He had been in Sing

---

4. Thomas Gray, "Elegy Written in a Country Churchyard."

Sing or one of those hardcore prisons, and he'd had a cellmate who would say the rosary and he taught him how to say it. And he said, "I started saying the rosary and one night I had a vision of the Virgin Mary. I didn't have good chances for parole, but I was released soon after." It changed his life and he was in Rome after a pilgrimage to Medjugorje. So sometimes people still do have these experiences with the rosary, even those who were not formerly Catholics.

Aaron: So the rosary offered him a rope to climb out of the pit. Someone like St. John of the Cross would connect his humbled condition to his capacity for spiritual experience.

Ann: I think Jung said that the defeat of the ego is always a gift to the Self. That's another thing I think is so strange right now. You need the ego to function in society as a mediating force, but right now we're living in a period of extreme narcissism. Yikes, look at our president. There's no concept of being related to anything larger. Jimmy Carter is a saint compared to narcissistic Trump.

Aaron: And where would you say art comes into the equation, especially in terms of the transcendent?

Ann: For me, art has always been a sacred task—a vocation. Early on, I was interested in all kinds of religious imagery. I read St. John of the Cross, and later Madame Blavatsky, and spent years reading alchemy. Then I got into the art world and everybody was reading Clement Greenberg. I couldn't stand it. When I met him, it was even worse. He was such a creep. I was always out of step with the art world. I always felt like a relic. My work, at the moment, is facing total rejection. It's difficult because a lot of people are terrified of work that deals with the unconscious and they're also terrified of work that deals with spirituality (**Figs. 22.2, 22.3**). That's why I thought your *Stations of the Cross* exhibition was brave and important. I don't want to only hear about *Piss Christ* [by Andres Serrano]. Or Chris Ofili. Or Maurizio Cattelan. I also want to hear about artists who aren't transgressive, who have a spiritual practice or who are trying to access one. The art world needs to open a door to it, because nobody can look at fifth-generation Abstract Expressionism or often contrived political art anymore. Social justice is important, but artists forget the original social justice warriors, like the Abolitionists, were divinely inspired. That's where Joseph Beuys was such an important model. He invented the Green Party. He was a social environmentalist, an activist. But he was also a deeply spiritual man.

Aaron: You met Beuys, right?

Ann: I met him in Germany in the late seventies, and I had a few conversations with him. He had thousands of people around him and I met him when he was doing the Documenta honey pumps. People like Benjamin Buchloh say he was a poser. He wasn't. He was one of the most completely authentic people I've ever met. There are some parts of his story, that like the Crimea crash, may be a symbolic myth, but I don't care. When you met Beuys you knew that something very bad had happened to him. He still had metal plates in his skull and his face was sunken, and very badly scarred. You knew when you looked into his eyes that this was a

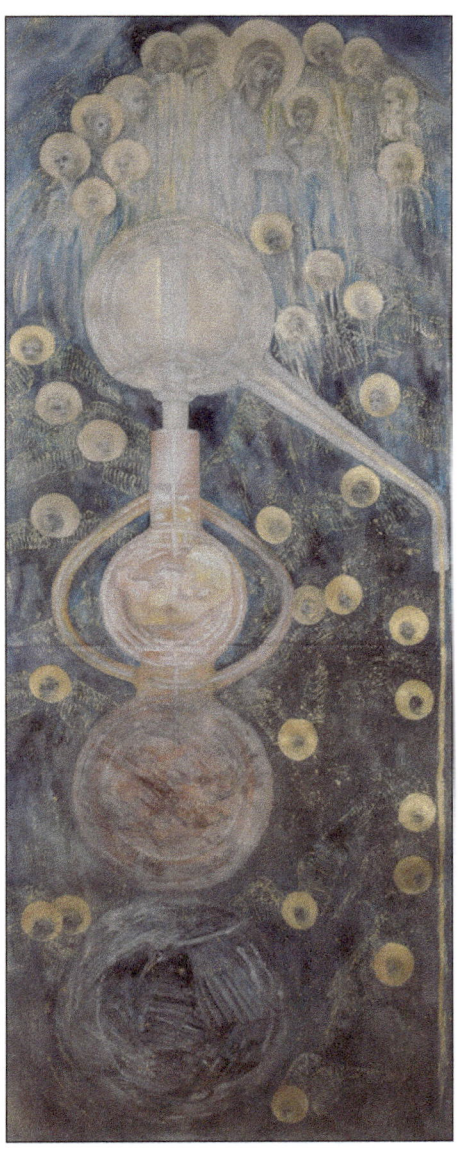

Figure 22.2

man who had literally been into the bowels of hell and had come out, like Jonah. It was like the night sea journey in alchemy where he had gone into the belly of the beast and emerged transformed, a different person. I think his conversations *What is Art?*, with a priest Volker Harlan, are great documents.

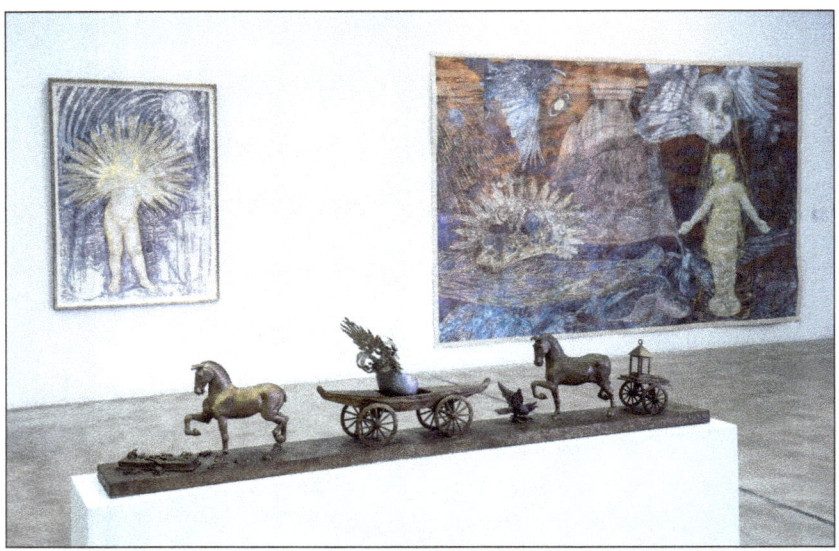

Figure 22.3

Aaron: Beuys himself was rather priestly, right?

Ann: He was priestly, but you also felt a fragility. I met him in '77 and even then he wasn't in great health, and you had a sense that this guy wasn't going to live forever. Kazantzakis, in his sequel to *The Odyssey*, describes Odysseus spending all of his energy and then sort of disappearing in a puff of smoke. That's how you felt about Beuys, that whatever this experience had been, he was using every ounce of whatever that energy was to transform life and himself and his art in every way possible. I wish I had that kind of energy. It's a kind of energy that only comes from a completely authentic religious experience.

Aaron: In a way, he was like Lazarus, raising himself embalmed in felt and honey.

Ann: There's something to be said about employing very simple arche-typal elements to express a political philosophy. Look at Mahat-ma Gandhi, an intellectual lawyer who communicated what he had to say to the Indian people by developing a spinning wheel, and using the elementary image of salt.

Aaron: It seems to take a tremendous spiritual as well as artistic sensitiv-ity to be able to recognize the power of these very basic elements, as if these symbols have been hiding in plain sight. Do you think there's a place for that kind of thinking in art schools today, or even seminaries?

Ann: I teach art history and mythology in the Graduate Design De-partment of the Yale School of Drama, which is better than most places. But what's disturbing me right now is that in art depart-ments across the country all students are getting is outdated cultural theory. Students who've never read Plato or Aristotle are suddenly trying to read Derrida, who's already out of favor; or are all assigned Adorno the atheist. Students are locked into this incredibly rigid system of critical theory and discouraged from reading anything about mysticism, spirituality, anything about religion. Let's all move on! I've had a lot of Yale art students take my classes and come up to me and say, "I couldn't discuss any of the things you're talking about in a crit."

Aaron: It seems like there's a disjunction, because a lot of artists are look-ing for the kind of source material you're talking about, but at the same time MFA programs are encouraging them to pin what they're doing to the same cadre of theorists, presumably to show they're "serious"—i.e., marketable.

Ann: The best thing you could do for art schools would be to remove all critical theory and start alternative reading lists. It'd be more interesting to have students, for example, read things like Chi-nese metaphysics. That would help open them up. Or maybe even choose their own reading. That would be a novel idea.

Aaron: It's interesting that in many ways the art world now encourages artists to go deeper into their cultural identities for material, and yet the language they're incentivized to use when talking about culture can be quite boundarized. It almost seems mandatory now for artists to use the word "hybridity" in their personal statements!

Ann: So true and sadly funny. I did an interview with William Kentridge and got to know him in Rome. He said that what saved him was that he didn't go to art school in America, and didn't hear about the New York School. He didn't read Greenberg. He said that he was interested in this black artist they called the Goya of Soweto, who did a kind of political painting, and he was interested in drawing. So he found his own path.

Right now, I'm writing about Harry E. Smith, who never went to art school. He was involved in all these American folk ways. He collected everything, from paper airplanes to recordings of Navajo chants. He had a vast library on subjects like alchemy and mysticism. The lack of independent thinking today is a problem. I mean, somebody like Leonora Carrington would never have survived a modern art school.

Aaron: Well, if you're not killed off by art school then at least there's the art market to finish you off!

Ann: Sadly this is so true. I think it's a very difficult time for visionary artists. I'm just trying to get through Holy Week, exhaustion at seventy-two, grinding poverty, and churning out writing.

Aaron: Well, hopefully you'll come out the other side resurrected.

Ann: Or at least on my feet.

23. Tobi Kahn: Healing Vision

Aaron: As you know, Tobi, you're featured in my book *Art and Religion in the 21st Century*. I put your work in a section I called "indwelling," about sacred spaces and embodied experiences. There was a critic who said that instead of themes they would've preferred to see the book divided up by religion, e.g. Jewish art, Christian art, Hindu art. It's funny, because for me the more interesting angle is to ask how artists from very different religious and cultural traditions triangulate their way towards certain shared questions. What do you think?

Tobi: Absolutely, I agree. I think of myself as an artist who is Jewish, but I think my work is based on spirituality at its core.

Aaron: *Spirituality* can sometimes be a bit diffuse as a term. Would it be fair to say that even within the wider category of spirituality that your work is often about healing?

Tobi: I've really always been interested in healing, in how art takes the viewer to a deeper, more meditative place. One of my first such works was called *Gathering of Seven*, created in 1980. It consisted of a group of poles that you walked through as a place to reflect. I always admired the work of Martin Puryear, whom I met that year. Years later, he created a piece that so inspired me entitled, *Ladder for Booker T. Washington* (1996), which went up four stories to the ceiling. I've always been interested in artists whose work was more than just the work. Brancusi is one of those artists for that reason as well.

Aaron: Your work with the poles interests me. It reminds me of the beautiful tradition of aboriginal burial poles, which leave the body open to the sky until it disappears.

Tobi: Exactly. And then I made shrines in the seventies and early eighties, which were about finding a place that you could rest your eye, in which you felt like you were coming to something larger than yourself. I am also interested in political art, however, that is not the work I want to create.

Aaron: You know, I think sometimes people believe there's a binary, and they can either do something political or religious, but something meditative can be the beginning of a mind-set that can allow one to think about politics in a different way. I'm thinking of someone like Thomas Merton, for instance.

Tobi: We're all put on this planet for a certain amount of time. I want to create spaces that can be uplifting. I get great satisfaction from creating hospice and memorial chapels. I was once asked, "How does it feel knowing that those works might be some of the last things that people see?" I responded by saying, "I hope it brings them a certain amount of comfort." I want to feel that I'm giving something back to people at all different stages of their lives.

Aaron: It's interesting that people might expect you to shy away from that context, as if death would stain art. But your work seems to insist that there's something sort of ennobling in the experience of dying. And that art—good art—should be able to respond to that moment.

Tobi: I've learned so much from people in hospice who know that they're not going to be around for the next ten or fifteen years. There's something very powerful about that. I feel like I'm on a continuum and I also believe that my best work becomes what it is because of what I'm going through. I have been asked, "Did you think of this particular thing when you did it?" And I sometimes say, "Not consciously." It takes me weeks, if not months, to finish something. There is something that I've always admired greatly when scribes create liturgical art—when you write a sacred text, for example—your mind is supposed to always be on that holiness. When I create art, it's about being in the zone of making something that I hope will resonate on many different levels (**Fig. 23.1**).

Aaron: Yeah, achieving that mindfulness is incredibly difficult. Personally, I've found working on a pottery wheel is one of the only times that I can achieve anything resembling that sense of immersion. One can see why many monastic traditions—especially the Trappists—built work into their rule. I like the idea of seeing work as integral to spirituality, rather than in opposition.

Tobi: See, this is why I enjoy talking to you. I do not want my work to just be beautiful. And it's not just to make you think about something other than yourself. It's about being at one in the world and knowing that you're part of something much larger than yourself.

Aaron: The language you're using reminds me of the titles of those Barnett Newman works from the late forties. He took the word *atonement*, and broke it down to *Onement*. Everything—art, Judaism, philosophy—was contained for him in that word.

Tobi: I could not say it better.

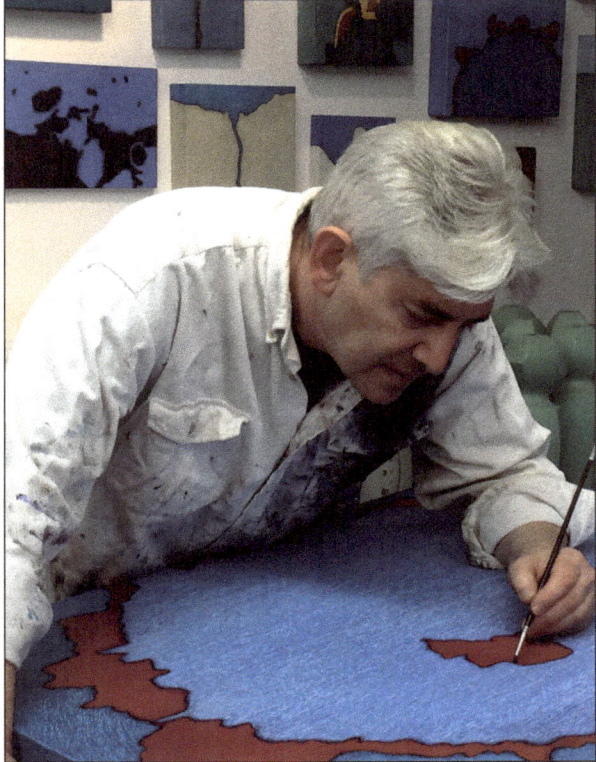

Figure 23.1

Aaron: Formally speaking, your work rarely has that sharp angularity of Newman's "zip" paintings, though I do see some parallels with his early works, especially the more cellular ones. More than that, though, I think Newman's great insight was that demarcating or delineating could also be an act of unifying. And I see that quite powerfully in your work, too. There's this palpable essence that's equal in all parts of your painting, whether we're looking at passages of sky or water or land.

Tobi: I'm very interested in the viewer's reaction. I was once asked, "Is this painting about a specific place?" And I said, "It is to me, but it doesn't have to be to you." I prefer the viewer to see my work and say, "That reminds me of when I was in this place or that," rather than "*Is* it this place or that?" I've never wanted to be a figurative painter even if the works are based on figurative elements. All my paintings are based on photographs that I've taken. I eliminate the obvious information that would refer to a particular place or time. The work is more about creating a sense of time in one's mind.

Aaron: That process of removing information to get to an abstract form reminds me of Ellsworth Kelly, who also took inspiration from his photographs, but generally didn't show them. It's fascinating to try to create forms that are both particular and universal enough to evoke specific—yet very different—connections from people. I see you playing with a form until you find something almost archetypal, where your experience can meet the viewer's, but in unexpected ways.

Tobi: I actually recently saw a show of Ellsworth Kelly's photographs at Matthew Marks Gallery in Chelsea. It was so powerful to see how he got his shapes, often based on shadows of buildings. And it made me appreciate his work even more.

Aaron: It's interesting that Kelly and his gallerists originally worried that such connections would make his work feel less meaningful. But to me, it's perhaps even more powerful that he was able to find abstraction in and through the world.

Tobi: I do understand why he did it. I always tell people I don't want to play "Where's Waldo?" with sources. I'm open about the fact that my paintings are based on places that I've seen, but I've also eliminated, as you said, most of the things that would look too specific. I have been asked, "Is that Maine or is that New Zealand?" I say, "I'm not sure. I've been to both places and I realize that they remind me of one another." I'm fascinated, too, with fractal geometry. I look at cell formations, for example, and I'm interested in the cell formations that remind me of aerial views as well. It is not about one or the other. It's about the amalgam or the way I see things that repeat in nature. I'd rather the work allude to something.

Aaron: Thinking about cells, I want to talk more about your connections not only to medicine, but also how people *experience* medical care. You have a number of works in hospitals and hospices, and have designed chapels for medical establishments (**Fig. 23.2**). So your viewers in those cases are experiencing your work in situations where their body has, to a certain extent, become medicalized. Those situations usually encourage people—for better or worse—to see and experience their own bodies less holistically, as clusters of cells, or a group of dysfunctional organs. So at the very moment when they are losing a certain kind of bodily coherence, your work offers them the chance to find another type of unity or meaning. When you paint something microcosmic it also looks macrocosmic. A neuron can also be a nebula.

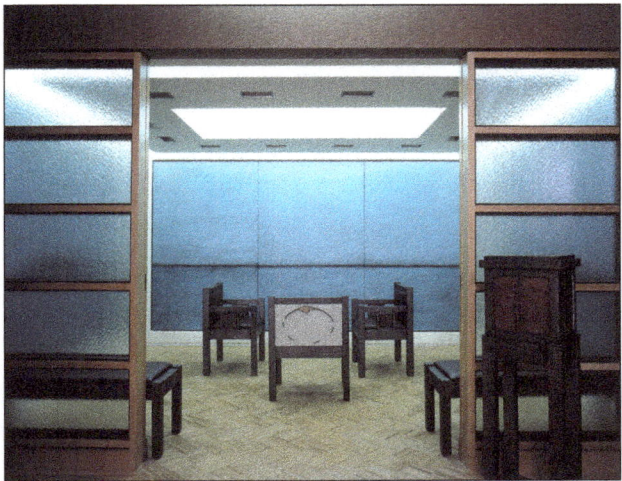

Figure 23.2

Tobi: Right.

Aaron: Maybe we could even take it a step further? As you're being medicalized, and shown evidence—perhaps by CT or MRI—of how your body is malfunctioning, you give people a way to see these strange, frightening images in different ways. They can see them as generative instead of degenerative; that something isn't just ending for them, it's also beginning. You provide a different window onto their experience, which isn't entirely bound by medical discourse.

Tobi: So true. People are so bewildered by the world. There's so much sorrow that they want a certain amount of solace.

Aaron: And slowness, too. Given how driven we are by the pace of our own technology, we really lack things that slow down how we process and reflect. To me, your works really draw people into a similarly gradual process of looking. So perhaps that's another form of rehabilitation. Are you exploring healing in any other commissions at the moment?

Tobi: I recently finished a project for the Auburn Seminary in New York (**Fig. 23.3**), whose mission is about interfaith dialogue on healing and social justice. I'm currently working with a hospital to create an outdoor sculptural meditative space. It will express what this hospital is trying to say about itself. It is a very exciting project with a lot of potential to help create a community on all different levels.

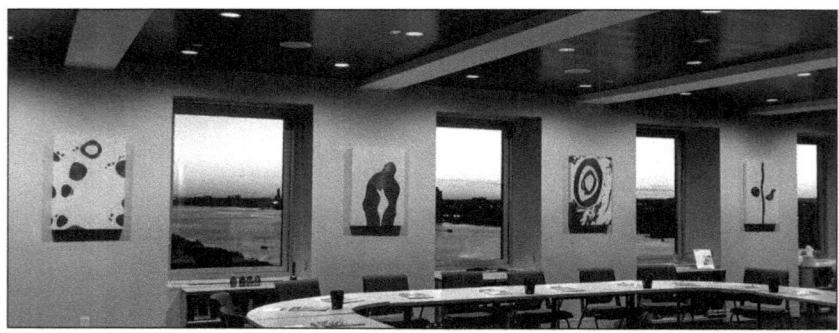

Figure 23.3

Aaron: It's interesting that we're entering this moment in the history of medical institutions where hospitals are really focusing on communicating their methodology, and the kind of phenomenological experience that they want to engender for patients and visitors. And even asking: what is the place of beauty in medicine? In the past—I think back to growing up, when I accompanied my dad on rounds—it seemed like hospitals often treated these questions as quite peripheral. And when images showed up in hospital hallways or patients' rooms, they were meant to be decorative. At best. But your hospital work seems to start from a really different premise. Instead of trying to distract people from where they are, you seem to say: "Well, you're in this space, but let's pretend that you didn't *have* to be here. What would make you *want* to be here? Is it possible to find some beauty even in the most difficult or painful moment?"

Tobi: What's interesting about this project is that potentially it will have elements outside as well as inside. Starting from the moment you enter the campus, I want you to feel like you've learned something about the place, even before you talk to someone. It is a campus that's used for teaching and healing—two things that I really believe in. I've been working on this project for over a year and have created over a dozen sculptural models.

Aaron: It sounds like Rothko doing all those different versions of his Seagram murals.

Tobi: Actually, a curator was here and said, "Let's do an exhibition of these models." I hadn't thought of them as a body of work. To me, it was just about figuring out what I was doing. Creating works changes over time. Some work you feel like you walk through, some you feel like you're just looking through. It's such a different way of thinking, and if I hadn't worked on this project for this amount of time, I don't know if I would've arrived at this place. Now I think I know which work I want the hospital to commission. It wasn't the first version and it wasn't the last, it was the work that I did in the middle.

Aaron: In a way it's about picking a moment in your own creative journey that you want people to experience as they enter the hospital campus. There's a sense of creating a gateway, with all the right rituals of entry. It seems like a lot of responsibility to create a space that will work equally well, in different ways, for the physician making a daily commute, or a patient entering apprehensively.

Tobi: It's been very powerful. Some of the sculptures look architectural and others looks like sacred spaces. I recently went to the Grant Wood exhibition at the Whitney Museum. His *American Gothic* (1930) wasn't really about the figures, it was about that window that he wanted to frame in the back. Now I find that fascinating. What's most important isn't necessarily what one thinks of first. And that makes perfect sense because it doesn't hit you over the head, it's just there. I want viewers to see my work in that way as well. What's joyful is when the work becomes its own narrative and its own story. When you look at it, you understand it more and more. You don't necessarily get everything all at once. I don't want it to be too obvious, where you walk away and say, "Oh, he did an x or a y." It's back to the first thing I told you: I want it to be the viewer's journey, not my journey. I want to help them on their journey.

24. Michael Takeo Magruder: Digital Horizons

Aaron: Right now, Michael, you have a show on at the Panacea Museum in Bedford, England. It's a reconfiguration of your *De/coding the Apocalypse* exhibition that you originally did in London, which grew out of conversations you had with me, Ben Quash, Michelle Fletcher, Edward Adams, and Natasha O'Hear. I want to talk a bit first about what you find compelling about collaborating with theologians. We aren't usually first on the Rolodex for contemporary artists!

Michael: Perhaps we should first talk about collaboration in general and producing artworks in dialogue. As you know, most of my projects involve extensive research across a wide range of disciplines. In shows like *De/coding*, I bring together different worlds: in this instance art, technology, and religion. As an artist, if I'm seeking to discuss and reflect on these kinds of intersections, it doesn't make sense for me to work alone because I'm not a specialist in those other disciplines. To thoroughly explore these areas, I need to collaborate with experts like you. If I didn't, I don't feel that I could produce quality artworks that are conceptually robust and can stand up to close critical examination.

Aaron: How savvy have you found theologians when it comes to understanding the challenges of technology? The great theologians of culture, like Paul Tillich, tend to offer powerful diagnoses of cultural problematics, but can lack a more granular sense of detail. With some notable exceptions, that gap seems to have increased, with contemporary theologians sometimes a bit hapless in the face of new technologies like augmented reality and blockchain. So, in a sense, in these collaborations you become an ambassador for a complex, rather hermetic technological world. Have you seen ways in which theologians have discovered new directions based on your discussions?

Michael: Yes, absolutely. Any good dialogue must be mutually beneficial, and I do think theologians have an appreciation for the artistic use of technology, both historically and in the present day. If we overlay the histories of art, technology, and religion, the connections and crossovers become quite apparent. The invention of the printing press and its subsequent use by artists to mass produce works with religious themes is a perfect example. The fact that my work takes the technologies of our time and explicitly grounds them in these kinds of art historical contexts certainly gives theologians a way to more accurately understand and better contextualize today's emerging forms of media within their own theological discourses.

Aaron: Right. And the same holds true for advances in stained glass as a tool of theological communication in the Middle Ages, or the codex in Christianity and Islam. There's a risk of falling into a false binary between religion and technology or science. At its best, one could argue that theology has often found ways to embrace new forms of knowledge. Still, you must find you encounter audiences that are uncomfortable with your work because they find it either "too religious" on the one hand, because of its subject matter, or irreverent on the other hand, because you bring in so many contemporary allusions.

Michael: Actually, my artworks that concern religion have never received those kinds of negative criticism, and I honestly don't think about these projects as being either religious or non-religious. What I'm trying to do with these works is take people on journeys that involve surfacing different narratives and new perspectives related to well-known religious subjects. The art world is very secular, but my pieces that reference religious themes have been embraced in that domain because they focus on wider geo/socio/eco-political contexts. They are not viewed as religious statements, but rather, as reflections on important contemporary issues through the frame of religion. Conversely, when I bring these projects to religious spaces, I don't attempt to align them to the actual practicing of faith, but I certainly seek to integrate them in ways that are sensitive and respectful to the faiths in question. My aim is always to produce experiences that are relevant and speak to both the religious and the non-religious equally, as I feel art should fundamentally address the human condition.

Aaron: I've watched you work very sensitively with clergy and congregations when you install pieces in religious spaces. You explain things to staff and different constituencies. In a way you're sort of your own John the Baptist, preparing the way for your work to be received by the community.

Michael: When an artist presents a work in a public space that has not been explicitly made for the showing of art, some important considerations arise. One must be mindful of the primary remits of such spaces and the communities who use them. In the case of churches and other places of worship, an artist needs to be aware of and sensitive to the beliefs and rituals of the host congregations. Art that is brought into these environments needs to provoke meaningful dialogue in ways that are respectful. If someone is offended by an artwork in a traditional gallery setting there is always the easy option of leaving the show. However, this isn't a reasonable solution for a person coming into their own place of worship. With this in mind, of course it's simpler to exhibit work within a white cube context, but for art projects that are clearly dialoging with religious subjects and narratives, removing them from these religious environments will often diminish many of their most compelling and provocative qualities.

Aaron: And there are things that are very unexpected. I look back at putting your *Lamentation for the Forsaken* video sculpture in the Church of the Epiphany in Washington, D. C., and we had challenges there that you simply don't have in galleries (**Fig. 24.1**). But you also had a much richer tapestry of society on view. We were exhibiting in a church that makes it a major part of its mission to serve the homeless population in central D. C., so there was an economic diversity that you don't often see in galleries. It was also used for *jummah* on Fridays by Muslims working in the capital. So once a week there were dozens of prayer rugs laid down right in front of your work. It reminded me that religious spaces can be these really dynamic ecosystems, which make the white cube feel kind of anesthetized.

Michael: I think that's a great example because Epiphany's socially diverse and multi-faith environment created an intriguing setting for the *Lamentation* installation. The artwork's focus on the plight of refugees fleeing the Syrian Civil War juxtaposed with one of the most important Christian narratives—Jesus' journey to and eventual death on the cross—was brought into dialogue with local hardships and issues concerning discrimination (e.g., the anti-Muslim rhetoric of the current US administration). Displayed in a white cube context, the artwork would have absolutely lost these real-world connections. I remember your co-curator, the Rev. Dr. Catriona Laing, asked if it bothered me that the sanctuary space was regularly shifting around and being used by different people, and my immediate response was: no, this is wonderful and exactly what I want. Walking into the church during Muslim prayer, or a quiet time when numerous homeless people were sleeping in the pews, certainly impacted how people approached and received the artwork. I wanted viewers not only to think about the problems in Syria, but to also consider those who face discrimination and disenfranchisement in their own communities. Given that the church is just a few blocks from the White House, and we are living at a pivotal moment when there is so much discussion about building walls and dehumanizing society's less fortunate, it was important to foster these associations. Churches can—and indeed should—provide platforms for more nuanced and reflective discourse. In that way, their position within society is not too dissimilar to that of artists, who are critiquing the moral and ethical problems of our time.

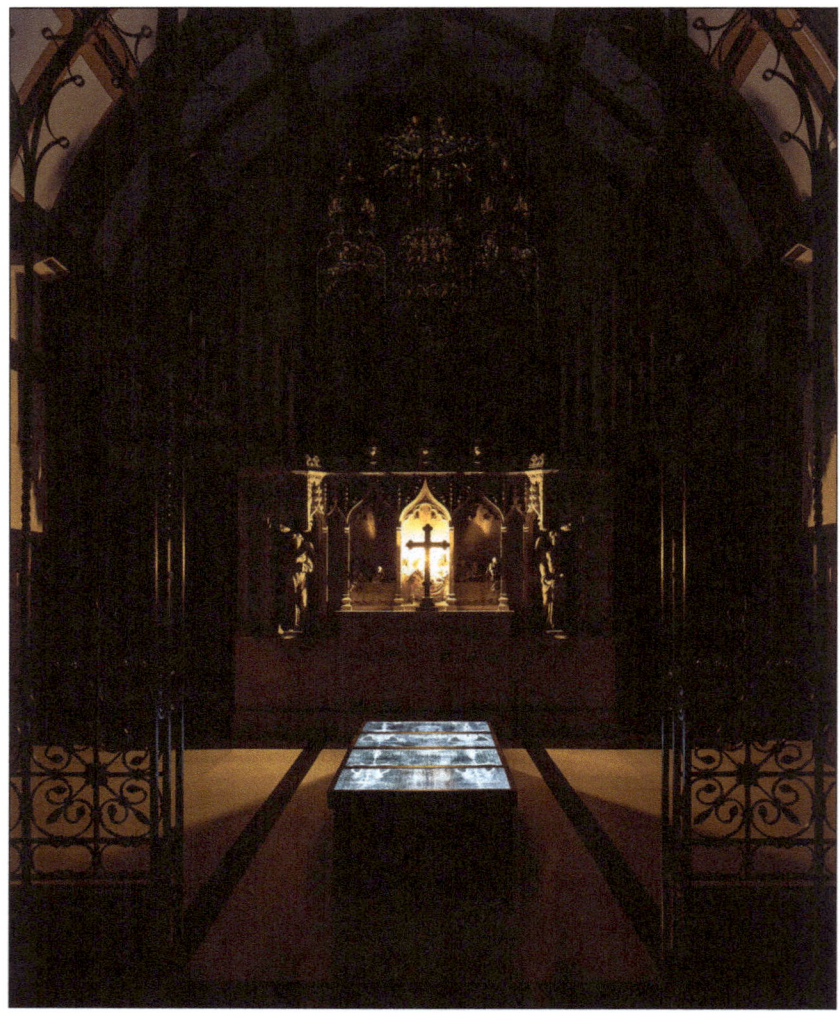

Figure 24.1

Aaron: It's interesting, in light of that, to think about how de-historicized and de-cultured our perception of museum spaces has become. We tend to forget, for example, that Tate Britain is on the same site where a prison used to be, or that its name is inextricably tied to the Tate sugar company, and thus Britain's colonial past. And of course activists at the Brooklyn Museum have called for its "de-colonization" recently, and there have been protests at the

196

Metropolitan Museum's Sackler Wing because of that family's role in the opioid crisis. So, in a way, coming from the church back into the museum, one is perhaps even more sensitized to the history and usages of exhibition spaces, and the responsibility to engage with past and present communities.

Michael: Yes, I firmly believe that art should not shy away from exploring uncomfortable histories and power relationships, especially when they concern our important cultural institutions. For me, being able to dialogue with a space's past enriches the work, even if there are significant challenges and sensitivities to overcome.

Aaron: As a curator, I'd definitely agree.

Michael: Well, you are in a rather unique position insofar as very few individuals have curated as many successful international art projects within religious spaces. Although it's the curator's job to help artists negotiate the kinds of challenges we've been discussing, to do this in religious settings requires a different knowledge base that extends well outside most contemporary art practices. I don't think one can just take any good art curator, task them with producing a show for a religious space, and expect the process and outcome to be the same as when they are working in their usual environment. Of course, the curator will rely deeply on their art knowledge and experience, but they will also need to have a good understanding of and sensitivity to the theological contexts in which they are working. And then, to add another layer of complexity, the curator must engage with artists who share those same qualities and are willing to adapt their works in ways that allow them to be effectively integrated into the religious space. Altogether, I think that makes for a quite rare situation.

Aaron: It strikes me how few religious institutions—aside from, say, large cathedrals—have staff with curatorial training. I think training in the arts needs to become a bigger part of divinity and seminary education. We need a certain threshold of visual literacy, especially among clergy.

Michael: I'd add courage as well. There should be a willingness on the part of religious gatekeepers to show art that comes from outside—and perhaps even questions—their faiths and traditions.

Such works, when presented in the right manner, can certainly provide provocative starting points for conversation within faith communities.

Aaron: That's a really interesting point. One of the pioneers in this line of thinking was Father Marie-Alain Couturier in France, who believed any great artist—regardless of their affiliation—was speaking in a religious key, or at least a language that would be relevant and appreciable by religious communities. It takes a quite radical hospitality to open not only one's space, but one's iconography, traditions, and texts to people who may not share those convictions.

Michael: I think that's one of the main reasons your *Art and Religion in the 21st Century* monograph is an important contribution in this area. I'm confident that most of the artists in the book are not religious, but with the eye of both a curator and a theologian, you've selected a wide range of works from contemporary practice and arranged them into groupings that explore central religious themes and questions. Sometimes the connections are very explicit in the artworks, sometimes not. But even in the latter, the implicit references are quite apparent, as is the case with my *Visions of Our Communal Dreams* project, which you included in the book.[5] In creating that work, I was indeed thinking about references to the creation story and notions of paradise, but at the time I launched the project I hadn't framed it according to these theological contexts.

Aaron: Even beyond the iconographical, I think in a way you're always asking questions with a theological dimension to them, because as you said earlier, you're interested in the human condition. That's what I see in a work like *Visions of Our Communal Dreams*. You're really asking how we create our social reality, and whether we're implicitly shaping something together that we don't yet understand. When we think about the Creation story, we usually ask what God creates, but we should also ask what world Adam and Eve make for themselves after Eden. After they're evicted, so to speak, how do they have the optimism to build a world?

5. Rosen, *Art and Religion in the 21st Century*, 39.

How do you continue after you've lost paradise? Do you try to build another paradise? Do you try to construct a Tower of Babel to reclaim your connection to the heavens? I think your work prompts these kinds of debates. Now that you've begun to address religious questions more explicitly in your recent work, do you look back at some of your earlier work and say, "Wow, that was actually a profoundly theological question that I was after, but I didn't see it that way at the time?"

Michael: In looking back on my practice I can see that my early work certainly incorporated some clear theological references. My first resolved body of artwork, which I produced during the late nineties, took the form of hybrid stained-glass windows (**Fig. 24.2**). At the time, I was interested in exploring notions of the sublime and the transcendental, and how such ideas were shifting in response to the pervasive information flows and rapid technological innovations of the Digital Age. My use of the window motif and stained-glass medium was very intentional as I wanted the works to dialogue with the history of Western religious aesthetics and their place in communicating spiritual narratives. This was because I wanted people to reflect on how modern technology was supplanting religion's long-standing position within society as the greatest herald of "truth."

However, even though I was explicitly connecting these artworks to forms and traditions that were unquestionably aligned to religion, I didn't consciously frame and relate my practice directly to theological questions. Returning to what you said about Couturier, I do think good art shares many of the same preoccupations as religion, and at present, I think these intersections become most apparent in areas relating to ethics and morality. Art, like religion, should be provocative and push us to engage with the social challenges of our time. Although as an artist I strive to produce conceptually beautiful and aesthetically seductive works, my primary aim is always to create experiences that are socially relevant. We live in a transitional time in which many of our enduring cultural and social norms are being rendered obsolete by the present technological revolution, and as an artist who has witnessed and understands the nature of these changes,

I feel it is my responsibility to use this knowledge and experience to help others negotiate these new issues and challenges.

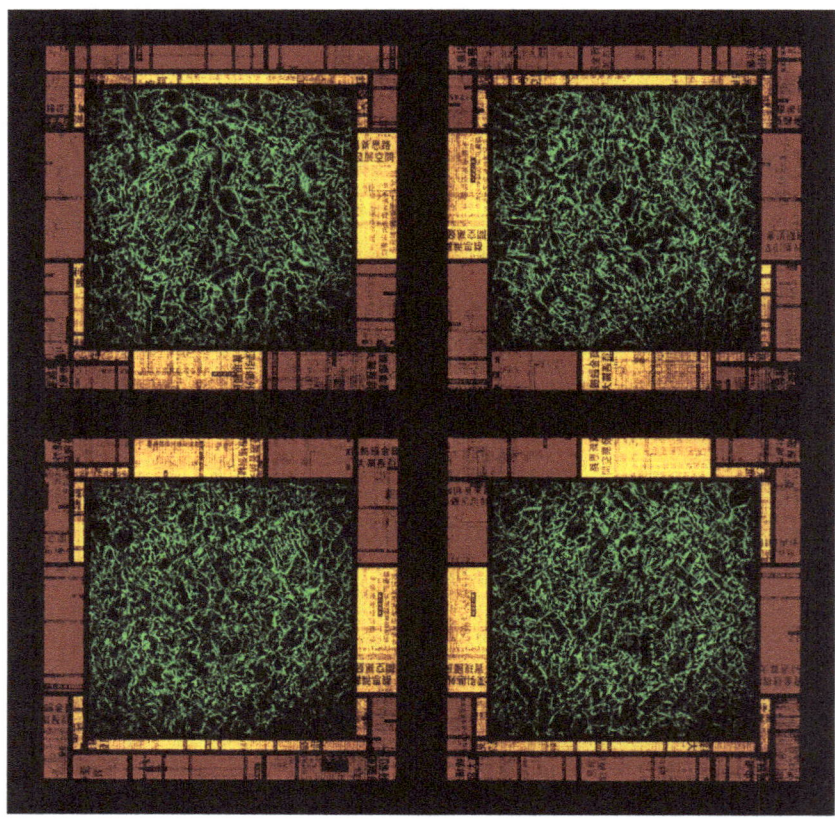

Figure 24.2

Aaron: It seems like digital technologies can be so intuitive to use that we often don't pay attention to the important meta-questions that underlie their usage. And there can be quite catastrophic effects when we use technology that outpaces our ability to think about it. It was interesting when Mark Zuckerberg testified before the US Congress and he appeared absolutely flummoxed by how big his product had become and that people would expect him to ask ethical questions about how it was evolving. It doesn't seem like he is the right person to reflect on these issues, but it's clear the senators interviewing him barely understood what the Internet was, so they weren't much help.

Michael: On the other hand, millennials might not be either.

Aaron: Right, even if social media has become their lingua franca, and they are thinking about their profiles, or how they make themselves appealing through these platforms. They aren't necessarily considering how it is reshaping their sense of self or community, for instance. It seems like we're on the verge of developments, especially in fields like biotechnology, that will be amazing and monstrous, probably in equal measure. As an artist, what questions do you think we aren't asking right now that we should be?

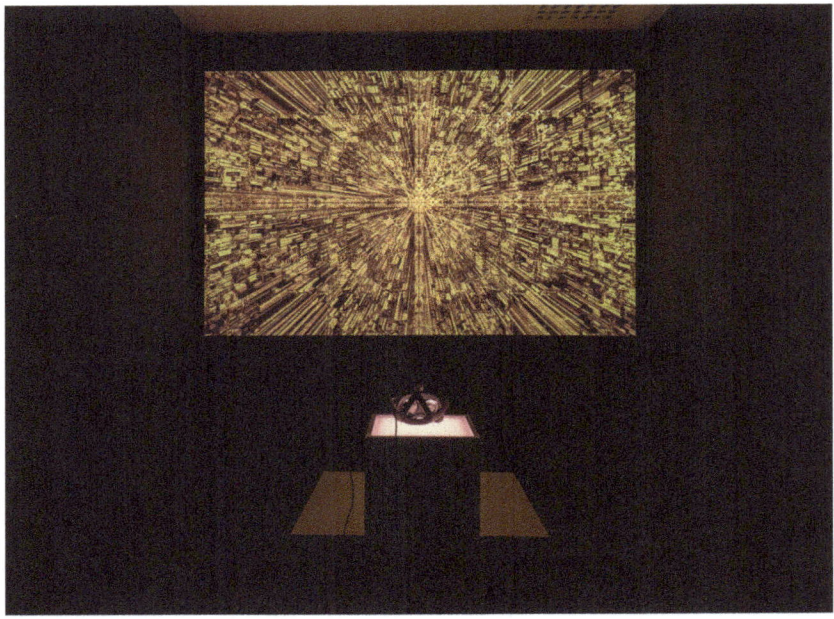

Figure 24.3

Michael: In my work, I'm always trying to provide people with different and hopefully more contemplative means to better understand the various systems that comprise current technological infrastructures. As you rightly point out, most of the leading-edge technologies of this time can be used in ways that will either enable great progress or create disastrous consequences for many—if not all—sections of society. Earlier we spoke about my *De/coding the Apocalypse* show (**Fig. 24.3**), and this project is a perfect example of how I create art that draws from and brings together both the seemingly positive and negative sides of technology. As with the original meaning of the word *apocalypse*, my desire is to construct journeys that offer an unveiling of our technologically informed world. I want my work to raise awareness about the many complex issues and contexts that are far too often portrayed in terms of simple binary choices.

Art should educate and provide experiences that encourage people to question their own lives and decisions. As with religion, it is a process of searching for "truths" that most likely can never be definitively answered.

Works Cited

Abdessemed, Adel. *Adel Abdessemed: Conversation with Pier Luigi Tazzi*. Arles, France: Actes Sud, 2012.

———. *Adel Abdessemed*. Translated by Lorna Scott. Paris: Manuella Editions, 2016.

———. "Adel Abdessemed in conversation with Elisabeth Lebovici." In *A l'attaque: Adel Abdessemed*, n.p. Zurich: JRP/Ringier, 2007.

———. *A l'attaque: Adel Abdessemed*. Zurich: JRP/Ringier, 2007.

Alloa, Emmanuel. "Portrait of the Artist as a Pagan." In *Adel Abdessemed: Je suis innocent*, edited by Philippe-Alain Michaud, 131–43. Göttingen: Steidl, 2012.

Amichai, Yehuda. "The Real Hero." In *The Selected Poetry of Yehuda Amichai*, translated by Chana Bloch and Stephen Mitchell, 156–57. Berkeley, CA: University of California Press, 2013.

Attar, Farid. *The Conference of the Birds*. London: Penguin, 1984.

Baseman, Gary. *Walking Through Walls*. Exhibition catalogue. New York: Jonathan Levine Gallery, 2011.

Bell, Julian. *Mirror of the World: A New History of Art*. London: Thames & Hudson, 2010.

Belting, Hans. "Cher Adel Abdessemed." In *Adel Abdessemed*, n.p. Paris: Manuella Editions, 2016.

Benjamin, Walter. *Berlin Childhood around 1900*. Translated by Howard Eiland. Cambridge, MA: Belknap Press of Harvard University Press, 2006.

Bhagavad Gita: As It Is. Translated by A. C. Bhaktivedanta Swami Prabhupada. Alachua, FL: Bhaktivedanta Book Trust, 1989.

Biermann, G. Roland, interviewed by Aaron Rosen. "Divine Apparitions." *Art & Christianity* (Winter 2013) 16–20.

Bois, Yve-Alain. "On Two Paintings by Barnett Newman." *October* 108 (Spring 2004) 3–34.

Bolton, Andrew, et al. *Heavenly Bodies*, Vol. 1 *Fashioning Worship*; Vol. 2 *Fashioning Devotion*. New Haven, CT: The Metropolitan Museum of Art and Yale University Press, 2018.

Buber, Martin. *The Eclipse of God: A Critique of the Key 20th Century Philosophies: Existentialism, Crisis Theology, and Jungian Psychology*. New York: Harper & Row, 1965.

Cixous, Hélène. *Insurrection de la poussiere: Adel Abdessemed*. Translated by Eric Prenowitz. Paris: Éditions Galilée, 2014.

Clarke, Arthur C. "The Star." In *The Collected Stories of Arthur C. Clarke*, accessed online. New York: RosettaBooks, 2016.

Danto, Arthur. *Beyond the Brillo Box*. New York: Farrar, Strauss and Giroux, 1992.

Derrida, Jacques. *The Gift of Death*. Translated by David Wills. Chicago: University of Chicago Press, 1995.

Dijkstra, Bram. *Idols of Perversity: Fantasies of Feminine Evil in Fin-de-Siècle Culture*. Oxford: Oxford University Press, 1986.

Eck, Diana. *Encountering God: A Spiritual Journey from Bozeman to Banaras*. Boston: Beacon, 2003.

Eliot, T. S. "The Waste Land." In *The Waste Land and Other Poems*, 21–49. New York: Modern Library, 2002.

Falguieres, Patricia. "State of Exception." In *Adel Abdessemed: Je suis innocent*, edited by Philippe-Alain Michaud, 205–11. Translated by Jane Marie Todd. Göttingen: Steidl, 2012.

de Fontenay, Elisabeth. "Urgence d'une decreation." In *Adel Abdessemed*, translated by Gila Walker, n.p. Paris: Manuella Editions, 2016.

Girard, René. *Violence and the Sacred*. Translated by Patrick Gregory. London: Continuum, 2009.

Gray, Thomas. "Elegy Written in a Country Churchyard." In *The Complete Poems of Thomas Gray*. https://www.thomasgray.org/cgi-bin/display.cgi?text=elcc.

Guston, Philip. "Philip Guston Talking." In *Philip Guston: Paintings 1969–1980*, 49–56. London: The Whitechapel Art Gallery, 1982.

Hall, Stuart. "Cultural Identity and Diaspora." In *Diaspora and Visual Culture: Representing Africans and Jews*, edited by Nicholas Mirzoeff, 21–33. New York: Routledge, 2000.

Jasper, David. *G. Roland Biermann: Apparitions: The Triptychs*. Exhibition catalogue. London: St Mary Bow Church, 2005.

JR, interviewed by Stephen Colbert. *The Colbert Report*. Comedy Central. August 28, 2014.

Kafka, Franz. *The Blue Octavo Notebooks*. Translated by Stanley Corngold. Cambridge, MA: Exact Change, 1991.

———. "The Great Wall and the Tower of Babel." In *Parables and Paradoxes*, translated by Willa and Edwin Muir, 25–27. New York: Schocken, 1974.

———. *Parables and Paradoxes*. Translated by Willa and Edwin Muir. New York: Schocken, 1974.

———. "Paradise." In *Parables and Paradoxes*. Translated by Willa and Edwin Muir. New York: Schocken, 1974.

———. "Selections from Diaries, 1911–1923." In *The Basic Kafka*, 255–68. New York: Pocket, 1979.

Kakutani, Michiko. "Portraying 9/11 as a Katzenjammer Catastrophe." *The New York Times*, August 31, 2004.

Kandinsky, Wassily. *Concerning the Spiritual in Art*. Translated by M. T. H. Sadler. Mineola, NY: Dover, 1977.

Katz, Dana. *The Jew in the Art of the Italian Renaissance*. Philadelphia: University of Pennsylvania Press, 2008.

Kentridge, William. *Six Drawing Lessons*. The Charles Eliot Norton Lectures. Cambridge, MA: Harvard University Press, 2014.

Kitaj, R. B. "Jewish Art—Indictment & Defence: A Personal Testimony by R. B. Kitaj." *Jewish Chronicle*, Color Magazine Supplement (November 30, 1984) 46.

Kristeva, Julia. "Le corps d'Adel (Conversation)." In *Adel Abdessemed*, translated by Lorna Scott, unpaginated. Paris: Manuella Editions, 2016.

Kundera, Milan. *The Unbearable Lightness of Being*. New York: Harper Perennial, 2009.

Lavin, Marilyn Aronberg. "The Altar of Corpus Domini in Urbino: Paolo Uccello, Joos Van Ghent, Piero della Francesca." *The Art Bulletin* 49.1 (March 1967) 1–24.

Lawlor, Clark. *Consumption and Literature: The Making of the Romantic Disease*. New York: Palgrave Macmillan, 2007.

Lee, Pamela. "Animal Feeling." In *Adel Abdessemed: Je suis innocent*, edited by Philippe-Alain Michaud, 169–76. Göttingen: Steidl, 2012.

Levenson, Jon. *The Death and Resurrection of the Beloved Son: The Transformation of Child Sacrifice in Judaism and Christianity*. New Haven, CT: Yale University Press, 1993.

Levi, Primo. *The Periodic Table*. Translated by Raymond Rosenthal. New York: Schocken, 1984.

———. *The Wrench*. Translated by William Weaver. London: Abacus, 1986.

McCarthy, Cormac. *The Road*. New York: Vintage, 2006.

Metzger, Gustav. *Damaged Nature, Auto-Destructive Art*. London: Coracle, 1999.

Michaud, Philippe-Alain, ed. *Adel Abdessemed: Je suis innocent*. Göttingen, Germany: Steidl, 2012.

Montaigne, Michel de. *The Complete Essays*. Translated by M. A. Screech. London: Penguin, 2003.

National Population and Housing Census. Kathmandu, Nepal: Secretariat Central Bureau of Statistics, 2012.

Newman, Barnett. *Barnett Newman: Selected Writings and Interviews*. Edited by John P. O'Neill. New York: Alfred A. Knopf, 1990.

———. "The Sublime is Now." *Tiger's Eye* 1.6 (1948) 51–53.

O'Hara, Frank. *The Collected Poems*. Edited by Donald Allen. Berkeley, CA: University of California Press, 1995.

Potok, Chaim. *My Name is Asher Lev*. London: Penguin, 1973.

Rosen, Aaron. *Art and Religion in the 21st Century*. London: Thames & Hudson, 2015.

———. *Imagining Jewish Art: Encounters with the Masters in Chagall, Guston, and Kitaj*. London: Legenda, 2009.

Rosen, Aaron, ed. *Encounters: The Art of Interfaith Dialogue*. Turnhout, Belgium: Brepols, 2018.

———. *Religion and Art in the Heart of Modern Manhattan: St. Peter's Church and the Louise Nevelson Chapel*. London: Routledge, 2018.

Rosenbaum, Thane. *Second Hand Smoke*. New York: St. Martin's Griffin, 2000.

Rosenblum, Robert. *Modern Painting and the Northern Romantic Tradition: Friedrich to Rothko*. New York: Harper & Row, 1975.

Roth, Philip. *Shop Talk: A Writer and His Colleagues and Their Work*. New York: Houghton Mifflin, 2001.

Rubinoff, Jeffrey. *Art Beyond War: A Discussion about Prehistoric War and the History of Art by Artists*. Hornby Island, BC: Jeffrey Rubinoff Sculpture Park, 2010.

———. *Existential Realities of Post Agriculture*. Hornby Island, BC: Jeffrey Rubinoff Sculpture Park, 2012.

———. *Through the Lens of the Endgame*. Hornby Island, BC: Jeffrey Rubinoff Sculpture Park, 2011.

Ruskin, John. *Modern Painters*. Vol. 1. London: George Allen, 1906. http://www.gutenberg.org/files/29907/29907-h/29907-h.htm#b2s3c1p1.

Sah, Govinda, interviewed by Gerard Houghton. *A Sense of Wonder*. Exhibition catalogue. London: October Gallery, 2013.

Scholem, Gershom. *On the Kabbalah and its Symbolism*. Translated by Ralph Manheim. New York: Schocken, 1996.

Schulz, Bruno. *The Street of Crocodiles and Other Stories*. Translated by Celina Wieniewska. New York: Penguin, 2008.

Sheets, Hilarie. "Emmett Till's Coffin, a Hangman's Scaffold and a Debate Over Cultural Appropriation." *New York Times*, May 31, 2017.

Smith, David. "Tradition and Identity." In *Art in Theory 1900–2000: An Anthology of Changing Ideas*, edited by Charles Harrison and Paul J. Wood, 766–67. Oxford: Blackwell, 2003.

Spang, Bently. "The Process of Self Definition within the Native North American Art Movement." *Journal of Multicultural and Cross-Cultural Research in Art Education* 13 (1996).

Spiegel, Shalom. *The Last Trial: On the Legends and Lore of the Command to Abraham to Offer Isaac as a Sacrifice: The Akedah*. Woodstock, VT: Jewish Lights, 1993.

Spiegelman, Art. *The Complete Maus*. New York: Pantheon, 1996.

———. *In the Shadow of No Towers*. London: Viking, 2004.

Spinoza, Benedict. *On the Improvement of The Understanding, The Ethics, Correspondence*. Translated from the Latin by R. H. M. Elwes. New York: Dover, 1955.

Taylor, Mark C. *Disfiguring: Art, Architecture, Religion*. Chicago: University of Chicago Press, 1992.

Turner, Denys. *The Darkness of God: Negativity in Christian Mysticism*. Cambridge: Cambridge University Press, 1999.

Turnham, Steve. "Donald Trump to Father of Fallen Soldier: 'I've Made a Lot of Sacrifices.'" *ABC News*, July 30, 2016.

Tutu, Desmond. "Who We Are: Human Uniqueness and the African Spirit of Ubuntu," Templeton Prize, 2013, YouTube.com.

Van Alphen, Ernst. *Caught by History: Holocaust Effects in Contemporary Art, Literature, and Theory*. Stanford, CA: Stanford University Press, 1997.

Withnall, Adam. "US Warns of Month of Violence by Isis during Ramadan." *The Independent*, June 9, 2016.